LABOUR UNIONS AND
THE THEORY OF INTERNATIONAL TRADE

# CONTRIBUTIONS
# TO
# ECONOMIC ANALYSIS

202

*Honorary Editor:*
J. TINBERGEN

*Editors:*
D. W. JORGENSON
J. WAELBROECK

NORTH-HOLLAND
AMSTERDAM • NEW YORK • OXFORD • TOKYO

# LABOUR UNIONS
# AND THE THEORY
# OF INTERNATIONAL TRADE

M.C. KEMP

*Department of Economics*
*The University of New South Wales*
*Kensington, Australia*

N.VAN LONG

*Department of Economics*
*Australian National University*
*Canberra, Australia*

K. SHIMOMURA

*Research Institute for Economics*
*and Business Administration*
*Kobe University*
*Kobe, Japan*

1991

NORTH-HOLLAND
AMSTERDAM • NEW YORK • OXFORD • TOKYO

ELSEVIER SCIENCE PUBLISHERS B.V.
Sara Burgerhartstraat 25
P.O. Box 211, 1000 AE Amsterdam, The Netherlands

Distributors for the United States and Canada:

ELSEVIER SCIENCE PUBLISHING COMPANY INC.
655 Avenue of the Americas
New York, N.Y. 10010, U.S.A.

Library of Congress Cataloging-in-Publication Data


Kemp, Murray C.
    Labour unions and the theory of international trade / M.C. Kemp,
N. van Long, K. Shimomura.
        p.   cm. -- (Contributions to economic analysis ; 202)
    Includes bibliographical references and index.
    ISBN 0-444-88480-7
    1. Trade unions and foreign policy.  2. International trade.
3. International economic relations.  4. Competition, International.
I. Long, Ngo van.  II. Shimomura, Kazun.  III. Title.  IV. Series.
HD6490.F58K45  1991
322'.2'0973--dc20                                            91-15462
                                                                  CIP

Typeset using the facilities of
the University of Illinois at Chicago
Office of Publication Services

ISBN: 0 444 88480 7

PRINTED IN THE NETHERLANDS

## Introduction to the Series

This series consists of a number of hitherto unpublished studies, which are introduced by the editors in the belief that they represent fresh contributions to economic science.

The term "economic analysis" as used in the title of the series has been adopted because it covers both the activities of the theoretical economist and the research worker.

Although the analytical methods used by the various contributors are not the same, they are nevertheless conditioned by the common origin of their studies, namely theoretical problems encountered in practical research. Since for this reason, business cycle research and national accounting, research work on behalf of economic policy, and problems of planning are the main sources of the subjects dealt with, they necessarily determine the manner of approach adopted by the authors. Their methods tend to be "practical" in the sense of not being too far remote from application to actual economic conditions. In addition, they are quantitative rather than qualitative.

It is the hope of the editors that the publication of these studies will help to stimulate the exchange of scientific information and to reinforce international cooperation in the field of economics.

*The Editors*

# PREFACE

When asked how long it took him to complete a painting, the portraitist Eric Bird replied: "Forty-four years and ten hours." Something like that is true of this book.

It is a very Australian book; at least it will seem so to an older generation of Australian economists. Thus underlying its more ambitious, culminating sections (contained in Chapters V–VII) is a model of an open, growing, two-class economy with centralized wage setting, a model which has its roots in the *Tariff Report* of 1929 and which, in Australia, informed both undergraduate teaching and public policy making throughout the 'thirties and for much of the 'forties.

However, our composition has taken rather more than Bird's ten hours. Serious work began after Kemp's visit to Kobe University in August–September 1983 and has continued intermittently since then, vigorous pulses coinciding with Shimomura's visits to the University of New South Wales in 1986 and 1989. Some of our early thoughts may be found in Kemp and Shimomura (1984b, 1985a, 1985b) and in Kemp and Long (1987).

We are greatly indebted to Kobe University and the University of New South Wales for their support over a long period and, in particular, for making possible Shimomura's two visits to Sydney; and it is a pleasure to acknowledge the encouragement and support of Professors Masahiro Fujita and Hiromasa Yamamoto and of Emeritus Professor Seiji Sasaki. We are indebted also to the Alexander von Humboldt Foundation which made possible Kemp's visits to Germany during the southern summers of 1987–1988 and 1988–1989. The warm hospitality of the Foundation and of the Universities of Kiel, Konstanz and Munich is gratefully acknowledged.

# CONTENTS

Preface . . . . . . . . . . . . . . . . . . . . . . . . . . . . . . . . vii

1. A PROSPECTUS . . . . . . . . . . . . . . . . . . . . . . . . 1

2. THE HECKSCHER-OHLIN MODEL . . . . . . . . . . . . . . . 5

3. THE SPECIFIC-FACTORS MODEL . . . . . . . . . . . . . . . . 59

4. A LABOUR UNION IN EVERY COUNTRY . . . . . . . . . . 155

5. UNION POWER IN THE LONG RUN . . . . . . . . . . . . 181

6. A DIFFERENTIAL GAME BETWEEN THE LABOUR
    UNIONS OF DIFFERENT COUNTRIES . . . . . . . . . . 215

7. A DIFFERENTIAL GAME BETWEEN ORGANIZED
    LABOUR AND ORGANIZED CAPITAL . . . . . . . . . 231

REFERENCES . . . . . . . . . . . . . . . . . . . . . . . . . . . . 279

INDEX . . . . . . . . . . . . . . . . . . . . . . . . . . . . . . . . 285

# CHAPTER ONE

## A PROSPECTUS

We now have at our disposal a fairly completely worked out theory of international trade under several types of price and quantity "distortions"; see, for example, Ohlin (1931), Haberler (1933, pp. 196-198; 1950), Hagen (1958), Fishlow and David (1961), Herberg and Kemp (1971, 1972), Herberg, Kemp and Magee (1971), Bhagwati and Srinivasan (1971), Jones (1971), Brecher (1974a), Magee (1976). For the most part, however, the distortions are simply taken as given; they are the data of the theory, not implications of it. Moreover, the theory is static.[1] Time plays no role; factor accumulation and decay are ruled out. What is needed is a more general dynamic theory to which at least some distortions are endogenous.

In the present essay we take some small and painful steps towards the required reconstruction of trade theory. We provide a theory of trade between countries in at least one of which the pattern of competitive markets is disturbed by a powerful national labour union and in which, therefore, wage distortions are endogenous; and then proceed to re-examine the several comparative-equilibrium questions of conventional trade theory. In addition, we confront several questions which can be posed only in the new framework. For example, we seek to discover whether there are circumstances in which, by imposing a minimum real wage, a labour union may so change the effective factor-endowment ratio of a country as to reverse the direction of its trade. That an arbitrary minimum wage can achieve a reversal is well known and easy to understand. The outstanding question is whether a rationally-chosen minimum wage can do so. As another example, we seek to discover whether a rational labour union, aware of the effect of its policies on business investment and of the feedback from investment to labour productivity, would ever judge market intervention to be unprofitable.

We shall find ourselves on what should be the common ground

of labour economics and the theory of international trade. For a long time, however, trade theorists and labour economists have had little to say to each other. Labour economics has tended to be partial-equilibrium in scope, and trade theory is rooted in the fiction of perfect competition. Thus each subject has lacked the principal strength of the other but, conversely, has something of value to impart. If we are exceptionally lucky, the pages that follow will mark an early stage in the process of rapprochement.

It remains only to provide the reader with some guidance through the chapters that follow. In Chapters II and III we take two well-known models of production and trade (the Heckscher-Ohlin model and the earlier specific-factors model), modify them by imposing a labour union on one of the trading partners and then proceed to the mundane but essential business of checking existence and uniqueness and making the promised sensitivity calculations. In Chapter IV we reconsider the analysis of Chapter II under the assumption that there is a strong labour union in each trading country. The new assumption suggests new questions: Is it possible for the workers in both countries to be better off in a union-ridden world than in a union-free world? Is it possible for the workers of the world to be worse off? Moreover the new assumption calls for new techniques of analysis. For if neither country is small, the unions will perceive that they stand in a strategic relationship to each other, and this suggests a game-theoretical analysis in which questions of existence and uniqueness become even more pressing. In Chapter V–VII we considerably broaden the scope of our analysis by allowing for capital accumulation and its interaction with union policies. These chapters also contain the most venturesome, experimental and fragile analysis of the book. In Chapter V, the labour union is the sole source of market imperfection. It is shown there that there are circumstances in which, in the long run, the union is powerless to help its members by market intervention. In Chapter VI, there is a union in each country, so that we are driven again to adopt a game-theoretic mode of analysis. It emerges that there are plausible circumstances in which, in the long run, neither union can help its members. Thus the conclusions of Chapter V are reinforced. In Chapter VII, on the other hand, the union interacts with the organized owners of capital. The recognition of organized capital forces us to substantially modify the conclusions of Chapter V. Indeed it emerges that the economy will stagnate for lack of savings and, in addition, will suffer from long-run unemployment. The chapter ends with some tentative suggestions concerning the directions which further research might take.

## FOOTNOTES

(1)   As partial exceptions to the rule, we may mention papers by Herberg and Kemp (1972) and Kemp, Kimura and Okuguchi (1977), in which intersectoral wage differentials adjust to sectoral labour shortages and surpluses.  To our present tastes, the adjustment process of those early papers is too mechanical, insufficiently tied to micro-maximizing.

CHAPTER TWO

## THE HECKSCHER-OHLIN MODEL

Throughout, our approach will be Heckscher-Ohlin, in the broad sense that much will be made of international disparities in factor endowments. In the present chapter the analysis is Heckscher-Ohlin in the narrower sense that it rests on the two-by-two model of production. We begin with a careful statement of assumptions, including those which define the two-by-two model.

## 1. PRINCIPAL ASSUMPTIONS

There are two trading countries, the home and the foreign, each endowed with given stocks of homogeneous labour ($\bar{N}$ for the home country, $\bar{N}^*$ for the foreign country) and capital (K for the home country, $K^*$ for the foreign). Within each country, both factors of production are free to move between sectors. Between countries, however, both factors are completely immobile. (The latter assumption will be relaxed in Section 7, where capital is taken to be internationally mobile.)

There are two consumption goods, the first of which will serve as numeraire. The two goods are produced by means of an internationally-common no-joint-products technology. The technology is described by concave, constant-returns production functions $F^i(K_i, N_i)$, where $K_i$ and $N_i$ are, respectively, the capital and labour inputs of the ith industry, $i = 1, 2$. Alternatively, and more conveniently for our purposes, the technology is described by the minimum unit-cost functions $c^i(w,r)$, $i = 1, 2$, where w and r are, respectively, the wage rate of labour and the rental rate of capital. The cost functions have the following conventional properties.

[c.1]   $c^i(w,r)$ is defined for all $(w,r) > 0$

[c.2]   $c^i(w,r)$ is twice-differentiable at all $(w,r) > 0$

[c.3]   $c^i(w,r) > 0$ for all $(w,r) > 0$

[c.4]   $c^i(\lambda w, \lambda r) = \lambda c^i(w,r)$ for all $\lambda > 0$ and all $(w,r) > 0$

[c.5]   For all $(w,r) > 0$,

$$c^i_w \equiv \partial c^i / \partial w > 0, \quad c^i_r \equiv \partial c^i / \partial r > 0$$

$$c^i_{ww} \equiv \partial^2 c^i / \partial w^2 < 0, \quad c^i_{rr} \equiv \partial^2 c^i / \partial r^2 < 0$$

$$c^i_{wr} \equiv \partial^2 c^i / \partial w \partial r > 0$$

[c.6]   For any given $r > 0$,

$$\lim_{w \to 0} c^i(w,r) = \tilde{K}_i r$$

$$\lim_{w \to \infty} c^i(w,r) = \infty$$

$$\lim_{w \to 0} c^i_w(w,r) = \infty$$

$$\lim_{w \to 0} c^i_r(w,r) = \tilde{K}_i$$

$$\lim_{w \to \infty} c^i_w(w,r) = \tilde{N}_i$$

$$\lim_{w \to \infty} c^i_r(w,r) = \infty$$

and, for any given $w > 0$,

$$\lim_{r \to 0} c^i(w,r) = \tilde{N}_i w$$

$$\lim_{r \to \infty} c^i(w,r) = \infty$$

$$\lim_{r \to 0} c^i_r(w,r) = \infty$$

$$\lim_{r \to 0} c^i_w(w,r) = \tilde{N}_i$$

$$\lim_{r \to \infty} c^i_r(w,r) = \tilde{K}_i$$

$$\lim_{r \to \infty} c^i_w(w,r) = \infty$$

where $\tilde{N}_i \equiv \lim\limits_{K_i \to \infty} N_i(K_i) \geq 0$, $N_i(K_i)$ defined by $F^i(K_i, N_i(K_i)) = 1$, and
where $\tilde{K}_i \equiv \lim\limits_{N_i \to \infty} K_i(N_i)$, $K_i(N_i)$ defined by $F^i(K_i(N_i), N_i) = 1$.

From the extremal nature of the cost functions, $c_w^i$ is the ith labour input (per unit of output) and $c_r^i$ is the ith capital input. Hence $c_w^i/c_r^i$ is the labour:capital ratio in the ith industry. The ith good is said to be more labour-intensive (less capital-intensive) than the jth if, for any $(w,r) > 0$ and for any $i,j = 1, 2$, $i \neq j$, $c_w^i(w,r)/c_r^i(w,r) > c_w^j(w,r)/c_r^j(w,r)$.

[c.7]   The first good is more labour-intensive than the second.

Let p be the price of the second good in terms of the first or numeraire good.

[c.8]   For any $p > 0$ the system of price-equals-average-cost equations

$$1 = c^1(w,r), \quad p = c^2(w,r)$$

has a unique and positive solution $(w(p), r(p))$.
Let $(\underline{p}, w(\underline{p}), r(\underline{p}))$ solve the system of equations

$$1 = c^1(w,r)$$

$$p = c^2(w,r)$$

$$c_w^1(w,r)/c_r^1(w,r) = \bar{N}/K$$

and let $(\bar{p}, w(\bar{p}), r(\bar{p}))$ solve the system

$$1 = c^1(w,r)$$

$$p = c^2(w,r)$$

$$c_w^2(w,r)/c_r^2(w,r) = \bar{N}/K$$

Evidently $\underline{p}$ and $\bar{p}$ depend on $\bar{N}/K$. Given $\bar{N}/K$, specialization must be incomplete if and only if $p \in (\underline{p}, \bar{p})$.

Individuals fall into one or the other of two mutually exclusive classes. Thus an individual is either a worker who owns no capital or a capitalist who provides no labour. All workers have the same homothetic preferences and the same endowment of labour; indeed, by choice of units, each worker controls exactly one unit of labour. Similarly, all capitalists have the same homothetic preferences and the same endowment of capital; again by choice of units, each capitalist owns one unit of capital. Each worker can provide either one unit of labour or nothing; it is not possible to provide, say, one-quarter of a unit of labour. Preferences are represented by the minimum expenditure functions $\bar{e}_x(p, v_x)$, $x = w, z, r$, where $v_w(v_z, v_r)$ is the non-negative well-being of the typical employed worker (unemployed worker, capitalist). However, given the homotheticity of preferences, utility can be so transformed that the function is homogeneous in utility. Thus, re-written, the expenditure function is $e_x(p)u_x$, $x = w, z, r$, where $u_x \equiv \varphi^x(v_x)$ and $\varphi^x$ is a non-negative and increasing function. The function $e_x(p)$ will be referred to as the unit expenditure function. It is assumed to have the following properties.

[e.1]  $e_x(p)$ is defined and positive for all $p > 0$

[e.2]  $e_x(p)$ is twice differentiable at all $p > 0$

[e.3]  $e'_x(p) \equiv de_x/dp > 0$ and $e''_x(p) \equiv d^2e_x/dp^2 < 0$ at all $p > 0$

[e.4]  $\lim_{p \to 0} e_x(p) = 0,$      $\lim_{p \to \infty} e_x(p) = \infty$

$\lim_{p \to 0} e'_x(p) = \infty,$      $\lim_{p \to \infty} e'_x(p) = 0$

In the home country there is a single labour union to which all workers, employed or unemployed, belong. Of course, we recognize that all-embracing craft unions are quite exceptional; but the explanation may be found in costs of organization and imperfections of information, aspects of reality from which we abstract. Internal consistency then drives us to the assumption of one big union. Moreover, to admit more than one union would confound the effects of unionism with those of union fragmentation.

The union sets a minimum wage to which competitive firms adjust. Specifically, each firm chooses the profit-maximizing level of employment at the prescribed wage; hours of work are taken as given, beyond analysis. All-or-nothing wage-employment contracts are ruled out, in spite of their attractive efficiency properties; similarly, we ignore the possibility of non-linear wage contracts. Since in the world we know each firm has its own technology, a national labour union would find itself obliged to negotiate as many distinct contracts as there are firms; practically speaking, the informational requirements of such a pattern of contracts would be impossible. Moreover, the attempt to negotiate all-or-nothing contracts would induce the formation of a countervailing employers' organization.

It is now customary, in theoretical labour economics, to endow unions with a utility function defined over the level of employment, the wage rate and the degree of support of the unemployed. In the typical formulation, the wage rate and the income of the unemployed are expressed in terms of money or some single-commodity numeraire. In the partial-equilibrium settings of traditional labour economics that formulation is unobjectionable. But for general-equilibrium analysis, with relative prices endogenous, both wages and the level of support of the unemployed must be deflated by the appropriate cost-of-living indices. Alternatively, and for our purposes more conveniently, the union's utility can be expressed as a function of the levels of well-being of the typical employed and unemployed workers, and of the level of employment, $N \equiv \sum N_i$. Thus we have

$$U = \bar{U}(N/\bar{N}, v_w, v_z)$$

$$= \bar{U}(N/\bar{N}, (\varphi^w)^{-1}(u_w), (\varphi^z)^{-1}(u_z))$$

$$(1) \qquad = \bar{\bar{U}}(N/\bar{N}, u_w, u_z)$$

Of course, if $v_z$ and $u_z$ are given constants (the utility value of leisure, perhaps) then (1) reduces to $U = U(N/\bar{N}, u_w)$.

Frequently $\bar{U}$ is assigned the more specific form

$$(1') \qquad U = \frac{N}{\bar{N}} v_w + \left(1 - \frac{N}{\bar{N}}\right) v_z$$

In support of this formulation it is assumed that there is a once-over random allocation of jobs to workers, so that $N/\bar{N}$ is the probability of any individual finding a job and U is the expected utility of the typical worker. However if jobs are allocated at random and if workers are averse to risk, as is usually assumed, then they will pool their earnings and seek to maximize the well-being of a typical worker, whether employed or unemployed; that is, the union will maximize not (1') but $Nu_w = N\varphi^w(v_w)$, where $v_w$ and $u_w$ retain their interpretations as the pre-pooling utility of a typical employed worker. To impose (1') on the union is to deny it a full quota of rationality. Henceforth, then, it will be assumed that

$$(2) \quad U = \frac{N}{\bar{N}} u_w = \frac{N}{\bar{N}} \frac{w}{e_w(p)}$$

If p is given, that is, if the home country is small, then the union maximizes U if and only if it maximizes the wage bill $N_w$. However for large-country analysis, and also for small-country comparative statics, it is essential that we retain the general formulation (2).

Of course, the assumed objective is not realistic. But it is unrealistic principally because of elements of seniority in accepted methods of hiring and firing, elements which are best ignored in a study of rational unionism.

## 2.   A SMALL OPEN ECONOMY: THE TWO TYPES OF EQUILIBRIUM

In this section, and in the two following it, attention is focussed on a small open economy for which the terms of trade are given, beyond control.   In the present section we describe in detail the union's problem of finding an *optimal* minimum wage, and we provide sufficient conditions for the solubility of that problem.   We also characterize the possible pre-union equilibria.   In Sections 3 and 4 it is explained how the union-ridden equilibrium responds to changes in the technological and other parameters of the economy.

### Pre-Union Equilibrium

Given the terms of trade, and assuming that production is incompletely specialized, so that $p \in (\underline{p}, \bar{p})$, the pre-union equilibrium wage and rental rates are uniquely determined by the two price-equals-average-cost equations

$$(3) \quad 1 = c^1(w,r)$$

$$(4) \quad p = c^2(w,r)$$

However each worker commands one unit of labour, and each capitalist owns one unit of capital.   Hence

$$(5) \quad w = e_w(p)u_w$$

$$(6) \quad r = e_r(p)u_r$$

Thus, indirectly, (3) and (4) determine the levels of well-being of workers and capitalists. Outputs are then determined by the requirement that each factor be fully employed:

(7)     $\bar{N} = Y_1 c_w^1(w,r) + Y_2 c_w^2(w,r)$

(8)     $K = Y_1 c_r^1(w,r) + Y_2 c_r^2(w,r)$

Equations (3)–(8) completely describe the diversified pre-union equilibrium.

If in the pre-union economy only one good is produced then the equations must be modified. Thus if p is so low that only the first good is produced then (4) must be deleted and the second-industry terms must be dropped from (7) and (8); and if p is so high that only the second good is produced then (3) must be deleted and the first-industry terms must be dropped from (7) and (8).

Figure 1 depicts the pre-union equilibrium in terms of factor rewards. In that figure $OT_1$ is the locus of points (w,r) such that $c_w^1(w,r)/c_r^1(w,r) = \bar{N}/K$ and $OT_2$ is the locus of points such that $c_w^2(w,r)/c_r^2(w,r) = \bar{N}/K$, where $\bar{N}/K$ is, of course, the factor endowment ratio. There also are displayed the locus of points such that $1 = c^1(w,r)$ and the loci of points such that $p^{(i)} = c^2(w,r)$, $i = 1, 2, 3$, where $p^{(1)} < p^{(2)} < p^{(3)}$. When $p = p^{(1)}$ only the first good is produced and $E^{(1)}$ is the equilibrium point; when $p = p^{(3)}$ only the second good is produced and $E^{(3)}$ is the equilibrium point; and when $p = p^{(2)}$ both goods are produced at the equilibrium point $E^{(2)}$. We shall write w(p) and r(p) to indicate the pre-union equilibrium wage and rental rates. And it will be assumed henceforth that in the pre-union equilibrium both goods are produced.

## Union-ridden Equilibrium

The equilibrium defined by equations (3)–(8) is disturbed by the formation of a labour union which sets a minimum wage. Suppose for the time being that the union were to choose a wage above the pre-union level w(p). Then, as Figure 1 makes clear, only the second or relatively capital-intensive good would be produced and, since $c_w^2/c_r^2 < \bar{N}/K$ for $w > w(p)$, unemployment would emerge and persist. Thus in any union-ridden equilibrium with $w > w(p)$ the following equations must be satisfied.

# Figure 1

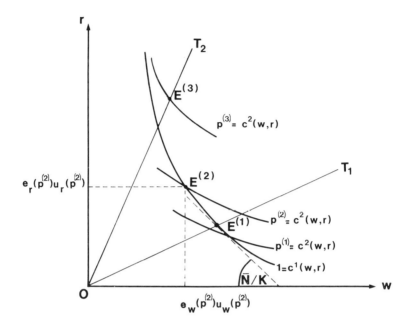

(9)    $p = c^2(w,r)$

(10)   $w = e_w(p)u_w$

(11)   $r = e_r(p)u_r$

(12)   $N = Y_2 c_w^2(w,r)$

(13)   $K = Y_2 c_r^2(w,r)$

This set of equations differs from (3)–(8) in the deletion of equation (3), in the modification of (7) and (8) to allow for the specialization of production, and in the abandonment of the requirement that labour be fully employed.

Equations (9)–(13) describe an economy subject to a minimum wage which is sufficiently high to create unemployment but otherwise quite arbitrary. The union, on the other hand, seeks to maximize $U = (N/\bar{N})u_w$, the utility of its typical member after the wage bill has been shared. Drawing on (9)–(13) and the homogeneity of the cost functions, U can be written as

$$U = \frac{K}{\bar{N}} \frac{c_w^2(w,r)}{c_r^2(w,r)} \frac{w}{e_w(p)}$$

(14)   $$U = \frac{K}{\bar{N}} \frac{c_w^2(\omega,r)}{c_r^2(\omega,r)} \frac{\omega}{e_w(p)} \frac{p}{c^2(\omega,1)} = \psi(\omega)$$

where $\omega \equiv w/r$, and the objective of the union is seen to be that of maximizing $\psi$ by choosing an appropriate $\omega$. If p is sufficiently low there may be only the boundary solution $\omega^0 = \omega(p) \equiv w(p)/r(p)$. Let us for the time being put aside that uninteresting case and assume that the union's problem has an interior solution $\omega^0 > \omega(p)$. Differentiating (14),

$$\frac{\omega}{U} \frac{dU}{d\omega} = 1 - \theta_2(\omega) - \sigma_2(\omega)$$

where $\theta_2(\omega) \equiv \omega c_w^2(\omega,1)/c^2(\omega,1)$ is the distributive share of labour and

$$\sigma_2(\omega) \equiv \frac{c^2(\omega,1)c_{wr}^2(\omega,1)}{c_w^2(\omega,1)c_r^2(\omega,1)}$$

is the elasticity of factor substitution in the second industry. It follows that an internal solution to the union's problem must satisfy

(15)        $1 - \theta_2(\omega) - \sigma_2(\omega) = 0$

Equation (15) has a solution if and only if there is a value of $\omega$ such that $\theta_2(\omega) + \sigma_2(\omega)$ is not less than one and a value of $\omega$ such that $\theta_2(\omega) + \sigma_2(\omega)$ is not greater than one. It suffices for uniqueness if, in addition, $\theta_2(\omega) + \sigma_2(\omega)$ is a monotone function. In particular, for existence and uniqueness it suffices that $\sigma_2$ be a constant less than one, for then $\theta_2(\omega)$ is an increasing function with $\lim_{\omega \to 0} \theta_2(\omega) = 0$ and $\lim_{\omega \to \infty} \theta_2(\omega) = 1$. However that condition is by no means necessary. Of course, at the equilibrium point, $\sigma_2 < 1$. But that is only common sense: if $\sigma_2$ were greater than one, a small reduction of the wage would increase both total output and labour's share of it. In the sequel we shall simply assume that (15) has a unique solution without committing ourselves to the special CES form. Then equations (9)–(15) describe a unique union-ridden equilibrium with $\omega = w^0 > \omega(p)$.

Some aspects of the foregoing discussion are illuminated by Figures 2–4. In Figure 2 the ray OT represents the optimal wage : rental ratio $\omega^0$, already determined by equation (15); and, of course, $p^{(1)} < p^{(2)} < p^{(3)} < p^{(4)}$. Evidently $\omega^0$ is optimal only for sufficiently large p. We begin by showing that the critical minimum value of p (the "switching" price) lies between $p^{(2)}$ and $p^{(4)}$. Consider $p^{(4)}$. If at $p^{(4)}$ it is not in the interest of the union to intervene in the labour market then the union will not intervene at any higher price. For as p rises above $p^{(4)}$ both the pre-union and the union-ridden wage rates rise in step, the former along the ray $OT_2$, the latter along OT, with only the second good produced in each case; hence the pre-union and union-distorted values of $w/e_w$ maintain a relationship of constant proportionality. Now consider $p^{(2)}$. At that price $\omega^0$ is the pre-union equilibrium wage : rental ratio. Moreover in that equilibrium both goods are produced. To specialize in producing the second commodity would entail a quantum jump in unemployment without compensating wage benefits and therefore would be suboptimal for the union. However, by assumption, a critical minimum p exists. Hence it must lie between $p^{(2)}$ and $p^{(4)}$.

We can go further and affirm that, if it exists, the switching price

# Figure 2

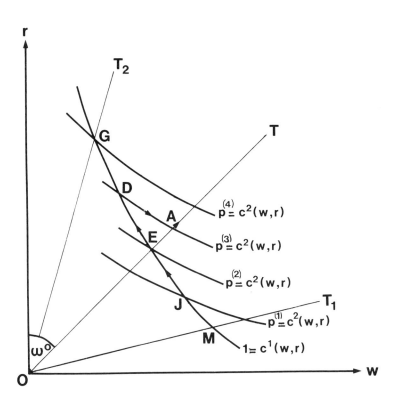

## Figure 3

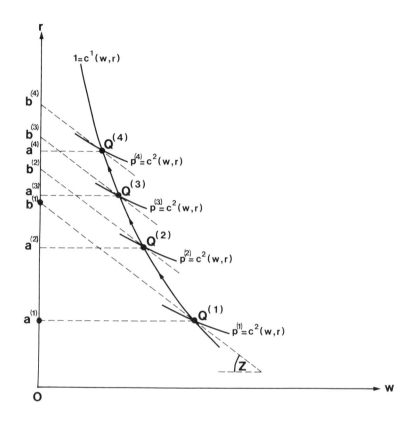

# Figure 4

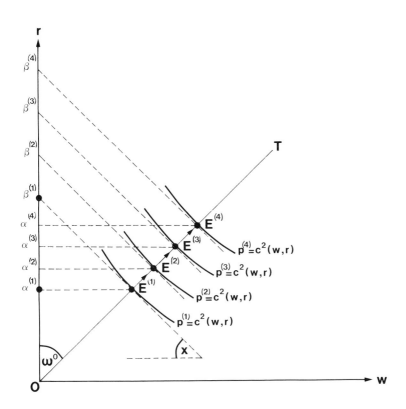

is unique. Our proof is in terms of Figures 3 and 4. In Figure 3 there is again displayed an array of pre-union equilibria $Q^{(1)}$, $Q^{(2)}$, $Q^{(3)}$, $Q^{(4)}$ associated respectively with the prices $p^{(1)}$, $p^{(2)}$, $p^{(3)}$, $p^{(4)}$, where $p^{(1)} < p^{(2)} < p^{(3)} < p^{(4)}$ and where each equilibrium lies within the cone of diversification ($T_1OT_2$ in Figure 2). Evidently the wage bill $wz$ at $Q^{(1)}$ is represented by the vertical distance $a^{(1)}b^{(1)}$. Similarly, the wage bill at $Q^{(i)}$ is represented by $a^{(i)}b^{(i)}$, $i = 2, 3, 4$. From the Stolper-Samuelson Theorem and the relative capital-intensity of the second industry, we may infer that $a^{(1)}b^{(1)} > a^{(2)}b^{(2)} > a^{(3)}b^{(3)} > a^{(4)}b^{(4)}$. In Figure 4, on the other hand, there is displayed an array of under-employment equilibria $E^{(1)}$, $E^{(2)}$, $E^{(3)}$, $E^{(4)}$, with only the second good produced. The wage bill $wx$ associated with $E^{(1)}$ is represented by $\alpha^{(1)}\beta^{(1)}$. Similarly, the wage bill associated with $E^{(i)}$ is represented by $\alpha^{(i)}\beta^{(i)}$, $i = 2, 3, 4$. By elementary geometry, $\alpha^{(1)}\beta^{(1)} < \alpha^{(2)}\beta^{(2)} < \alpha^{(3)}\beta^{(3)} < \alpha^{(4)}\beta^{(4)}$. Thus the pre-union wage bill is a monotone-decreasing function of $p$ and the wage bill associated with specialized production is a monotone-increasing function of $p$. Hence the switch price is unique.

Let $p^{(3)}$ of Figure 2 be the uniquely-determined switch price. If $p > p^{(3)}$ it is optimal for the union to intervene and impose $\omega^0 > \omega(p)$, the higher wage more than compensating for the jump in unemployment; if $p < p^{(3)}$ the balance swings the other way and it is optimal for the union to passively accept the pre-union wage $w(p)$; and if $p = p^{(3)}$ it is a matter of indifference to the union whether it accepts the pre-union wage or imposes $\omega^0$. At $p = p^{(1)}$, for example, the equilibrium lies at J in Figure 2, with full employment, incomplete specialization of production and a value of $\omega$ represented by the slope of the ray OJ. As the price rises from $p^{(1)}$, the union-ridden equilibrium moves from J to D through E, with full employment and diversified production but with the ratio of outputs $Y_2/Y_1$ steadily increasing; it then jumps to A on OT and thereafter moves outward along OT. In contrast, as $p$ increases, the pre-union wage moves gradually from D to G and then outward along $OT_2$.

In this section we have found that, if the union demands a minimum wage in excess of the pre-union level, the economy completely abandons production of the relatively labour-intensive commodity. The extreme form of the change in productive structure is disconcerting. However it is peculiar to the small-country version of the two-by-two model. The response of production to the exercise of union power is much less extreme in the large-country version of the model, which will be studied in Sections 5 and 6; and the same is true of the specific-factors model of Chapter III.

## 3. THE COMPARATIVE STATICS OF SMALL-COUNTRY EQUILIBRIA (I)

In this and the following section we subject the union-ridden equilibrium of Section 2 to systematic comparative statics manipulation. In the present section we examine the impact on employment, output, factor rewards and the welfare of workers and capitalists of exogenous changes in the terms of trade, factor endowments and technology of the small country. In Section 4 we consider the impact of protective tariffs on the same list of variables.

Given $\omega^0$, the solution to (15), we have, from (9)–(14),

$$(16) \quad U^0 = \frac{K}{\overline{N}} \frac{p}{e_w(p)} \frac{c_w^2(\omega^0,1)\omega^0}{c_r^2(\omega^0,1)c^2(\omega^0,1)} > u_w(p)$$

$$(17) \quad u_r^0 = \frac{p}{e_r(p)c^2(\omega^0,1)}$$

$$(18) \quad w^0 = \frac{p\omega^0}{c^2(\omega^0,1)}$$

$$(19) \quad r^0 = \frac{p}{c^2(\omega^0,1)}$$

$$(20) \quad Y_2^0 = \frac{K}{c_r^2(\omega^0,1)}$$

$$(21) \quad N^0 = \frac{c_w^2(\omega^0,1)}{c_r^2(\omega^0,1)}$$

Differentiating (16)–(21) totally, we obtain

$$(22) \quad \hat{U}^0 = \hat{K} - \hat{\overline{N}} + (1 - \varepsilon_e^w)\hat{p}$$

$$(23) \quad \hat{u}_r^0 = (1 - \varepsilon_e^w)\hat{p}$$

(24)  $\hat{w}^0 = \hat{p}$

(25)  $\hat{r}^0 = \hat{p}$

(26)  $\hat{Y}_2^0 = \hat{K}$

(27)  $\hat{N}^0 = \hat{K}$

where $\hat{x} \equiv dx/x$ and $\varepsilon_e^w \equiv pe_w'(p)/e_w(p)$ is the proportion of their budgets devoted by workers to the second or exported commodity, with $0 < \varepsilon_e^w < 1$ for all $p > 0$.

Equations (22)–(27) describe the response of the endogenous variables to small changes in the terms of trade and factor endowments. We want to know also how those variables respond to technological improvements. Let us consider then the simplest Mill-Edgeworth or factor-neutral improvements confined to the second industry. To this end we introduce the parameter $\mu$, increases in which represent technical improvements and which initially is equal to one. The basic equations (9)–(14) are then modified by dividing $c^2$ and its derivatives by $\mu$, so that the solutions (16)–(21) become

$$(28) \quad U^0 = \frac{K}{\overline{N}} \; \frac{\mu p}{e_w(p)} \; \frac{c_w^2(\omega^0,1)\omega^0}{c_r^2(\omega^0,1)c^2(\omega^0,1)}$$

$$(29) \quad u_r^0 = \frac{\mu p}{e_r(p)c^2(\omega^0,1)}$$

$$(30) \quad w^0 = \frac{\mu p \omega^0}{c^2(\omega^0,1)}$$

$$(31) \quad r^0 = \frac{\mu p}{c^2(\omega^0,1)}$$

$$(32) \quad Y_2^0 = \frac{\mu K}{c_r^2(\omega^0,1)}$$

$$(33) \quad N^0 = \frac{K c_w^2(\omega^0,1)}{c_r^2(\omega^0,1)}$$

Differentiating (28)–(33) with respect to $\mu$, we find that

(34)     $\hat{U}^0 = \hat{u}_r^0 = \hat{w}^0 = \hat{r}^0 = \hat{Y}_2^0 = \hat{\mu}$

(35)     $\hat{N}^0 = 0$

An important key to the comparative static propositions (22)–(27), (34) and (35) is the fact, implicit in Figure 2, that in the union-ridden equilibrium $\omega$ depends only on conditions of production in the active second industry and is independent of other exogenous factors. It follows that the same is true of $N/K$, which is equal to $c_w^2(\omega,1)/c_r^2(\omega,1)$, and therefore of $N\omega/K = Nw/Kr$, the ratio of distributive shares. Thus the labour union sets both the wage : rental ratio and the two distributive shares at levels which are independent of the terms of trade, of the two factor endowments, and even of factor-neutral changes in the conditions of production. Moreover, since $\omega$ is independent of p, w and r are proportional to p.

Let us consider further the effects of changes in the two factor endowments. We have noted already that the union-ridden equilibrium value of $\omega$ is independent of endowments. Since w and r are determined by $p = rc^2(\omega,1)$ and $w = \omega r$, they too are independent of endowments; the same is true of $u_r$. We have noted also that $N/K$ is independent of endowments. This implies that employment responds equi-proportionately to changes in the stock of capital; given that w is independent of endowments, it then follows that U responds positively to increases in K. Similarly, since wN is independent of $\bar{N}$, an increase in the work force, perhaps the result of immigration, causes the well-being of each worker to decline.

## 4.     THE COMPARATIVE STATICS OF SMALL-COUNTRY EQUILIBRIA (II)

In the present section we consider the impact of a small import duty on the union-ridden equilibrium. In particular, we wish to know whether a protective tariff tends to raise worker well-being and whether it tends to reduce the level of unemployment.

The latter question goes back to the Mercantilists, was much debated between the two world wars, especially in the United Kingdom, and recently has been the subject of further intensive study; see, for example, Brecher (1974a, b), Chan (1978), Das (1982), Eichengreen

(1981, 1983), Johansson and Löfgren (1980, 1981) and Kumcu (1985). However recent discussion of the question has been highly fragmentary, based on a great variety of mutually incompatible models. Moreover, without exception, the models have been partial equilibrium, in the sense that wage rates, nominal or real, have been treated as data, not as products of the analysis. There is need of a fresh analysis which treats the wage rate as a variable to be determined. For that reason we have felt justified in devoting an entire section to the topic.

As our starting point we take again the union-ridden equilibrium of Section 2, with only the second good produced and with the first good fully imported. The equilibrium is disturbed by the imposition of a small duty on imports. If $p$ now denotes the domestic price ratio, $\bar{p}$ the world price ratio and $\tau$ the $ad$ $valorem$ rate of import duty, we can write $p(1+\tau) = \bar{p}$. Initially, $\tau = 0$. The proceeds of the tariff are returned to the public in a lumpsum fashion. Specifically, the proceeds are divided between workers and capitalists in the same manner as earned income; thus, if the tariff proceeds are denoted by $\Delta$ and that part of it accruing to labour by $\Delta_w$,

(36)    $\Delta_w / \Delta = wN/(wN + rK) = \theta_2(\omega)$

Recalling that $\varepsilon_e^w(p)$ and $\varepsilon_e^r(p)$ are, respectively, the proportions of wage-earners' and capitalists' incomes spent on the second commodity, we have

$$\Delta = \frac{\tau}{1 + \tau} \left[ (1 - \varepsilon_e^w)(wN + \theta_2\Delta) + (1 - \varepsilon_e^r)(rK + (1 - \theta_2)\Delta) \right]$$

or, solving,

(37)    $\Delta = \dfrac{b}{1 - b} (wN + rK)$

where

(38)    $b(\omega,\tau) \equiv \dfrac{\tau}{1 + \tau} \left[ \theta_2(\omega)(1 - \varepsilon_e^w(p)) + (1 - \theta_2(\omega))(1 - \varepsilon_e^r(p)) \right]$

It follows from (36) and (37) that

$$U = \frac{wN + \Delta_w}{\bar{N}e_w(p)}$$

$$= \frac{p}{e_w(p)} \frac{K}{\bar{\bar{N}}} \frac{\omega c_w^2(\omega,1)}{c^2(\omega,1)c_r^2(\omega,1)} \Big/ (1 - b(\omega,\tau))$$

(39)     $= \psi(\omega,\tau)/(1 - b(\omega,\tau)) \equiv \eta(\omega,\tau)$

The union seeks that value of $\omega$ for which U is a maximum, given $\tau$. Differentiating (39) with respect to w, we obtain

$$\frac{1}{U} \frac{\partial U}{\partial \omega} = \frac{c^2(\omega,1)c_r^2(\omega,1)}{\omega c_w^2(\omega,1)} \frac{d}{d\omega} \Big( \frac{\omega c_w^2(\omega,1)}{c^2(\omega,1)c_r^2(\omega,1)} \Big)$$

(40)     $$+ \frac{1}{1 - b} \frac{\tau}{1 + \tau} (\varepsilon_e^r(p) - \varepsilon_e^w(p)) \frac{d\theta_2(\omega)}{d\omega}$$

where[1]

(41)   $$\frac{\omega}{\theta_2(\omega)} \frac{d\theta_2(\omega)}{d\omega} = (1 - \theta_2(\omega))(1 - \sigma_2(\omega)) > 0$$

Since $\tau = 0$, $\partial U/\partial \omega = 0$ when $\omega = \omega^0$.

The initial free-trade equilibrium is disturbed by the imposition of a small import duty. Equating (40) to zero, differentiating totally, evaluating at $\tau = 0$, $\omega = \omega^0$, and making use of (41), we obtain

$$\frac{c^2(\omega^0,1)c_r^2(\omega^0,1)}{\omega^0 c_w^2(\omega,1)} \frac{d^2}{d\omega^2} \Big( \frac{\omega c_w^2(\omega,1)}{c^2(\omega,1)c_r^2(\omega,1)} \Big)\Big|_{\omega=0} \cdot \frac{d\omega}{d\tau}\Big|_{\tau=0}$$

(42)     $$+ (\varepsilon_e^r(\bar{p}) - \varepsilon_e^w(\bar{p})) \frac{d\theta_2(\omega)}{d\omega} = 0$$

Since $1 - \sigma_2(\omega^0) = \theta_2(\omega^0)$ is positive and since the term

$$\frac{d^2}{d\omega^2} \Big( \frac{\omega c_w^2(\omega,1)}{c^2(\omega,1)c_r^2(\omega,1)} \Big)\Big|_{\omega=\omega^0}$$

is negative, we can infer from (41) and (42) that

(43)   $\text{sign} \Big( \dfrac{d\omega}{d\tau}\Big|_{\tau=0} \Big) = \text{sign} (\varepsilon_e^r(\bar{p}) - \varepsilon_e^w(\bar{p}))$

Thus the response of the wage : rental ratio to a small import duty depends solely on the proportions of their incomes spent on the second or exported good by wage earners and capitalists. Given (43), we can easily complete our calculations:

$$
(44) \quad \frac{1}{U} \frac{dU}{d\tau}\bigg|_{\tau=0} = \frac{1}{U} \frac{\partial U}{\partial \tau}\bigg|_{\tau=0} = (\varepsilon_e^w(\bar{p}) - \varepsilon_e^r(\bar{p}))(1 - \theta_2)
$$

$$
(45) \quad \frac{1}{r} \frac{dr}{d\tau}\bigg|_{\tau=0} = -\left(1 + \theta_2(\omega^0)\right) \frac{1}{\omega^0} \frac{d\omega}{d\tau}\bigg|_{\tau=0}
$$

$$
(46) \quad \frac{1}{w} \frac{dw}{d\tau}\bigg|_{\tau=0} = -\left(1 - (1 - \theta_2(\omega^0))\right) \frac{1}{\omega^0} \frac{d\omega}{d\tau}\bigg|_{\tau=0}
$$

$$
(47) \quad \frac{1}{u_r} \frac{du_r}{d\tau}\bigg|_{\tau=0} = -\theta_2(\omega^0)(\varepsilon_e^w(\bar{p}) - \varepsilon_e^r(\bar{p})) + \frac{1}{\omega^0} \frac{d\omega}{d\tau}\bigg|_{\tau=0}
$$

$$
(48) \quad \frac{1}{Y_2} \frac{dY_2}{d\tau}\bigg|_{\tau=0} = -\theta_2(\omega^0)\sigma_2(\omega^0) \frac{1}{\omega^0} \frac{d\omega}{d\tau}\bigg|_{\tau=0}
$$

$$
(49) \quad \frac{1}{N} \frac{dN}{d\tau}\bigg|_{\tau=0} = -\sigma_2(\omega^0) \frac{1}{\omega^0} \frac{d\omega}{d\tau}\bigg|_{\tau=0}
$$

Given (43)–(49), and assuming that $\varepsilon_e^r(\bar{p}) - \varepsilon_e^w(\bar{p})$ is sufficiently small but not zero, so that the preferences of workers and capitalists are alike but not identical, we can immediately infer the direction of response of each variable to the imposition of a small tariff. Most of these results are intuitively appealing. For example, (44) tells us that home workers benefit from a small tariff if and only if they spend a greater proportion of their incomes on the second or untaxed commodity than do capitalists, that is, if and only if the proportion of their incomes syphoned off by the tax collector is smaller than the proportion of their incomes received from the tax collector. Similarly, (47) tells us that the well-being of home capitalists changes in a manner determined partly by the change in the wage : rental ratio (and hence in the rental of capital) and partly by the patterns of expenditure of workers and capitalists (and hence by the balance of capitalists' tax payments and tax reimbursements).

What is not immediately clear is why the wage : rental ratio and the

level of employment are so closely related to the expenditure patterns
of workers and capitalists. We therefore pause to offer a diagrammatical illustration of our results, especially those embodied in (43)
and (49). The illustration is based on an alternative, more intuitive
but equivalent formulation of the union's problem. We continue to
assume that $\varepsilon_e^r(\bar{p}) \neq \varepsilon_e^w(\bar{p})$.

Let $K = 1$, and consider the "production function" defined by the
system of equations[2]

$$N = Y_2 c_w^2(\omega,1)$$

$$1 = Y_2 c_r^2(\omega,1)$$

Then, recalling that $c^2(\omega,1) = p/r$, (39) can be re-written as

$$(50) \quad U = \frac{1}{\overline{N}} \frac{Nu_w}{1 - \dfrac{\tau}{1+\tau}\left[\theta_2(N)(1 - \varepsilon_e^w(p)) + (1 - \theta_2(N))(1 - \varepsilon_e^r(p))\right]}$$

where $\theta_2(N) = Nf_2'(N)/f_2(N)$ and, since $N = c_w^2(\omega,1)/c_r^2(\omega,1)$, is equal
to $\theta_2(\omega)$, and where $u_w$ must now be interpreted as an employed
worker's utility before wage-sharing and before the distribution of
tariff revenue. The union's task is to find that $(N,u_w)$ which maximizes (50) subject to

$$(51) \quad u_w = \frac{p}{e_w(p)} f_2'(N)$$

Equation (51) defines the upper boundary of the union's constraint
set. It is depicted as the negatively-sloped curve AB of Figure 5. If
the rate of import duty increases then $p = \bar{p}/(1+\tau)$ must decline, implying that AB shifts down, becoming A'B'.

From (50), on the other hand, we obtain a family of indifference
curves for the union. By calculation, the slope of the typical curve is

$$\left.\frac{d\log u_w}{d\log N}\right|_U = -1 + \frac{\dfrac{\tau}{1+\tau}\theta_2'(N)[\varepsilon_e^w(p) - \varepsilon_e^r(p)]N}{1 - b}$$

where $\theta_2'(N) \equiv d\theta_2/dN < 0$. It follows that if $\varepsilon_e^w(p) > \varepsilon_e^r(p)$ then the
imposition of a small tariff will cause the slope of the curve to

## Figure 5

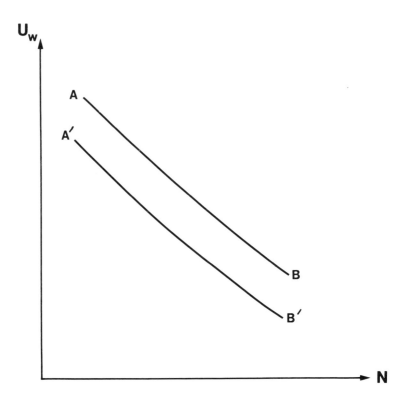

increase in absolute value and that if $\varepsilon_e^w(p) < \varepsilon_e^r(p)$ then the tariff will cause the slope to decrease. Thus in Figure 6 the pretariff indifference curve through point H is GJ and the post-tariff curve through H is G'J' if $\varepsilon_e^w(p) > \varepsilon_e^r(p)$ and G"J" if $\varepsilon_e^w(p) < \varepsilon_e^r(p)$. Combining Figures 5 and 6, we obtain Figure 7, the promised illustration of (43) and (49). If $\varepsilon_e^w(p) > \varepsilon_e^r(p)$, the new equilibrium is at H', with a higher level of employment and therefore a lower value of $\omega$; and if $\varepsilon_e^w(p) < \varepsilon_e^r(p)$ the new equilibrium is at H", with a lower level of employment and therefore a greater value of $\omega$. Notice that, consistent with (44), the indifference curve G'J' passes to the left of H.

It has been assumed that $\varepsilon_e^w(\bar{p}) \neq \varepsilon_e^r(\bar{p})$. If $\varepsilon_e^w(\bar{p}) = \varepsilon_e^r(\bar{p})$ so that, locally at least, the preferences of the two groups are identical, it is still possible to infer the direction in which the wage and rental rates move in response to the tariff; they decline. To determine the manner in which the other variables respond, however, one must examine the second derivatives $d^2x/d\tau^2$, $x = \omega, U, u, Y, N$. It can be verified that if $\varepsilon_e^w(\bar{p}) = \varepsilon_e^r(\bar{p})$ then $d^2x/d\tau^2 = 0$ for $x = \omega, u_r, Y_2, N$; to ascertain the responses of those variables it is necessary to consider the third and possibly higher derivatives. In the case of worker well-being U, however, matters are different. Thus, when $\varepsilon_e^w(\bar{p}) = \varepsilon_e^r(\bar{p})$, (39) can be re-written as

$$(52) \quad U = (\frac{p}{e} \frac{K}{\bar{N}} \frac{\omega c_w^2}{c^2 c_r^2})/(1 - \frac{\tau}{1 + \tau}(1 - \varepsilon_e))$$

where $\varepsilon_e \equiv pe'/e$. It follows that

$$\frac{\partial U}{\partial \tau} =$$

$$\frac{\frac{p}{e} \frac{K}{\bar{N}} \frac{\omega c_w^2}{c^2 c_r^2} \{-(1-\varepsilon_e)[(1 - \frac{\tau}{1 + \tau}(1-\varepsilon_e)] + \frac{1 - \varepsilon_e}{1 + \tau} + \frac{\tau}{1 + \tau} p\varepsilon_e'\}}{(1 - \frac{\tau}{1 + \tau}(1 - \varepsilon_e))^2}$$

where $\varepsilon_e' \equiv d\varepsilon_e/dp$ and that

$$(54) \quad \frac{1}{U} \frac{\partial^2 U}{\partial \tau^2}\bigg|_{\tau = 0} = -\varepsilon_e(1 - \varepsilon_e) < 0$$

CHAPTER 2

## Figure 6

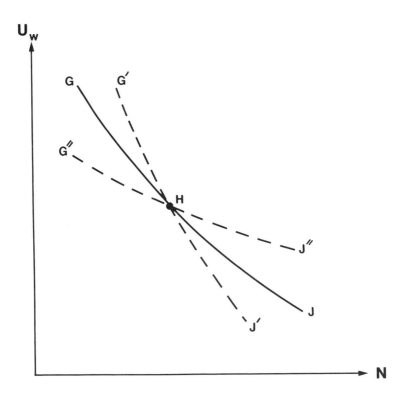

## Figure 7

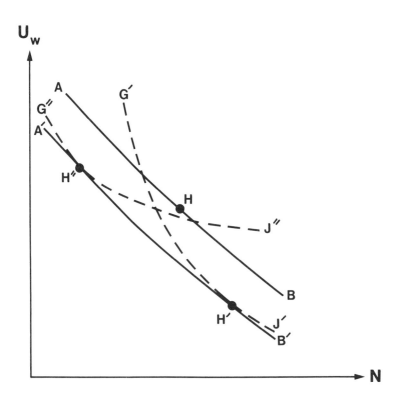

Hence $\Delta U/\Delta \tau < 0$. Thus if workers and capitalists have the same preferences then a small import duty reduces the well-being of each worker but, at least to a second-order approximation, fails to bring about any change in the level of employment.

## 5.    UNION-RIDDEN WORLD EQUILIBRIUM

The discussion to this point has been greatly eased by the small-country assumption. Now we must abandon that crutch and rework our analysis on the assumption that each of two countries, the home or union-ridden country and the foreign or union-free country (which may be an aggregate of several countries), has some influence on the terms of international trade. For simplicity it will be assumed henceforth that all households have the same homothetic preferences, so that $e_w(p) \equiv e_r(p) \equiv e(p)$, and that the two countries share a common technology.

### The Union-distorted Excess-demand Curve

We begin by constructing an important tool of analysis, the union-distorted excess-demand curve for the second commodity. To this end we define $(w_i(\bar{N}/K), r_i(\bar{N}/K))$ as the solution to the system of equations

$$1 = c^1(w,r)$$

$$\bar{N}/K = c_w^i(w,r)/c_w^i(w,r) \qquad i = 1 \text{ or } 2$$

Thus, given the assumption that the first good is relatively labour-intensive, $w_1(\bar{N}/K)$ is the least upper bound, and $w_2(\bar{N}/K)$ is the greatest lower bound, on wage rates consistent with the incomplete specialization of production. Let us denote by $\bar{w}$ the minimum wage rate set by the union. There are three cases to consider.

Case I:    $\bar{w} \geq w_1(\bar{N}/K)$

Case II:   $w_1(\bar{N}/K) > \bar{w} \geq w_2(\bar{N}/K)$

Case III:  $\bar{w} < w_2(\bar{N}/K)$

We shall concentrate on Case II. That case behind us, it will be possible to deal with the remaining cases quite briefly.

Suppose then that the union sets $\bar{w}$ between $w_1$ and $w_2$. Defining $p(\bar{N}/K, \bar{w})$ as the solution to the equations

$$p = c^2(\bar{w},r)$$

$$\bar{N}/K = c_w^2(\bar{w},r)/c_r^2(\bar{w},r)$$

and defining $p(\bar{w})$ as the solution to the equation $\bar{w} = w(p)$, we can distinguish three subcases.

(i) If $p \leq p(\bar{w})$ then the preunion equilibrium lies somewhere in the segment AB of the locus $1 = c^1(w,r)$ depicted in Figure 8; in particular, the equilibrium wage rate $w(p)$ exceeds $\bar{w}$, which therefore is non-binding. At A only the first good is produced; elsewhere on the segment production is diversified.

(ii) If $p(\bar{N}/K, \bar{w}) > p > p(\bar{w})$ then $\bar{w}$ is binding and the union-ridden equilibrium lies in the open segment BD, with only the second good produced and some unemployment. The complete system consists of the equations

$$p = c^2(w,r)$$

$$K = Y_2 c_r^2(w,r)$$

$$N = Y_2 c_w^2(w,r) < \bar{N}$$

$$w = \bar{w}$$

with unknowns $r$, $Y_2$ and $N$.

(iii) If $p \geq p(\bar{N}/K, \bar{w})$ then the equilibrium lies beyond D in the ray $OT_2$, with labour fully employed and only the second good produced; moreover, if $p > p(\bar{N}/K, \bar{w})$ then $\bar{w}$ is non-binding. The complete system consists of the equations

$$p = c^2(w,r)$$

$$K = Y_2 c_r^2(w,r)$$

$$\bar{N} = Y_2 c_w^2(w,r)$$

$$w \geq \bar{w}$$

with unknowns $w$, $r$, and $Y_2$.

## Figure 8

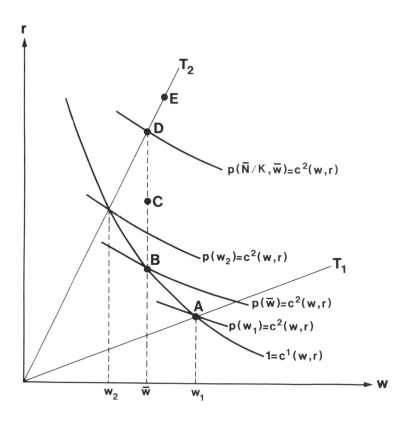

Now consider Figure 9. Depicted in that figure is the preunion excess-demand curve for the second commodity ABCD, the segments AB and CD corresponding to complete specialization in the production of the second and first commodities, respectively, and the segment BC corresponding to diversified production. (Our assumptions do not imply that the excess-demand curve consists of jointed straight-line segments; nor do any of our conclusions depend on that manner of drawing the curve. The curve is drawn in that way for ease in distinguishing its several phases.) Also depicted is the union-distorted excess-demand curve $AA_0B_0C_0CD$ associated with the minimum wage $\bar{w}$. As we have seen, for very high price ratios $(p \geq p(\bar{N}/K, \bar{w}))$ the minimum wage is ineffective, so that the preunion and union-distorted curves coincide; and the same is true for sufficiently low prices $(p \leq p(\bar{w}))$. On the other hand, as $p$ passes from just below to just above the critical value $p(\bar{w})$ there is an abrupt change in the level of employment and in the pattern of specialization, from full employment and diversification to less-than-full employment and complete specialization in producing the second commodity; in terms of Figure 9, the jump is from near $C_0$ in $C_0C$ to near $B_0$ in $A_0B_0$. Suppose that $p = p(\bar{w})$. Then the union-distorted excess demand is represented by $C_0$ which, as we have seen, is associated with full employment and diversified production. No other point in the closed interval $B_0C_0$ is part of the union-distorted excess-demand curve. Nevertheless any point in $B_0C_0$ is a potential world equilibrium. To see that this is so, imagine that the foreign excess-supply curve for the second commodity cuts $B_0C_0$, say at the interior point P, and that, to force the home country's excess demand to P, factors are moved from the first to the second industry. In the absence of a union such an allocation could not be sustained; the associated unemployment would force down the wage. But $\bar{w}$ is a union-enforced *minimum* wage; hence the allocation can be maintained and P is a potential equilibrium. For this reason we shall find it convenient to pretend that the interval $B_0C_0$ is part of the union-distorted excess-demand curve.

If the minimum wage increases from $\bar{w}$ to $\bar{w} + \Delta\bar{w}$, the vertical arm of the path ABDE of Figure 8 moves to the right, the anchor point B sliding down the locus $1 = c^1(w,r)$. As Figure 10 makes clear, $p(\bar{w} + \Delta\bar{w}) < p(\bar{w})$ and $p(\bar{N}/K, \bar{w} + \Delta\bar{w}) > p(\bar{N}/K, \bar{w})$. It follows that the excess-demand curve shifts in the manner depicted by Figure 9, from $AA_0B_0C_0CD$ to $AA_1B_1C_1CD$.

CHAPTER 2

## Figure 9

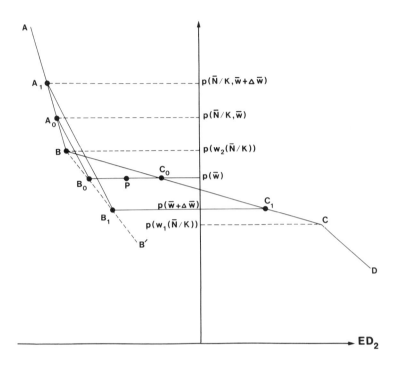

# Figure 10

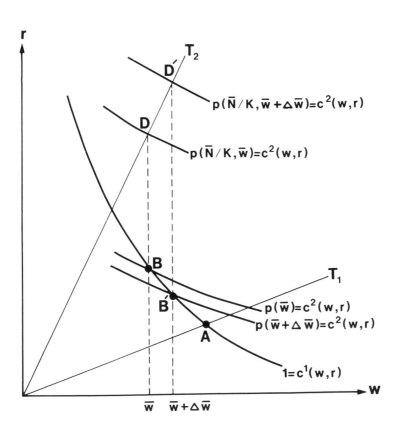

That completes our discussion of Case II, in which $w_1(\bar{N}/K) > \bar{w} \geq w_2(\bar{N}/K)$. Concerning Case I we need only add that if $\bar{w} > w_1$ and if $p \leq p(w_1)$ then the union-distorted excess-demand curve lies to the left of the preunion curve. In Case III, on the other hand, the two excess-demand curves coincide for all $p > 0$, implying that the union's wage policy is completely unworkable.

Figure 11 displays four union-distorted excess-demand curves. Between them the curves cover all possibilities of interest. Thus those subscripted 0 and 1 are for Case II and are simply copied from Figure 9, while those subscripted 2 and 3 are for Case I with $p \leq p(w_1)$. With each part of the union-distorted excess-demand curve there is associated a particular pattern of specialization and employment. Consider, for example, the curve $AA_1B_1C_1CD$. On the initial segment $AA_1$ only the second good is produced, under conditions of full employment; on the segment $A_1B_1$ only the second good is produced, with some unemployment; on $C_1C$ both goods are produced, with full employment; and on $CD$ only the first good is produced, with full employment. As a second example, we take the curve $AA_3B_3C_3D_3$. On the initial segment $AA_3$ only the second good is produced, with full employment; on $A_3B_3$ only the second good is produced with some unemployment; and on $C_3D_3$ only the first good is produced with some unemployment.

## World Equilibrium with an Arbitrary Minimum Wage

That completes our discussion of the union-distorted excess-demand curve. We shall make use of it in describing the world trading equilibrium. In the present subsection we simply take $\bar{w}$ as given and consider the properties of the equilibrium associated with it. The choice of $\bar{w}$ by an optimizing union will be considered in the following subsection.

For the time being it is assumed not only that the two countries have identical homothetic preferences and share a common technology but also that they have the same factor endowments, so that they differ only in the presence or absence of a union. This radical assumption eases the exposition; but it also serves the purpose of isolating the role of the union in creating trade. The assumption will be discarded after it has done its job.

# Figure 11

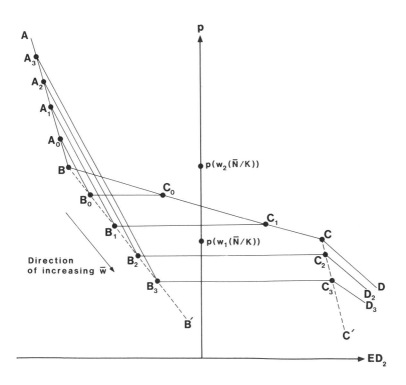

Consider Figure 12. The preunion excess-demand curve ABCD is reproduced from Figure 9. In view of the above assumptions it can be viewed as the excess-demand curve of the *foreign* country. For later convenience, the segment $C_1C_3$ is re-drawn, symmetrically with respect to the price axis, as $C_1B_3$; thus, for example, $B_3J = JC_3$. The position of the home or union-distorted excess-demand curve, on the other hand, depends on the value of the minimum wage. Figure 12 displays five possible curves with, for example, $A_0B_0C_0CD$ associated with the minimum wage $\bar{w}_0$ and $A_4B_4C_4D_4$ with $\bar{w}_4$ and with $w_0 < w_1 < w_2 < w_3 < w_4$.

We can now show that, whatever the value of $\bar{w}$, the world equilibrium must lie on the segment $B_3C_1$. Suppose that $\bar{w} = \bar{w}_1$. The world equilibrium then lies at $C_1$, with no trade and with the home country producing both commodities at full employment. As the minimum wage rises from $\bar{w}_1$ to $\bar{w}_3$ the equilibrium moves along $B_3C_1$ from $C_1$. Thus when $\bar{w} = \bar{w}_2$ the equilibrium lies at P, with the home country producing both commodities, exporting the second, and suffering some unemployment; and when $\bar{w} = \bar{w}_3$ the equilibrium lies at $B_3$, with the home country producing only the second commodity under conditions of partial unemployment. As $\bar{w}$ rises beyond $\bar{w}_3$ the equilibrium point moves back along $B_3C_1$. On the return journey, however, the economy displays a quite different pattern of production. Thus when $\bar{w} = \bar{w}_4$ so that the equilibrium again lies at P, the home excess-demand curve is $A_4B_4C_4D_4$ and only the second good is produced. Finally, it is obvious that if $\bar{w} < \bar{w}_1$ then the equilibrium point is $C_1$; there is no trade and the minimum wage is not binding. Thus, summarizing, if the two countries have the same preferences, technology and endowments then (i) as the minimum wage goes from zero to infinity each price between J and $C_1$ twice emerges as the unique equilibrium price; (ii) if the union chooses a minimum wage smaller than $\bar{w}_1$ the wage is not binding, the union's policy is ineffective and there is no trade; (iii) if the union chooses a wage between $\bar{w}_1$ and $\bar{w}_3$, the home country produces both commodities, exports the second, and suffers some unemployment (in effect, the unemployment provides the home country with a comparative advantage in producing the relatively capital-intensive second commodity); and (iv) if the union chooses a wage in excess of $\bar{w}_3$ the home country produces only the second commodity, therefore exports the second commodity, and suffers some unemployment.

# Figure 12

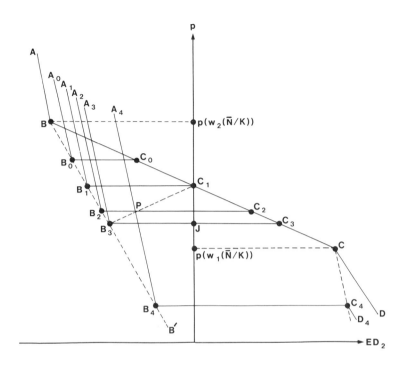

It follows from (i) that, in any world equilibrium, the foreign country is incompletely specialized. If the minimum wage lies between $\bar{w}_1$ and $\bar{w}_3$ production is incompletely specialized at home also, implying that factor rewards are the same in both countries. Thus, in that case, the effect of the union is to force up wages in both countries; since foreign workers remain fully employed, the union does more for them than for its own members. Of course it remains to be seen whether the union would ever optimally choose a wage rate between $\bar{w}_1$ and $\bar{w}_3$.

We have assumed that the two countries are distinguishable only in terms of the degree of unionization. It is time to adopt a more orthodox stance and allow for the possibility that the factor endowment ratio differs from country to country. If the ratios are not too disparate the preceding analysis carries through virtually unchanged. Thus suppose that the home country is relatively labour-abundant so that in the preunion world equilibrium it exports the labour-intensive first commodity. In Figure 13 BC and $B^*C^*$ are, respectively, those parts of the preunion home and foreign excess-demand curves which correspond to incomplete specialization. The preunion world equilibrium is then at E, with the home country importing $EC_1$ of the second commodity at the price $p^{nu} = OE$. By familiar reasoning, all possible equilibrium points lie on $B_3C_1$ the slope of which is equal in magnitude to that of $C_1C$. If the union chooses $\bar{w} \leq w(p^{nu})$ then the union's policy is ineffective and the world equilibrium is that of the preunion situation. If the union chooses a wage between $w(p^{nu})$ and $w(p^J)$, where $p^J = OJ$, then the equilibrium point lies in the interval $C_1B_3$, with both goods produced and some unemployment. As the wage increases from $w(p^{nu})$ to $w(p^J)$ it passes through $w(p^D)$, where $p^D = OD$, at which point the home country switches from the Heckscher-Ohlin pattern of exporting the first commodity to the anti-Heckscher-Ohlin pattern of exporting the second. Finally, if the union chooses a wage higher than $w(p^J)$ then at home only the second good is produced and there is some unemployment; the equilibrium lies in the segment $B_3D$ and the pattern of trade is anti-Heckscher-Ohlin. Thus each point in $B_3D$ (but not each point in $B_3C_1$) is an equilibrium for two different values of the minimum wage.

Figure 13

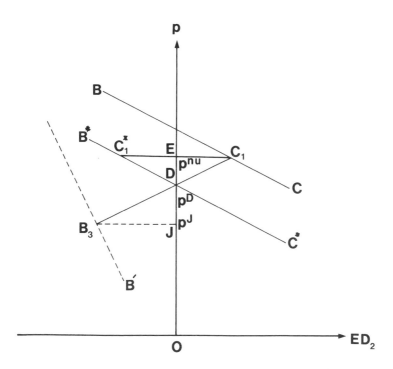

## World Equilibrium with an Optimal Minimum Wage

We can now take the final step of restricting $\bar{w}$ to be optimal from the viewpoint of the union and examining the existence and properties of the equilibrium. For this part of our analysis we revert to a more explicitly mathematical mode. Let us define $z = \bar{N}/K$, $z^* = \bar{N}^*/K^*$, $x = N/K$ and $h = K^*/K$, where $\bar{N}^*$ and $K^*$ are the foreign factor endowments. Then we can write down two alternative descriptions of world equilibrium, one for the case in which $w(p^{nu}) \leq \bar{w} < w(p^J)$, the other for the case in which $\bar{w} \geq w(p^J)$.

**Case A: $w(p^{nu}) \leq \bar{w} < w(p^J)$**  As we have noted, in this case production is diversified in both countries and factor rewards are everywhere the same. Hence (Diewert (1982))

$$Y_2/K = w'(p)x + r'(p)$$

$$Y_2^*/K^* = w'(p)z^* + r'(p)$$

and we can write down the system of equilibrium conditions

$$(55) \quad \{ \frac{e'(p)}{e(p)} [w(p)x + r(p)] - [w'(p)x + r'(p)]\}$$

$$+ h \{ \frac{e'(p)}{e(p)} [w(p)z^* + r(p)] - [w'(p)z^* + r'(p)]\} = 0$$

$$(56) \quad \bar{w} = w(p)$$

with p and x as unknowns. (Equation (55) states that, for the second commodity, world demand equals world supply.)

**Case B: $\bar{w} \geq w(p^J)$**  In this case only the second good is produced at home and the world equilibrium is determined by the system

$$(57) \quad - [1 - \varepsilon_e(p)] \frac{Y_2}{K}$$

$$+ h \{ \frac{e'(p)}{e(p)} [w(p)z^* + r(p)] - [w'(p)z^* + r'(p)]\} = 0$$

$$(58) \quad K = Y_2 c_r^2(\bar{w},r)$$

(59)  $N = Y_2 c_w^2(\bar{w}, r)$

(60)  $p = c^2(\bar{w}, r)$

with $Y_2$, $p$, $N$ and $r$ as unknowns.

The task of the union, then, is to solve the problem

$(P_0)$  $\max_{\bar{w}} U = \dfrac{\bar{w}x}{ze(p)}$

s.t. (55)–(56) if $\bar{w} < w(p^J)$,  (57)–(60) if $\bar{w} \geq w(p^J)$

It is possible that $(P_0)$ has no solution. However sufficient conditions for a solution can be provided.

**PROPOSITION 1:** For $(P_0)$ to have a solution it suffices that

$$zw(p^{nu}) \geq \frac{e(p^{nu})}{e(p^D)} \lim_{\omega \to \infty} \frac{\omega c_w^2(\omega,1)}{c_r^2(\omega,1)c^2(\omega,1)}$$

**PROOF**  We need only consider Case B.  Suppose then that $\bar{w}$ increases from an initial value $w(p^J)$.  The home country produces only the second commodity, with some unemployment; and, in terms of Figure 13, $p$ approaches $D$ along $B_3D$.  Consider the locus $p^D = c^2(w,r)$.  There may or may not exist a finite value of $w$, say $\hat{w}$, such that $p^D = c^2(\hat{w},0)$; but, whether or not $\hat{w}$ exists, $(dr/dw)\big|_{p^D=c^2}$ must converge to zero as $w$ goes to infinity.  It follows that $\lim_{\bar{w} \to \infty} Y_2 = 0$ and, therefore, $\lim_{\bar{w} \to \infty} p = p^D$.  From (58)–(60) therefore,

$$\lim_{\bar{w} \to \infty} U = \lim_{\bar{w} \to \infty} \frac{\bar{w}x}{e(p)z}$$

$$= \frac{1}{e(p^D)z} \lim_{\bar{w} \to \infty} \bar{w}x$$

$$= \frac{1}{e(p^D)z} \lim_{\bar{w} \to \infty} \frac{\omega c_w^2(\omega,1)}{c_r^2(\omega,1)c^2(\omega,1)}$$

for, if that condition is satisfied, $\bar{w} = w(p^{nu})$ is a solution.  ◊

**COROLLARY:** For $(P_0)$ to have a solution it suffices that (15) has a solution and that $\theta_2(\omega) + \sigma_2(\omega)$ is an increasing function; it therefore suffices also that $\sigma_2$ be constant and less than one.

Given that $(P_0)$ has a solution, is the solution characterized by unemployment and, if so, is the unemployment severe enough to cause the direction of trade to reverse?

Let us consider first the question of unemployment. Evidently there is unemployment if $dU/d\bar{w} > 0$ in the pre-union world equilibrium. What we seek then are interesting sufficient conditions for that inequality to hold. Now it can be verified from (3) and (4) that $d\log p/d\log\bar{w} = -(\theta_1 - \theta_2)/(1 - \theta_1)$ which, since the first industry is relatively labour-intensive, is negative. Hence the sign of

$$\frac{d\log U}{d\log \bar{w}} = \frac{d\log U}{d\log p}\frac{d\log p}{d\log \bar{w}}$$

is opposite to that of $d\log U/d\log p$. Rearranging the equilibrium condition (55) and recalling the definitions of $\theta_i$ and $\varepsilon_e$, we obtain

$$(61) \quad \frac{x + hz^*}{1 + h} = \frac{r(p)}{w(p)} \frac{[(1 - \varepsilon_e(p))\theta_1(p) + \varepsilon_3\theta_2(p)]}{\{1 - [(1 - \varepsilon_e(p))\theta_1(p) + \varepsilon_e(p)\theta_2(p)]\}} \equiv g(p)$$

Hence

$$(62) \quad U = \frac{w(p)x}{ze(p)} = \frac{w(p)}{ze(p)}\left[(1 + h)g(p) - hz^*\right]$$

Differentiating (62) with respect to $p$,

$$(63) \quad \frac{d\log U}{d\log p} = \frac{-(1 - \theta_1)}{\theta_1 - \theta_2} - \varepsilon_e + \frac{(1 + h)g(p)}{(1 + h)g(p) - hz^*}\frac{pg'(p)}{g(p)}$$

From (60), however,

$$(64) \quad \frac{pg'(p)}{g(p)} =$$

$$\frac{\sigma_1\theta_1(1 - \theta_1)(1 - \varepsilon_e) + \theta_2(1 - \theta_2)\varepsilon_e\sigma_2 + \varepsilon_e(1 - \varepsilon_e)(\theta_1 - \theta_2)\sigma_e}{(\theta_1 - \theta_2)\{1 - \varepsilon_e)\theta_1 + \varepsilon_e\theta_2\}\{1 - [(1 - \varepsilon_e)\theta_1 + \varepsilon_e\theta_2]\}}$$

where

$$\sigma_e = -\frac{e'}{pe''}(1 - \varepsilon_e)$$

is the "elasticity of consumption substitution". One notices immediately that if $\sigma_1$, $\sigma_2$ and $\sigma_e$ are sufficiently small then $d\log U / d\log p < 0$, implying that $d\log U / d\log \bar{w} > 0$. However, a more definite result is available. Thus if $\sigma_1 = \sigma_2 = \sigma_e \equiv \sigma$ then $pg'/g = \sigma/(\theta_1 - \theta_2)$, implying that

$$(65) \quad \frac{d\log U}{d\log p} = \frac{-(1 - \theta_1)}{\theta_1 - \theta_2} - \varepsilon_e + \frac{(1 + h)g(p)}{(1 + h)g(p) - hz^*} \cdot \frac{\sigma}{\theta_1 - \theta_2}$$

In the preunion world equilibrium, however, $(1 + h)g(p) = z + hz^*$. Hence,

$$(66) \quad \frac{d\log U}{d\log p}\bigg|_{p^{nu}} = \frac{(1 + hz^*/z)}{\theta_1 - \theta_2} \left\{ \sigma - \frac{1 - [(1 - \varepsilon_e)\theta_1 + \varepsilon_e\theta_2]}{1 + hz^*/z} \right\}.$$

Moreover, from (61),

$$1 - [(1 - \varepsilon_e)\theta_1 + \varepsilon_e\theta_2] = \frac{\dfrac{w}{r}\dfrac{z + hz^*}{1 + h}}{1 + \dfrac{w}{r}\dfrac{z + hz^*}{1 + h}}$$

$$= \theta_W,$$

labour's share of world income; and, since $1 + hz^*/z = (\bar{N} + \bar{N}^*)/\bar{N}$,

$$\frac{1}{1 + hz^*/z}\left\{1 - [(1 - \varepsilon_e)\theta_1 + \varepsilon_e\theta_2]\right\} = \frac{\bar{N}}{\bar{N} + \bar{N}^*}\theta_W$$

is the share of home workers in world income. Thus (66) shows that if

$$(67) \quad \sigma < \frac{\bar{N}}{\bar{N} + \bar{N}^*}\theta_W$$

that is, if the elasticity of substitution is smaller than the share of workers in world income, then $d\log U / d\log \bar{w}\big|_{p^{nu}} > 0$, implying that the union-ridden world equilibrium (the solution to $(P_0)$) involves some unemployment.

We turn now to the related question of trade reversal. Suppose that $(P_0)$ has a solution with some unemployment. Then, from (63),

$$(68) \quad -\frac{1 - \theta_1}{\theta_1 - \theta_2} - \varepsilon_e + \left(1 + \frac{hz^*}{x}\right) \frac{pg'(p)}{g(p)} = 0$$

Now trade reverses if and only if $x < z^*$ or, in view of (68), if and only if

$$(69) \quad \varepsilon_e + \frac{1 - \theta_1}{\theta_1 - \theta_2} - (1 + h) \frac{pg'(p)}{g(p)} > 0$$

If $\sigma_1 = \sigma_2 = \sigma_e \equiv \sigma$, (69) is equivalent to

$$(70) \quad \sigma < \frac{K}{K + K^*} \theta_W$$

Since the home country is relatively well endowed with labour, this restriction is tighter than (67).


## 6.    WORLD EQUILIBRIUM: COMPARATIVE STATICS

Our discussion of existence completed, we proceed to consider some related comparative statics questions. Specifically, we consider the impact of small changes in the factor endowments of the two countries on the equilibrium values of the factor rentals, the welfare of workers and the welfare of capitalists. For brevity, we confine ourselves to equilibria with production diversified in each country so that, in the notation of Figure 13, $\bar{w}$ lies between $w(p^{nu})$ and $w(p^J)$.

With production incompletely specialized everywhere, the response of factor rewards and capitalist well-being to a small disturbance is the same in each country. The nature of the response can be determined once it is known how the commodity price ratio changes. Thus, from (3)–(6),

$$(71) \quad \frac{dw}{w} = -\frac{1 - \theta_1}{\theta_1 - \theta_2} \frac{dp}{p}$$

$$(72) \quad \frac{dr}{r} = -\frac{\theta_1}{\theta_1 - \theta_2} \frac{dp}{p}$$

$$(73) \quad \frac{du_w}{u_w} = - \left[ \frac{1 - \theta_1}{\theta_1 - \theta_2} + \varepsilon_e(p) \right] \frac{dp}{p}$$

$$(74) \quad \frac{du_r}{u_r} = \left[ \frac{\theta_1}{\theta_1 - \theta_2} - \varepsilon_e(p) \right] \frac{dp}{p}$$

For the time being, then, we focus on the response of p. From (63) we obtain the equilibrium condition

$$(75) \quad \Delta \equiv - \frac{1 - \theta_1(p)}{\theta_1(p) - \theta_2(p)} - \varepsilon_e(p) + \frac{(1 + h)g(p)}{(1 + h)g(p) - hz^*} \frac{pg'(p)}{g(p)} = 0$$

Differentiating (75) totally and evaluating at $\Delta = 0$, we find that

$$(76) \quad \frac{dp}{p} = \alpha \left( \frac{dh}{h} + (1 + h) \frac{dz^*}{z^*} \right)$$

where

$$(77) \quad \alpha \equiv \frac{1}{-p(\partial\Delta/\partial p)} \frac{pg'(p)hz^*}{\left[ (1 + h)g(p) - hz^* \right]^2}$$

From the second-order condition for ($P_0$), $\partial\Delta/\partial p < 0$. Moreover, setting $x = z$ in (55) we obtain the condition of preunion equilibrium,

$$ED_2^{nu}(p) \equiv \left\{ \frac{e'(p)}{e(p)} \left[ w(p)z + r(p) \right] - \left[ w'(p)z + r'(p) \right] \right\}$$

$$+ h \left\{ \frac{e'(p)}{e(p)} \left[ w(p)z^* + r(p) \right] - \left[ w'(p)z^* + r'(p) \right] \right\} = 0,$$

with stability condition $dED_2^{nu}/dp < 0$ which, as calculation shows, implies that

$$\sigma_1\theta_1(1 - \theta_1)(1 - \varepsilon_e) + \theta_2(1 - \theta_2)\varepsilon_e\theta_2 + \varepsilon_e(1 - \varepsilon_e)(\theta_1 - \theta_2)\sigma_e > 0$$

From (64), therefore, sign $g'(p) = $ sign $(\theta_1 - \theta_2)$. Hence

$$(78) \quad \text{sign } \alpha = \text{sign } (\theta_1 - \theta_2)$$

Given the definitions of h, z and $z^*$, it is now a simple matter to relate w, r, $u_w$ and $u_r$ to the ultimate disturbances in $\bar{N}$, $\bar{N}^*$, K and $K^*$. The results of that exercise are summarized in Table 1.

### Table 1

THE COMPARATIVE STATICS OF WORLD EQUILIBRIUM:
PRODUCTION DIVERSIFIED IN BOTH COUNTRIES

| Endogenous Variable / Parameter | $\hat{p}$ | | $\hat{w}$ | $\hat{r}$ | $\hat{U}$ | $\hat{u}_w^*$ | $\hat{u}_r$ |
|---|---|---|---|---|---|---|---|
| | $\theta_1 > \theta_2$ | $\theta_2 > \theta_1$ | | | | | |
| $\hat{K}$ | − | + | + | − | + | + | − |
| $\hat{K}^*$ | − | + | + | − | + | + | − |
| $\hat{\bar{N}}$ | 0 | 0 | 0 | 0 | − | 0 | 0 |
| $\hat{N}^*$ | + | − | − | + | − | − | + |

The most notable feature of those results is their incomplete symmetry. Given the assumptions of incomplete specialization and uniformly homothetic preferences, it was to be expected that any change in the world stock of capital, wherever the change took place, would affect the listed variables in the same way. It was to be expected also that the incomplete unionization of the world work force would introduce an asymmetry into the effects of changes in the two national work forces. What is surprising, perhaps, is the extent of the asymmetry. Thus a change in the foreign work force has the usual Rybczynski effects on foreign outputs; and these in turn force the commodity price ratio and therefore factor rewards to change. A change in the home work force, on the other hand, has no effect on any of the variables. To understand why this is so, recall that, given commodity prices, the union seeks to maximize the wage bill and that, if there is unemployment, the wage bill is independent of the work force. From these facts we may infer that, given commodity prices, employment and outputs are unaffected by a change in the work force. The change therefore leaves commodity prices unchanged.

It remains to consider how the well-being of union members responds to each of the several disturbances. Bearing in mind that, for any parameter $\lambda$, $dU/d\lambda = \partial u/\partial \lambda$, we calculate from (62) that

$$(79) \quad \frac{dU}{U} = -\frac{dz}{z} + \frac{h(g(p) - z^*)}{(1 + h)g(p) - hz^*} \frac{dh}{h}$$

$$-\frac{hz^*}{(1 + h)g(p) - hz^*} \frac{dz^*}{z^*}$$

Recalling the definitions $z \equiv \bar{N}/K$, $z^* \equiv \bar{N}^*/K^*$ and $h \equiv K^*/K$, (79) reduces to

$$(80) \quad \frac{dU}{U} = -\frac{d\bar{N}}{\bar{N}} + \frac{g}{(1 + h)g - hz^*} \frac{dK}{K}$$

$$-\frac{hz^*}{(1 + h)g - hz^*} \frac{d\bar{N}^*}{\bar{N}^*} + \frac{hg}{(1 + h)g - hz^*} \frac{dK^*}{K^*}$$

Evidently U is negatively related to the size of the home work force, an increase in which spreads a given wage bill more thinly. On the other hand, an increase in the foreign work force (or a decline in the foreign stock of capital) raises the relative world output of the labour-intensive commodity, depresses the price of that commodity and reduces the well-being of labour.

An alternative diagrammatical formulation of the union's problem will serve to clarify the results summarized by Table 1. From (61) and (62) the union's problem is to maximize $U = (N/\bar{N})w(p)/e(p)$ subject to $N = (K + K^*)g(p) - \bar{N}^*$. From the Stolper-Samuelson Theorem, however, p is a function of $u_w$. Hence the union's problem can be re-written as

$$(P_0') \quad \max_{u_w, N} \quad U = (N/\bar{N})u_w$$

$$\text{s.t.} \quad N = (K + K^*)G(u_w) - \bar{N}^*$$

where $G(u_w) \equiv g(p(u_w))$.

**LEMMA:** If the preunion world equilibrium is stable for all factor endowments then $G'(u_w) < 0$.

**PROOF** If the preunion equilibrium is stable then the numerator of (64) is positive and, therefore, sign $[g'(p)]$ = sign $[\theta_1 - \theta_2]$. On the other hand, from the Stolper-Samuelson Theorem, sign $[du_w/dp]$ = sign $[d(w(p)/e(p))/dp]$ = sign $[\theta_1 - \theta_2]$. Thus

$$\text{sign } [G(u_w)] = \text{sign } [g'(p)] \text{ sign } \frac{d}{dp} \left( \frac{w(p)}{e(p)} \right) < 0$$

Now consider Figure 14, in which AB depicts the constraint of $(P'_0)$, $U'U'$ is a contour line of $U = (N/\bar{N})u_w$ and E represents an initial union-ridden equilibrium. It is a simple matter to determine how the constraint set, and therefore $u_w$ and N, respond to changes in the several factor endowments. Going a step farther, one can determine the response of p to any disturbance. Suppose, for example, that $\bar{N}^*$ increases. Inspection of the constraint of $(P'_0)$ shows that AB shifts vertically down by a constant amount $\Delta \bar{N}^*$. Thus the slope of the new curve A'B' at E' is the same as that of the old curve AB at E. Since the contour lines of U are hyperbolic the new equilibrium value of $u_w$ must be smaller than its initial value $u_w^0$. It then follows from the Stolper-Samuelson Theorem that p must increase or decrease according as $\theta_1$ is less than or greater than $\theta_2$.                    ◊

## 7.    INTERNATIONALLY-MOBILE CAPITAL

To this point in our discourse it has been assumed that both labour and capital are internationally immobile. We now relax that assumption and consider some of the implications of capital mobility. To make the contrasts as sharp as possible, it is assumed that capital is perfectly mobile, implying that, if some capital is employed in each country, earnings are equalized between countries. As in Sections 5 and 6 it is assumed that there is a common world technology and that preferences are everywhere the same and homothetic. It is assumed also that each country has the same population; however this assumption is a matter of convenience only.

### Equilibrium

Consider the preunion equilibrium. Since capital is mobile and the same constant-returns technology prevails everywhere, the two econo-

**Figure 14**

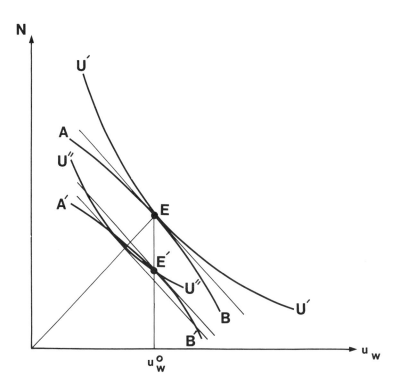

mies behave like one. In particular, the world stock of capital is divided between the two countries in such a way that each country is incompletely specialized, at least incipiently. Of course, the allocation is not unique. Formally, the market-clearing condition is

$$(81) \quad \frac{e'(p)}{e(p)} \left[ (\bar{N} + \bar{N})w(p) + (K + K^*)r(p) \right]$$

$$- \left[ (\bar{N} + \bar{N})w'(p) + (K + K^*)r'(p) \right] = 0$$

Let us continue to denote by $p^{nu}$ the preunion world equilibrium price ratio. Thus $p^{nu}$ is the solution to (81).

It will be convenient to refer also to $p^0$, the solution to the market-clearing equation

$$(82) \quad \frac{e'(p)}{e(p)} \left[ \bar{N}w(p) + (K + K^*)r(p) \right] - \left[ \bar{N}w'(p) + (K + K^*)r'(p) \right] = 0$$

Evidently $p^0$ would be the equilibrium price ratio if the entire world stock of capital were employed in one country. Let us recall that $\omega_i(z)$ is the solution to $z = c_w^i(\omega,1)/c_r^i(\omega,1)$ and define

$$\underline{p}(z) = \min_{i=1,2} \frac{c^2(\omega_i(z),1)}{c^1(\omega_i(z),1)}$$

$$\bar{p}(z) = \max_{i=1,2} \frac{c^2(\omega_i(z),1)}{c^1(\omega_i(z),1)}$$

It will be assumed that

$$(83) \quad \max \left\{ \underline{p}\left( \frac{\bar{N}}{K + K^*} \right), \underline{p}\left( \frac{2\bar{N}}{K + K^*} \right) \right\} < p^{nu},$$

$$p^0 < \min \left\{ \bar{p}\left( \frac{\bar{N}}{K + K^*} \right), \bar{p}\left( \frac{2\bar{N}}{K + K^*} \right) \right\}$$

This condition ensures that, whatever the union's choice of wage rate, there is incomplete specialization of home production. Given incomplete specialization,

$$(84) \quad \text{sign } (p^{nu} - p^0) = \text{sign } (\theta_1 - \theta_2) > 0$$

Now consider Figure 15. The preunion equilibrium at A is disturbed by the imposition by the union of a minimum wage $\bar{w}$. If $\bar{w}$ is less than $w(p^{nu})$ then it is ineffective and the equilibrium remains at A; and if $\bar{w}$ is greater than $w(p^0)$ then the entire stock of capital flows to the foreign country and the equilibrium moves to B. Suppose then that the union sets $\bar{w} = \bar{w}_E$, where $\bar{w}_E$ lies between $w(p^{nu})$ and $w(p^0)$. The commodity price ratio must fall to $p^E$, defined by $\bar{w}_E = w(p^E)$. For suppose that $p > p^E$; specifically, suppose that $p = p^{nu}$. Then the home rental rate would be $F\bar{w}_E$, which is lower than the foreign rental rate $r(p^{nu})$, and the entire world stock of capital would flow to the foreign country. But in that event there would be an excess supply of the relatively capital-intensive second commodity and the commodity price ratio would fall. (We have confirmed already that $p^0 < p^{nu}$.) Suppose alternatively that $p < p^E$; specifically, suppose that $p = p^0$. Then the home rental rate would be $G\bar{w}_E$, which is greater than the foreign rate $r(p^0)$, and the entire world stock of capital would flow to the home first industry, creating an excess demand for the second good.

We can now formulate the union's problem as that of finding

$$(P_3) \quad \max_{N,\, p} \quad U = \frac{w(p)N}{e(p)\bar{N}}$$

subject to

$$(85) \quad \frac{e'(p)}{e(p)} \left[ (N + \bar{N})w(p) + (K + K^*)r(p) \right]$$

$$- \left[ (N + \bar{N})w'(p) + (K + K^*)r'(p) \right] = 0$$

However, recalling (61), we can rewrite (85) as

$$(85') \quad N = g(p)(K + K^*) - \bar{N}$$

Substituting for N in $(P_3)$, the latter reduces to

$$(P_3') \quad \max_p \quad U = \frac{w(p)}{\bar{z}e(p)} \left[ g(p) - \bar{z} \right]$$

where $\bar{z} \equiv \bar{N}/(K + K^*)$. As we have just noticed, the chosen value of p must lie in the compact interval $[p^0, p^{nu}]$. Hence the problem has a solution.

CHAPTER 2

# Figure 15

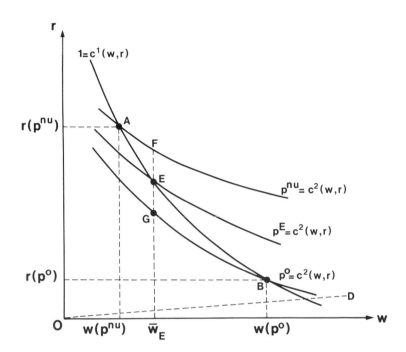

Does the solution to (P'$_3$) involve unemployment? One sees intuitively that there will be unemployment if the several elasticities of substitution are sufficiently small. For a more precise condition, however, one must resort to calculation. Thus, differentiating (P'$_3$),

$$(86) \quad \frac{d\log U}{d\log p} = \frac{1 - \theta_1(p)}{\theta_1(p) - \theta_2(p)} - \varepsilon_e(p) + \frac{g(p)}{g(p) - \bar{z}} \frac{pg'(p)}{g(p)}$$

Evidently the union-ridden equilibrium involves some unemployment if

$$(87) \quad \left. \frac{d\log U}{d\log p} \right|_{p=p^{nu}} < 0$$

Now, at $p = p^{nu}$, $g = 2\bar{N}/(K + K^*)$, and (87) is equivalent to

$$(88) \quad - \frac{1 - \theta_1(p^{nu})}{\theta_1(p^{nu}) - \theta_2(p^{nu})} - \varepsilon_e(p^{nu}) + \frac{2\bar{N}}{K + K^*} \frac{g'(p^{nu})}{g(p^{nu})} < 0$$

Moreover, if $\sigma_1 = \sigma_2 = \sigma_e = \sigma$ then $pg'/g = \sigma/(\theta_1 - \theta_2)$ and (88) reduces to

$$(89) \quad \frac{2\bar{z}\sigma - \{1 - [(1 - \varepsilon_e)\theta_1 + \varepsilon_e\theta_2]\}}{\theta_1 - \theta_2} < 0$$

From (61), however,

$$(90) \quad 1 - [(1 - \varepsilon_e)\theta_1 + \varepsilon_e\theta_2] = \frac{(K + K^*)r}{2\bar{N}w + (K + K^*)r} \equiv 1 - \theta$$

where $\theta$ is the world wage bill as a proportion of world income. It follows from (89) and (90) that if $\theta_1 > \theta_2$ and $\sigma < \theta/(2\bar{z})$ then the union-ridden equilibrium must involve some unemployment.

Suppose that in the union-ridden equilibrium there is some unemployment. Then the effect of the union is to raise the real wage everywhere, to raise the well-being of workers at home and abroad, but especially abroad $(\Delta u_w/u_w > \Delta U/U = \Delta U/u_w)$, to depress the real rental of capital and the well-being of capitalists everywhere, to force the relative price of the second commodity up or down according as $\theta_1$ is less than or greater than $\theta_2$, and therefore to raise or lower the relative world output of the second commodity according as $\theta_1$ is greater than or less than $\theta_2$. These propositions either are inherent in the preceding discussion or follow straightforwardly from the assumption of uniform homothetic preferences.

## Comparative Statics

We now calculate the responses of the equilibrium values to small changes in the national factor endowments. The results of the calculations are not at all surprising and, for that reason, are presented without comment.

Recalling (86) we see that, in any union-ridden equilibrium with unemployment,

$$(91) \quad \Delta \equiv \frac{g(p)}{g(p) - \bar{z}} \frac{pg'(p)}{g(p)} - \frac{\theta_1(p)}{\theta_1(p) - \theta_2(p)} - \varepsilon_e(p) = 0$$

Differentiating, we obtain

$$(92) \quad \frac{dp}{d\bar{z}} = \frac{pg'(p)}{-(\partial\Delta/\partial p)(g(p) - \bar{z})^2}$$

where $\partial\Delta/\partial p < 0$ and, in view of (64),

$$(93) \quad \text{sign} \left( \frac{dp}{d\bar{z}} \right) = \text{sign} \ (\theta_1 - \theta_2) > 0$$

Given the sign of $dp/d\bar{z}$, it is a simple matter to calculate the direction in which the remaining variables move. Thus

$$(94) \quad \text{sign} \left( \frac{dw}{d\bar{z}} \right) = \text{sign} \left( \frac{dw}{dp} \right) \text{sign} \left( \frac{dp}{d\bar{z}} \right) < 0$$

$$(95) \quad \text{sign} \left( \frac{dr}{d\bar{z}} \right) = \text{sign} \left( \frac{dr}{dp} \right) \text{sign} \left( \frac{dp}{d\bar{z}} \right) > 0$$

$$(96) \quad \text{sign} \left( \frac{du_w}{d\bar{z}} \right) < 0$$

$$(97) \quad \text{sign} \left( \frac{du_r}{d\bar{z}} \right) > 0$$

and, resorting to the envelope theorem,

$$(98) \quad \frac{dU}{U} = -\frac{g(p)}{g(p) - \bar{z}} \frac{d\bar{z}}{\bar{z}}$$

Finally, substituting into (93)–(98) from the definition $\bar{z} \equiv \bar{N}/(K + K^*)$, we obtain Table 2.

### Table 2

### THE COMPARATIVE STATICS OF WORLD EQUILIBRIUM: CAPITAL INTERNATIONALLY MOBILE

| Endogenous Variable | $\hat{p}$ | | $\hat{w}$ | $\hat{r}$ | $\hat{U}$ | $\hat{u}_w^*$ | $\hat{u}_r$ |
|---|---|---|---|---|---|---|---|
| Parameter | $\theta_1 > \theta_2$ | $\theta_2 > \theta_1$ | | | | | |
| $\hat{z} = \hat{\bar{N}} - \hat{K}$ | + | − | − | + | − | − | + |

## FOOTNOTES

(1) Since $\theta_2(\omega) \equiv \omega c_w^2(\omega,1)/c^2(\omega,1)$,

$$\frac{\omega}{\theta_2(\omega)} \frac{d\theta_2(\omega)}{d\omega} = 1 + \frac{\omega c_{ww}^2(\omega,1)}{c_w^2(\omega,1)} - \frac{\omega c_w^2(\omega,1)}{\omega c^2(\omega,1)}$$

$$= 1 - \theta_2(\omega) - \frac{c_{wr}^2(\omega,1)}{c_w^2(\omega,1)} \quad \text{[homogeneity of } c^2\text{]}$$

$$= 1 - \theta_2(\omega) - \frac{c_r^2(\omega,1)}{c^2(\omega,1)} \frac{c^2(\omega,1)c_{wr}^2(\omega,1)}{c_r^2(\omega,1)c_w^2(\omega,1)}$$

$$= (1 - \theta_2) - (1 - \theta_2)\sigma_2$$

$$= (1 - \theta_2)(1 - \sigma_2)$$

(2) From these two equations, $N = N(\omega) \equiv c_w^2(\omega,1)/c_r^2(\omega,1)$. Then $f_2(N) \equiv 1/c_r^2(\omega(N),1)$.

CHAPTER THREE

THE SPECIFIC-FACTORS MODEL


The analysis of Chapter II was, deliberately, as conventional as possible. It was conducted in terms of the familiar Heckscher-Ohlin model modified to accommodate an all-embracing labour union. The model proved to be productive, in the sense of providing unambiguous answers to most of the questions put to it. However some implausible characteristics of the model, notably the jump discontinuity in the employment relation, left a residual uneasiness. Accordingly, in the present chapter we look at an alternative model. Specifically, we return to an older tradition and pose our questions to a suitably revised version of the turn-of-the-century specific-factors model of production and trade.


## 1.    ASSUMPTIONS

As in Chapter II, there are two trading countries, the home country and the foreign, with each country potentially producing $n$ ($n \geq 2$) tradeable consumption goods by means of a no-joint-products constant-returns technology. Each country is endowed with a homogeneous and intersectorally mobile work force of given size and with given stocks of $n$ other homogeneous factors, each specific to an industry in the sense that it cannot be moved from one industry to another. The assumption that there is only one mobile factor is highly restrictive; it reduces the field of application of the theory to the short run. However there are compensations for, if the home country is small, the assumption makes it possible to handle two hundred products as easily as two. For the most part, nothing is assumed about the physical characteristics of the $n$ specific factors. At one extreme, the factor specific to the jth industry might be a bundle of physically heterogeneous factors with the common property that each is quite useless in industries other than the jth. At another extreme, it is possible that some of the specific factors are physically identical; for example, the first pair may be machines installed (bolted down) in the first industry and machines of the same type installed in the second industry.

The unit cost functions are now written $c^i(w,r_i)$, where $r_i$ is the rental of the ith specific factor. All cost functions satisfy conditions [II.c.1]–[II.c.6].

Again as in Chapter II, individuals fall into one of two mutually exclusive classes. Thus an individual is either a worker who owns no capital or a capitalist who provides no labour. All workers have the same homothetic preferences and the same endowment of labour; by choice of units, each worker controls one unit of labour. Similarly, all capitalists have the same homothetic preferences and the same endowment of each of the n specific factors; again by choice of units, each capitalist owns one unit of each specific factor. The preferences of workers and capitalists have the properties assigned to them in Chapter II; in particular, the two expenditure functions satisfy [II.e.1]–[II.e.4].

In the home country there is a single labour union to which all workers belong. As in Chapter II, the objective of the union is to maximize $(N/\bar{N})u_w$.

Finally, throughout this chapter it is assumed that in each country all goods are produced. This amounts to assuming that the equilibrium commodity prices fall within certain bounds. If the production functions satisfy the Inada condition, that in each industry the marginal product of labour goes to infinity as the input of labour goes to zero, production will be diversified for all positive prices.


## 2.    EQUILIBRIUM OF A SMALL OPEN ECONOMY

In this section and the next two, we confine our attention to a small open economy. In the present section we consider some familiar questions about the existence and uniqueness of a union-ridden equilibrium. Then, in Sections 3 and 4, we pass on to questions of a comparative statics kind.

We begin by re-writing the union's objective as a function of the variable it controls, viz. the wage rate w. Since all goods are produced, we have the n price-equals-average-cost equations

(1)     $p_i = c^i(w, r_i)$          $i = 1, 2, ..., n$

To these we add the n full-employment conditions

(2)     $K_i = Y_i c_r^i(w, r_i)$          $i = 1, 2, ..., n$

where $K_i$ is the available stock of the ith specific factor and $c_r^i(w, r_i)$ $\equiv \partial c^i(w, r_i)/\partial r_i$. The level of employment is given by

$$N = \sum_{i=1}^{n} Y_i c_w^i(w, r_i)$$

or, in view of (1) and (2), by

(3)     $$N = \sum_{i=1}^{n} \frac{c_w^i(w, r_i)}{c_r^i(w, r_i)} K_i$$

Substituting from (3) into the union's objective function (II.2), we obtain

(4)     $$U = \frac{w}{e_w(\underline{p})\bar{N}} \sum_{i=1}^{n} \frac{c_w^i(w, r_i)}{c_r^i(w, r_i)} K_i$$

where $\underline{p} \equiv (p_1, ..., p_n)$ is the vector of commodity prices. Let us define $\omega_i \equiv w/r_i$, $i = 1, 2, ..., n$. Then, from (1) and the homogeneity of $c^i$, $\omega_i$ is a function of $w/p_i$, with

(5)     $$\frac{w/p_i}{\omega_i(w/p_i)} \frac{d\omega_i(w/p_i)}{d(w/p_i)} \equiv \frac{w/p_i}{\omega_i(w/p_i)} \omega_i'(w/p_i)$$

$$= \frac{1}{1 - \theta_i(\omega_i(w/p_i))}$$

Moreover, (4) can be re-written as

(4')     $$U = \frac{w}{e_w(\underline{p})\bar{N}} \sum \frac{c_w^i(w, r_i)}{c_r^i(w, r_i)} K_i$$

The union seeks that value of w which, given $p_i$, $K_i$ and $\bar{N}$, maximizes (4'). Differentiating (4') with respect to w, we obtain

(6)     $$\frac{\partial U}{\partial w} = \frac{1}{e_w(\underline{p})\bar{N}} \sum \gamma_i(w/p_i)K_i$$

where

$$\gamma_i(w/p_i) = \frac{c_w^i(\omega_i(w/p_i), 1)}{c_r^i(\omega_i(w/p_i), 1)} \left[ 1 - \frac{\sigma_i(\omega_i(w/p_i))}{1 - \theta_i(\omega_i(w/p_i))} \right]$$

What are the properties of $\gamma_i$? In Chapter II it was assumed that the equation $1 - \theta_2(\omega) - \sigma_2(\omega) = 0$ has a unique solution and that $\theta_2'(\omega) + \sigma_2'(\omega) > 0$. Let us now assume that similar conditions are satisfied in each industry; specifically, let us assume that

[a.1]   the equation $1 - \theta_i(\omega_i) - \sigma_i(\omega_i) = 0$ has a unique solution $\omega_i^0$, $i = 1, 2$,

and that

[a.2]   $\theta_i'(\omega_i) + \sigma_i'(\omega_i) > 0$,      $i = 1, 2$.

Given [a.1] and [a.2], we can be sure that

$$\gamma_i(w_i/p_i) \gtreqless 0 \text{ as } w \gtreqless w_i^0$$

where $w_i^0 \equiv p_i \omega_i^0$.  Hence

$$\sum \gamma_i(w/p_i)K_i \gtreqless 0 \text{ as } w \begin{cases} < \min \{w_1^0, ..., w_n^0\} \\ > \max \{w_1^0, ..., w_n^0\} \end{cases}$$

It follows from this inequality and the continuity of $\gamma_i(w/p_i)$ that there is a value of $w$, say $w^0$, which maximizes U.  Thus

(7)   $$\left. \frac{\partial U}{\partial w} \right|_{w = w^0} = \frac{1}{e_w(p)\bar{N}} \sum \gamma_i(w^0/p_i)K_i = 0$$

and

(8)   $$\left. \frac{\partial^2 U}{\partial w^2} \right|_{w = w^0} = \frac{1}{e_w(p)\bar{N}} \sum \frac{1}{p_i} \gamma_i'(w^0/p_i)K_i \leq 0$$

where $\gamma_i'(w/p_i) \equiv d\gamma_i(w/p_i)/d(w/p_i)$.
   The following propositions are almost immediate.

**PROPOSITION 1:** A small open economy has a union-ridden equilibrium if [a.1] and [a.2] are satisfied.

**PROPOSITION 2:** If [a.1] and [a.2] are satisfied and if either

(i)     $\max \{w_1^0, ..., w_n^0\}$ and $\min \{w_1^0, ..., w_n^0\}$ are sufficiently close or

(ii)    $\gamma_i'(w/p_i) < 0$ for $w/p_i > 0$ and $i = 1, 2$

then a small open economy has a unique union-ridden equilibrium.

Henceforth, it will be assumed that [a.1], [a.2] and at least one of (i) and (ii) are satisfied, so that there is a unique $w^0$ such that (7) and (8) are satisfied, (8) as a strict inequality.

That completes our formal discussion of existence. Let us pause, however, to clarify the meaning of the equilibrium condition (7). Given the definition of $\gamma_i(w/p_i)$, (7) implies that

(9)     $1 - \sum \lambda_i \dfrac{\sigma_i}{1 - \theta_i} = 0$

where $\lambda_i \equiv N_i/N$. Thus, in the union-ridden equilibrium, the weighted average over the n industries of the elasticity of the marginal product of labour $(\sigma_i/(1 - \theta_i))$ is equal to one. On the other hand, it is a condition of union-ridden equilibrium in the Heckscher-Ohlin model of Chapter II that $1 = \sigma_2/(1 - \theta_2)$; see (II.15). The similarity of (9) and (II.15) flows from the fact that the elasticity of any contour of U is minus one.

## 3.     THE COMPARATIVE STATICS OF SMALL-COUNTRY EQUILIBRIA (I)

As in Section II.3, we seek to pin down the response of employment, outputs, factor rewards and the welfare of workers and capitalists to exogenous changes in the terms of trade, factor endowments and technology. Re-introducing the Mill-Edgeworth parameter $\mu_i$, with $\mu_i = 1$ initially, the complete small-country model can be written as

(10)    $\sum \gamma_i \left[ \dfrac{w^0}{\mu_i p_i} \right] K_i = 0$

(11)    $r_i^0 = \dfrac{w^0}{\omega_i \left[ \dfrac{w^0}{\mu_i p_i} \right]}$

(12) $\quad N^0 = \sum N_i^0 = \sum \dfrac{c_w^i \left[ \omega_i \left[ \dfrac{w^0}{\mu_i p_i} \right], 1 \right]}{c_r^i \left[ \omega_i \left[ \dfrac{w^0}{\mu_i p_i} \right], 1 \right]} K_i$

(13) $\quad Y_i^0 = \dfrac{\mu_i K_i}{c_r^i \left[ \omega_i \left[ \dfrac{w^0}{\mu_i p_i} \right], 1 \right]}$

(14) $\quad U^0 = \dfrac{w^0 N^0}{r_w(p)\bar{N}}$

(15) $\quad u_r^0 = \dfrac{1}{e_r(p)} \sum K_i r_i^0$

where $u_r$ is proportional to the well-being of the typical capitalist.

## Changes in commodity prices

Differentiating (10) with respect to $p_j$, and recalling that $\mu_j = 1$, we obtain

(16) $\quad \dfrac{p_j dw^0}{w^0 dp_j} = \dfrac{\dfrac{1}{p_j} \gamma_j' \left[ \dfrac{w^0}{p_j} \right] K_j}{\sum \dfrac{1}{p_i} \gamma_i' \left[ \dfrac{w^0}{p_i} \right] K_i}$

which, in view of [a.2], implies that

(17) $\quad 0 < \dfrac{p_j}{w^0} \dfrac{dw^0}{dp_j} < 1$

Similarly, from (11),

(18) $\quad \dfrac{p_j}{r_i^0} \dfrac{dr_i^0}{dp_j} = - \dfrac{\theta_i}{1 - \theta_i} \dfrac{p_j}{w^0} \dfrac{dw^0}{dp_j} < 0 \quad (i \neq j)$

and

(19) $\dfrac{p_j}{r_j^0}\dfrac{dr_j^0}{dp_j} = \dfrac{1 - \theta_j \dfrac{p_j}{w^0}\dfrac{dw^0}{dp_j}}{1 - \theta_j} > 1$

Thus, collating the results described by (17)–(19),

(20) $\dfrac{dr_j^0}{r_j^0} > \dfrac{dp_j}{p_j} > \dfrac{dw^0}{w^0} > 0 > \dfrac{dr_i^0}{r_i^0}$

This set of inequalities has long been known to hold for union-free economies; see Haberler (1936, especially pp.193-198) and Jones (1971). What we have shown is that it holds for union-ridden economies too.

Having pinned down the impact of a change in $p_j$ on factor rewards let us now consider the response of sectoral and total employment. From (12),

(21) $\dfrac{p_j}{N_i^0}\dfrac{dN_i^0}{dp_j} = -\dfrac{\sigma_i}{1 - \theta_i}\dfrac{p_j}{w^0}\dfrac{dw^0}{dp_j} < 0 \qquad (i \neq j)$

(22) $\dfrac{p_j}{N_j^0}\dfrac{dN_j^0}{dp_j} = -\dfrac{\sigma_j}{1 - \theta_j}\left[1 - \dfrac{p_j}{w^0}\dfrac{dw^0}{dp_j}\right] > 0$

$\dfrac{p_j}{N^0}\dfrac{dN^0}{dp_j} = \dfrac{N_j^0}{N^0}\dfrac{\sigma_j}{1 - \theta_j} - \dfrac{p_j}{w^0}\dfrac{dw^0}{dp_j}\sum \dfrac{N_i^0}{N^0}\dfrac{\sigma_i}{1 - \theta_i}$

(23) $\qquad = \dfrac{N_j^0}{N^0}\dfrac{\sigma_j}{1 - \theta_j} - \dfrac{p_j}{w^0}\dfrac{dw^0}{dp_j}$

where the last equality follows from (9). Equations (21) and (22) show that employment in the jth industry increases and that employment in each of the other industries declines, as in a union-free economy. The response of total employment is of indeterminate sign.

The response of outputs to a change in $p_j$ can be inferred from (21) and (22). Alternatively, we can compute from (13) that

(24) $\dfrac{p_j}{Y_i^0}\dfrac{dY_i^0}{dp_j} = -\dfrac{\theta_i\sigma_i}{1 - \theta_i}\dfrac{p_j}{w^0}\dfrac{dw^0}{dp_j} < 0 \qquad (i \neq j)$

and

$$(25) \quad \frac{p_j}{Y_j^0} \frac{dY_j^0}{dp_j} = \frac{\theta_j \sigma_j}{1 - \theta_j} \left[ 1 - \frac{p_j}{w^0} \frac{dw^0}{dp_j} \right] > 0$$

There remains the task of determining the changes in the welfare of workers and capitalists induced by a change in commodity prices. Let us begin with the response of workers' welfare. We know that, without special restrictions on the technology, the directions in which the real wage and the level of employment change are ambiguous. It is to be expected, therefore, that the response of $U^0$ may be hard to pin down. From (12) and (14), with $\mu_i = 1$,

$$(26) \quad U^0 = \frac{w^0}{e_w(p)\bar{N}} \sum \frac{c_w^i(\omega_i(w^0/p_i), 1)}{c_r^i(\omega_i(w^0/p_i), 1)} K_i$$

Differentiating with respect to $p_i$, and appealing to the envelope theorem,

$$\frac{p_j}{U^0} \frac{dU^0}{dp_j} = \frac{p_j}{U^0} \frac{\partial U^0}{\partial p_j}$$

$$(27) \qquad\qquad = \frac{\sigma_j}{1 - \theta_j} \frac{N_j^0}{N^0} - \varepsilon_e^{wj}$$

where $\varepsilon_e^{wj} \equiv (p_j/e_w)(\partial e_w/\partial p_j)$. As expected, the sign of (27) is indeterminate. To remove the indeterminacy we introduce several additional assumptions about the technology available to the economy and about the preferences of workers and capitalists. Similar assumptions were made by Jones and Ruffin (1977) in their study of a union-free specific-factors economy. First, it is assumed that the jth industry is technologically unbiased in the double sense that (a) the elasticity of labour's marginal product in the jth industry, $\sigma_j/(1 - \theta_j)$, is precisely equal to the economy-wide average, so that, making use of (9),

$$(28) \quad \frac{\sigma_j}{1 - \theta_j} = \sum \frac{N_i^0}{N^0} \frac{\sigma_i}{1 - \theta_i} = 1;$$

and that (b) the proportion of the labour force employed by the jth industry is precisely equal to the proportion of national income contributed by the jth industry:

$$(29) \quad \frac{N_j^0}{N^0} = \frac{p_j Y_j^0}{\Sigma \, p_i Y_i^0}$$

Second, it is assumed that workers spend on the jth good precisely the same proportion of their income as the rest of the community:

$$(30) \quad \varepsilon_e^{wj} = \frac{p_j D_j^0}{\Sigma \, p_i Y_i^0}$$

Given these assumptions, (27) reduces to

$$(27') \quad \frac{p_j}{U^0} \frac{dU^0}{dp_j} = \frac{p_j}{\Sigma \, p_i Y_i^0} (Y_j^0 - D_j^0)$$

Thus if the preferences of workers are typical of the community as a whole and if the technology available to the jth industry is average in the sense of (28) and (29) then a small increase in the price of the jth good causes the welfare of workers to improve or deteriorate according as the jth good is exported or imported. Thus the Jones-Ruffin restrictions are efficacious both in union-ridden and in union-free economies. However those restrictions are very strict indeed.

Finally, let us see how the welfare of a typical capitalist responds to a change in $p_j$. Differentiating (15) with respect to $p_j$, and recalling (18) and (19), we obtain

$$\frac{p_j}{u_r^0} \frac{\partial u_r^0}{\partial p_j} = \sum_h \left[ \frac{r_h^0 K_h}{\Sigma \, r_i^0 K_i} \right] \left[ \frac{p_j}{r_h^0} \frac{\partial r_h^0}{\partial p_j} \right] - \varepsilon_e^{rj}$$

$$= \frac{r_j^0 K_j}{\Sigma r_i^0 K_i} \frac{1}{(1 - \theta_j)} - \left[ \frac{p_j}{w^0} \frac{\partial w^0}{\partial p_j} \right] \sum_h \frac{w^0 N_h^0}{\Sigma \, r_i^0 K_i} - \varepsilon_e^{rj}$$

$$(31) \qquad = \frac{1}{1 - \theta} \left[ \frac{p_j Y_j^0}{Y^0} - \left[ \frac{p_j}{w^0} \frac{\partial w^0}{\partial p_j} \right] \theta - \varepsilon_e^{rj} (1 - \theta) \right]$$

where $Y^0 \equiv \Sigma p_i Y_i^0$ and $\theta \equiv w^0 N^0 / Y^0$. The sign of (31) is indeterminate. To remove the indeterminacy we again resort to special assumptions about the available technology and about the preferences of workers and capitalists. Thus it is assumed that the jth industry is technologically unbiased in the double sense that

$$(32) \quad \frac{1}{p_j} \gamma_j' \left[ \frac{w^0}{p_j} \right] = \Sigma \frac{1}{p_i} \gamma_i' \left[ \frac{w^0}{p_i} \right] \frac{K_i}{\bar{K}} \quad (\bar{K} \equiv \Sigma K_i)$$

and that

$$(33) \quad \frac{p_j Y_j^0}{K_j} = \frac{Y^0}{\bar{K}}$$

(Here $\bar{K}$ can be interpreted as an index of aggregate capital. However it is assumed neither that the index can be inserted into an aggregate production function nor, even, that all $K_i$ have the same physical characteristics.) We revert also to the assumption that capitalists spend on the jth good exactly the same proportion of their incomes as the rest of the community:

$$(30') \quad \varepsilon_e^{rj} = \frac{p_j D_j^0}{\Sigma p_i Y_i^0}$$

Given these assumptions, (31) reduces to

$$(34) \quad \frac{p_j}{u_r^0} \frac{\partial u_r^0}{\partial p_j} = \frac{p_j}{Y^0} (Y_j^0 - D_j^0)$$

Thus if the preferences of capitalists are typical of the community as a whole and if the technology available to the jth industry is average in the sense of (32) and (33) then a small increase in the price of the jth good causes the welfare of capitalists to improve or deteriorate according as the jth good is exported or imported. However, again, the conditions are very strict.

## Changes in specific factor endowments

Consider first some of the implications of a small change in the endowment of one of the specific factors. Differentiating (10) with respect to $K_j$, and setting $\mu_j = 1$, we obtain

$$(35) \quad \frac{K_j}{w^0} \frac{dw^0}{dK_j} = - \frac{\gamma_j'(w^0/p_j)K_j}{\Sigma(w^0/p_i)\gamma_i'(w^0/p_i)K_i}$$

It follows that

$$\text{sign}\left[\ \frac{K_j}{w^0}\frac{dw^0}{dK_j}\ \right] = \text{sign}\left[\ \gamma_j\left[\ \frac{w^0}{P_j}\ \right]\right]$$

$$= \text{sign}\left[\ 1 - \frac{\sigma_j}{1 - \theta_j}\ \right]$$

$$(36)\qquad = \text{sign}\left[\ \sum \lambda_i\ \frac{\sigma_i}{1 - \theta_i} - \frac{\sigma_j}{1 - \theta_j}\ \right]\qquad [\text{from (9)}]$$

From (1), on the other hand,

$$(37)\qquad \frac{dw}{dr_i} = -\ \frac{c_w^i}{c_r^i} = -\ \frac{N_i}{K_i} < 0$$

so that, recalling (36),

$$(38)\qquad \text{sign}\left[\ \frac{K_j}{r_i}\frac{dr_i}{dK_j}\ \right] = \text{sign}\left[\ \frac{\sigma_j}{1 - \theta_j} - \sum \lambda_i\ \frac{\sigma_i}{1 - \theta_i}\ \right]$$

Thus the wage rate increases or decreases (and the rental of each specific factor decreases or increases) according as the elasticity of the marginal product of labour in the jth industry is, respectively, smaller or greater than the economy-wide average. (If the jth industry is unbiased in the sense of (28) then (36) is zero.) This conclusion contrasts sharply with the corresponding result for union-free economies. In the absence of a labour union, an increase in the endowment of a specific factor necessarily forces up the wage rate and, therefore, forces down the rentals of all specific factors. The reason for the disparity of conclusions is not hard to find. In a union-free economy the level of employment is independent of changes in the endowments of specific factors. But in a union-ridden economy the level of employment is at the discretion of the union. In response to a change in $K_j$ the union might choose to raise employment to such a level that the wage rate falls. Indeed, switching our attention to the level of employment, we calculate from (12) that

$$(39)\qquad \frac{K_j}{N_i^0}\frac{dN_i^0}{dK_j} = -\ \frac{\sigma_i}{1 - \theta_i}\ \frac{K_j}{w^0}\frac{dw^0}{dK_j}\qquad (i \neq j)$$

(40) $\dfrac{K_j}{N_j^0} \dfrac{dN_j^0}{dK_j} = 1 - \dfrac{\sigma_j}{1 - \theta_j} \dfrac{K_j}{w^0} \dfrac{dw^0}{dK_j}$

and

$$\dfrac{K_j}{N^0} \dfrac{dN^0}{dK_j} = \dfrac{N_j^0}{N^0} - \dfrac{K_j}{w^0} \dfrac{dw^0}{dk_j} \sum \left[ \dfrac{N_j^0}{N^0} \right] \dfrac{\sigma_i}{1 - \theta_i}$$

(41)     $= \dfrac{N_j^0}{N^0} - \dfrac{K_j}{w^0} \dfrac{dw^0}{dK_j}$       [from (9)]

Thus if the elasticity of the marginal productivity of labour in the jth industry is at least as great as the economy-wide average, so that the wage rate fails to increase, then not only total employment but also employment in each industry will increase. It is easy to see that, under the same sufficient condition, the output of each industry will increase. In the absence of a union, that outcome is impossible.

Finally, we consider the implications of a change in $K_j$ for the well-being of workers and capitalists. (The number of capitalists is held constant.)

We know that the real wage may go up or down in response to an increase in $K_j$. This suggests that the direction of the response of workers' well-being may be ambiguous. However we also know that if the real wage declines then the level of employment must increase. Indeed we know that the level of employment must increase even when the real wage rises moderately; and this suggests that workers' well-being must rise. In fact, from (12) and (14),

(42)   $U^0 = \dfrac{w^0}{e_w(p)\bar{N}} \sum \dfrac{c_w^i(\omega_i(w^0/p_i),\, 1)}{c_r^i(\omega_i(w^0/p_i),\, 1)} K_i$

so that, differentiating with respect to $K_j$,

(43)   $\dfrac{K_j}{U^0} \dfrac{dU^0}{dK_j} = \dfrac{K_j}{U^0} \dfrac{\partial U^0}{\partial K_j} = \dfrac{N_j^0}{N^0}$

This implies that

(44)   $0 < \dfrac{K_j}{U^0} \dfrac{dU^0}{dK_j} < 1$

This finding may be understood by pretending that adjustment to the injection of capital takes place in two stages. In the first stage, the union holds employment at a constant level, allowing the real wage and the workers' well-being to rise. In the second stage, the union adjusts the level of employment in the direction which further increases the well-being of its members.

Switching our attention to the capitalists, we calculate from (15) that

$$(45) \quad \frac{K_j}{u_r^0} \frac{du_r^0}{dK_j} = \frac{1}{(\Sigma \, r_h^0 \, K_h)} \left[ w^0 N^0 \left[ \frac{K_j}{w^0} \frac{dw^0}{dK_j} \right] + r_j^0 K_j \right]$$

As was to be expected, the sign is indeterminate; it depends on the elasticity of the marginal productivity of labour in each industry. If the jth industry is unbiased in the sense of (28) then, from (36), $dw^0/dK_j = 0$ and (45) reduces to

$$(46) \quad 0 < \frac{K_j}{u_r^0} \frac{du_r^0}{dK_j} = \frac{r_j^0 K_j}{(\Sigma \, r_h^0 \, K_h)} < 1$$

Moreover the indeterminacy of response disappears if the endowments of all specific factors increase in the same proportion. Thus, differentiating (15) with respect to $K_j$, with $dK_i/K_i = dK_j/K_j$, $i \neq j$, we obtain

$$(47) \quad \frac{du_r^0}{u_r^0} = \frac{1}{\Sigma \, r_h^0 K_h} \Sigma \, r_i^0 K_i \frac{dK_i}{K_i} + \frac{1}{\Sigma \, r_h^0 K_h} \Sigma \, r_i^0 K_i \frac{dr_i^0}{r_i^0}$$

However, from (6), $w^0$ is homogeneous of degree zero in the vector $(K_1, ..., K_n)$. It follows that an equiproportionate change in all $K_i$ does not change $w^0$ and therefore does not change $r_i^0$. Applying this result to (47), we find that

$$(48) \quad \frac{K}{u_r^0} \frac{du_r^0}{dK} = 1$$

where $dK/K = dK_i/K_i$ $(i = 1, ..., n)$.

## Changes in the work force

Simple inspection of (10)–(15) reveals that an increase in the work force leaves unchanged the equilibrium values of all variables except workers' welfare. This outcome contrasts sharply with its counterpart in a union-free economy. The response of workers' welfare can be calculated, from (42) and the envelope theorem, to be

$$(49) \quad \frac{\bar{N}}{U^0} \frac{dU^0}{d\bar{N}} = \frac{\bar{N}}{U^0} \frac{\partial U^0}{\partial \bar{N}} = -1$$

Any addition to the work force means that the unchanged optimal $Nu_w$ must be more thinly shared.

## Technical improvements

Inspection of (10)–(15) reveals that an increase in $\mu_j$ has the same implications for factor rewards, for sectoral and total employment levels, and for the output of the ith commodity $(i \neq j)$ as does an increase in $p_j$. We may concentrate therefore on the responses of $U^0$, $u_r$ and $Y_j$. The last of these may be disposed of at once. Thus, from (13),

$$(50) \quad \frac{\mu_j}{Y_j^0} \frac{dY_j}{d\mu_j} = 1 + \frac{\sigma_j\theta_j}{1 - \theta_j} \left[ 1 - \frac{\mu_j}{w^0} \frac{dw^0}{d\mu_j} \right] > 1$$

As for $U^0$, we have, from (14) and (23),

$$\frac{\mu_j}{U^0} \frac{dU^0}{d\mu_j} = \frac{\mu_j}{w^0} \frac{dw^0}{d\mu_j} + \frac{\mu_j}{N^0} \frac{dN^0}{d\mu_j}$$

$$(51) \quad = \frac{N_j^0}{N^0} \frac{\sigma_j}{1 - \theta_j} > 0$$

Finally, from (15), then (18) and (19),

$$\frac{\mu_j}{u_r^0} \frac{du_r^0}{d\mu_j} = \frac{1}{e_r u_r^0} \sum K_i r_i^0 \left[ \frac{\mu_j}{r_i^0} \frac{dr_i^0}{d\mu_j} \right]$$

$$= \frac{1}{\sum K_i r_i^0} \sum K_i r_i^0 \left[ \frac{p_j}{r_i^0} \frac{dr_i^0}{dp_j} \right]$$

$$(52) \quad = \frac{1}{1 - \theta} \left[ \frac{p_j Y_j^0}{Y^0} - \theta \left[ \frac{p_j}{w^0} \frac{dw^0}{dp_j} \right] \right]$$

This expression is of indeterminate sign. However, a technical improvement which is evenly shared by all industries gives rise to an unambiguous improvement in the well-being of capitalists; in fact, the well-being of capitalists moves in step with efficiency. Thus, if $d\mu_j/\mu_j = d\mu/\mu$ $(j = 1, ..., n)$ then, by inspection of (10)–(15),

$$(53) \quad \frac{dw^0}{w^0} = \frac{d_i^r}{r_i^0} = \frac{dU^0}{U^0} = \frac{du_r^0}{u_r^0} = \frac{dY_i^0}{Y_i^0} = \frac{d\mu}{\mu}$$

$$(54) \quad \frac{dN_i^0}{N_i^0} = \frac{dN^0}{N^0} = 0$$

## 4. THE COMPARARIVE STATICS OF SMALL-COUNTRY EQUILIBRIA (II)

In Section II.4 we examined some of the implications of an import-duty in the context of a union-modified Heckscher-Ohlin model. In particular, we set out the conditions under which a protective tariff would reduce unemployment and enhance the well-being of workers. We now repeat the performance in the context of specific factors.

The basic assumptions remain the same as in Section II.4. In particular, it is assumed that the tariff proceeds are divided between workers and capitalists in the same manner as earned income. Thus if the tariff proceeds, in terms of the arbitrary unit of account, are denoted by $\Delta$, and that part of them accruing to labour by $\Delta_w$, we have

$$(55) \quad \Delta_w/\Delta = wN/(wN + \Sigma K_i r_i)$$

Then, recalling that $\varepsilon_e^{wj}$ and $\varepsilon_e^{rj}$ are the proportions of their expenditures allocated by wage-earners and capitalists to the jth commodity,

$$(56) \quad \Delta = \frac{\tau}{1 + \tau} \left\{ \varepsilon_e^{wj}(p)(wN + \theta\Delta) + \varepsilon_e^{rj}(p) [\Sigma K_i r_i + (1 - \theta)\Delta] - p_j Y_j \right\}$$

or, solving,

$$(57) \quad \Delta = \frac{\dfrac{\tau}{1 + \tau} \left\{ \dfrac{p_j Y_j}{Y} - [\varepsilon_e^{wj} \theta + \varepsilon_e^{rj} (1 - \theta)] \right\} Y}{\dfrac{\tau}{1 + \tau} [\varepsilon_e^{wj} \theta + \varepsilon_e^{rj} (1 - \theta)] - 1}$$

From (56) and (57),

$$
(58) \quad \Delta_w = \frac{\dfrac{\tau}{1+\tau}\left\{\dfrac{p_j Y_j}{Y} - [\varepsilon_e^{wj}\theta + \varepsilon_e^{rj}(1-\theta)]\right\}wN}{\dfrac{\tau}{1+\tau}[\varepsilon_e^{wj}\theta + \varepsilon_e^{rj}(1-\theta)] - 1}
$$

It follows from (4) and (58) that

$$
U = \frac{wN + \Delta_w}{e_w(\underset{\sim}{p})\bar{N}}
$$

$$
(59) \quad = \frac{\dfrac{w}{e_w(\underset{\sim}{p})\bar{N}}\left[\sum \dfrac{c_w^i(\omega_i(w/p_i),1)}{c_r^i(\omega_i(w/p_i),1)}K_i\right]\left[\dfrac{\tau}{1+\tau}\left[\dfrac{p_j Y_j}{Y}\right] - 1\right]}{\dfrac{\tau}{1+\tau}\left[\varepsilon_e^{wj}\theta + \varepsilon_e^{rj}(1-\theta)\right] - 1}
$$

The union seeks that value of w for which U is a maximum, given
τ. Differentiating (59) with respect to w, we find that

$$
\frac{w}{U}\frac{\partial U}{\partial w} = \frac{1}{N}\sum \gamma_i(w/p_i)K_i + \frac{\dfrac{\tau}{1+\tau}\left[\dfrac{p_j Y_j}{Y}\right]}{\dfrac{\tau}{1+\tau}\left[\dfrac{p_j Y_j}{Y}\right] - 1}\frac{\partial \log\left[\dfrac{p_j Y_j}{Y}\right]}{\partial \log w}
$$

$$
(60) \quad - \frac{\dfrac{\tau}{1+\tau}\left[\varepsilon_e^{wj} - \varepsilon_e^{rj}\right]\theta}{\dfrac{\tau}{1+\tau}\left[\varepsilon_e^{wj}\theta + \varepsilon_e^{rj}(1-\theta)\right] - 1}\frac{\partial \log \theta}{\partial \log w}
$$

Suppose that $\partial U/\partial w = 0$ when $w = w^0$ and $\tau = 0$.

An initial free-trade equilibrium is disturbed by the imposition of
a small tariff. Equating (60) to zero, differentiating totally, and evaluating at $w = w^0$ and $\tau = 0$, we obtain

$$\frac{dw}{d\tau}\bigg|_{\tau=0} = \frac{-N}{[\sum \frac{1}{p_i} \gamma_i'(w^0/p_i)K_i]} \left\{ -\left[\frac{p_jY_j}{Y}\right] \frac{\partial\log(p_jY_j/Y)}{\partial\log w} \right.$$

$$\left. + (\varepsilon_e^{wj} - \varepsilon_e^{rj}) \, \theta \, \frac{\partial\log \theta}{\partial\log N} \right\}$$

(61)
$$= \frac{-N}{[\sum \frac{1}{p_i} \gamma_i'(w^0/p_i)K_i]} \left\{ -\left[\frac{p_jY_j}{Y}\right] \frac{\partial\log(p_jY_j/Y)}{\partial\log N} \right.$$

$$\left. + (\varepsilon_e^{wj} - \varepsilon_e^{rj}) \, \theta \, \frac{\partial\log \theta}{\partial\log N} \right\} \frac{\partial\log N}{\partial\log w}$$

This formidable expression can be simplified by appealing to properties of the national income function $Y(p_1, ..., p_n, N, K_1, ..., K_n)$. It is well known that

$$\partial Y/\partial p_i = Y_i, \quad \partial Y/\partial N = w, \quad \partial Y/\partial K_i = r_i$$

By further calculation,

(62a) $\partial^2 Y/\partial N^2 = \partial w/\partial N = -w^2/H < 0$

(62b) $\partial^2 Y/\partial N\partial p_i = \partial w/\partial p_i = \partial Y_i/\partial N = \dfrac{1}{H} \dfrac{\sigma_i\theta_i}{1-\theta_i} Y_i w > 0$

(62c) $\partial^2 Y/\partial p_i\partial p_j = \partial Y_j/\partial p_i = \partial Y_i/\partial p_j = -\dfrac{1}{H} \dfrac{\sigma_i\theta_i}{1-\theta_i} \dfrac{\sigma_j\theta_j}{1-\theta_j} Y_iY_j < 0$

(62d) $\partial^2 Y/\partial p_i^2 = \partial Y_i/\partial p_i$

$$= \frac{Y_i}{p_i} \frac{\sigma_i\theta_i}{1-\theta_i} \left[1 - \frac{1}{H}\left[\frac{\sigma_i\theta_i}{1-\theta_i}\right] p_iY_i\right] > 0$$

where

$$H \equiv \sum \frac{\sigma_i \theta_i}{1 - \theta_i} p_i Y_i$$

$$= wN \sum \frac{\sigma_i}{1 - \theta_i} \frac{N_i}{N}$$

(62e)      $= wN$                              [from (9)]

From (62a) and (62b),

$$\frac{\partial \log (p_j Y_j / Y)}{\partial \log N} = \frac{\theta Y}{H} \frac{\sigma_j \theta_j}{1 - \theta_j} - \theta$$

$$\frac{\partial \log \theta}{\log N} = \frac{\partial \log (Nw/Y)}{\partial \log N}$$

$$= -\theta \quad [\text{since } \partial \log(wN)/\partial \log N = 0 \text{ in equilibrium}]$$

and

$$\frac{\partial \log N}{\partial \log w} = -\frac{H}{Nw}$$

Hence (61) can be re-written as

$$(61') \quad \frac{dw}{d\tau}\bigg|_{\tau=0} = \frac{-N\theta}{[\sum \frac{1}{p_i} \gamma_i'(w^0/p_i)K_i]} \left\{ \frac{p_j Y_j}{Y} \left[ \frac{\sigma_j}{1 - \theta_j} \frac{\theta_j}{\theta} - 1 \right] \right.$$

$$\left. + \theta \left[ \varepsilon_e^{wj} - \varepsilon_e^{rj} \right] \right\}$$

which is the fundamental equation of this section.

The sign of (61') is indeterminate without further assumptions. Let us return therefore to the special assumptions of Section 3. We notice first that if the jth industry is technologically unbiased in the sense of (31) and (32) then $\sigma_j/(1 - \theta_j) = 1$, $\theta_j = \theta$ and, from (61'),

$$(62) \quad \text{sign} \left[ \left. \frac{dw}{d\tau} \right|_{\tau=0} \right] = \text{sign} \left( \varepsilon_e^{wj} - \varepsilon_e^{rj} \right)$$

Thus a protective tariff on imports of the jth commodity raises the union-ridden equilibrium wage rate if and only if wage-earners spend on the jth commodity a greater proportion of their incomes than do capitalists. Equation (62) may be compared with eq. (II.43). Thus, bearing in mind that $\varepsilon_e^w$ and $\varepsilon_e^r$ of Chapter II are the proportions of their total expenditures allocated by workers and capitalists to the exported and therefore *untaxed* second commodity, (II.43) can be rewritten in the notation of this chapter as

$$\text{sign} \left[ \left. \frac{d\omega_i}{d\tau} \right|_{\tau=0} \right] = \text{sign} \left[ \left. \frac{dw}{d\tau} \right|_{\tau=0} \right]$$

$$= \text{sign} \left( \varepsilon_e^{wj} - \varepsilon_e^{rj} \right) \qquad (i \neq j)$$

We notice next that if the jth industry is technologically unbiased in the sense of (31) and if workers' preferences for the jth commodity are neutral in the sense of (33) then, from (61'),

$$(63) \quad \text{sign} \left[ \left. \frac{dw}{d\tau} \right|_{\tau=0} \right] = \text{sign} \left( \theta_j - \theta \right)$$

That is, the tariff forces the wage rate up or down as the jth industry is more or less labour-intensive than the average over all industries.

Finally, we notice that if the jth commodity is atypical by criterion (31) but not by criteria (32) and (33) then, from (61'),

$$\text{sign} \left[ \left. \frac{dw}{d\tau} \right|_{\tau=0} \right] = \text{sign} \left[ \frac{\sigma_j}{1 - \theta_j} - 1 \right]$$

$$(64) \qquad = \text{sign} \left[ \frac{\sigma_j}{1 - \theta_j} - \sum \left[ \frac{N_i}{N} \right] \left[ \frac{\sigma_i}{1 - \theta_i} \right] \right]$$

That is, the tariff forces the wage rate up or down as the elasticity of labour's marginal product in the jth industry is above or below the economy-wide average.

Let us now switch our attention from the wage rate to the other variables of our model. From (11)–(13) and (59) we calculate that

$$(65a) \quad \frac{1}{r_i^0} \frac{dr_i^0}{d\tau}\bigg|_{\tau=0} = \frac{-\theta_i}{1-\theta_i} \frac{1}{w^0} \frac{dw^0}{d\tau}\bigg|_{\tau=0} \qquad (i \neq j)$$

$$(65b) \quad \frac{1}{r_j^0} \frac{dr_j^0}{d\tau}\bigg|_{\tau=0} = 1 - \frac{-\theta_j}{1-\theta_j} \frac{1}{w^0} \frac{dw^0}{d\tau}\bigg|_{\tau=0}$$

$$(66a) \quad \frac{1}{N_i^0} \frac{dN_i^0}{d\tau}\bigg|_{\tau=0} = \frac{-\sigma_i}{1-\theta_i} \frac{1}{w^0} \frac{dw^0}{d\tau}\bigg|_{\tau=0} \qquad (i \neq j)$$

$$(66b) \quad \frac{1}{N_j^0} \frac{dN_j^0}{d\tau}\bigg|_{\tau=0} = \frac{-\sigma_j}{1-\theta_j} \left[ 1 - \frac{1}{w^0} \frac{dw^0}{d\tau}\bigg|_{\tau=0} \right]$$

$$\frac{1}{N^0} \frac{dN^0}{d\tau}\bigg|_{\tau=0} = \sum \frac{N_i^0}{N^0} \left[ \frac{1}{N_i^0} \frac{dN_i^0}{d\tau}\bigg|_{\tau=0} \right]$$

$$= \frac{\sigma_j}{1-\theta_j} \frac{N_j^0}{N^0} - \left[ \sum \frac{N_i^0}{N^0} \frac{\sigma_i}{1-\theta_i} \right] \left[ \frac{1}{w^0} \frac{dw^0}{d\tau}\bigg|_{\tau=0} \right]$$

$$(66c) \qquad = \frac{\sigma_j}{1-\theta_j} \frac{N_j^0}{N^0} - \frac{1}{w^0} \frac{dw^0}{d\tau}\bigg|_{\tau=0}$$

$$(67a) \quad \frac{1}{Y_i^0} \frac{dY_i^0}{d\tau}\bigg|_{\tau=0} = - \frac{\sigma_i\theta_i}{1-\theta_i} \frac{1}{w^0} \frac{dw^0}{d\tau}\bigg|_{\tau=0} \qquad (i \neq j)$$

$$(67b) \quad \frac{1}{Y_j^0} \frac{dY_j^0}{d\tau}\bigg|_{\tau=0} = \frac{\sigma_j\theta_j}{1-\theta_j} \left[ 1 - \frac{1}{w^0} \frac{dw^0}{d\tau}\bigg|_{\tau=0} \right]$$

$$(68) \quad \frac{1}{U^0} \frac{dU^0}{d\tau}\bigg|_{\tau=0} = (1-\theta)(\varepsilon_e^{rj} - \varepsilon_e^{wj}) - \frac{p_j Y_j}{Y} + \frac{\sigma_j}{1-\theta_j} \frac{N_j^0}{N^0}$$

On the other hand,

$$u_r^0 = \frac{1}{e_r(p)} (\sum K_i r_i^0 + \Delta - \Delta_w)$$

(69)    $\quad = \dfrac{\Sigma K_i r_i}{e_r(p)} \left[ 1 + \dfrac{\Delta}{Y} \right] \qquad$ [since $\Delta - \Delta_w = \dfrac{\Sigma K_i r_i^0}{Y} \Delta$]

Hence

$$\dfrac{1}{u_r^0} \dfrac{du_r^0}{d\tau} \bigg|_{\tau=0} = - \varepsilon_e^{rj} + \left[ \dfrac{1}{\Sigma K_i r_i^0} \right] \left[ \Sigma K_i r_i^0 \left[ \dfrac{1}{r_i^0} \dfrac{dr_i^0}{d\tau} \bigg|_{\tau=0} \right] \right]$$

$$- \left\{ \dfrac{p_j Y_j}{Y} - [\varepsilon_e^{wj} \theta + \varepsilon_e^{rj}(1 - \theta)] \right\} \qquad \text{[from (57)]}$$

$$= \theta\,(\varepsilon_e^{wj} - \varepsilon_e^{rj}) - \dfrac{p_j Y_j}{Y} \left[ 1 - \dfrac{1 - \theta_j}{1 - \theta} \right] - \dfrac{\Sigma w^0 N_i^0}{\Sigma K_i r_i^0} \left[ \dfrac{1}{w^0} \dfrac{dw^0}{d\tau} \bigg|_{\tau=0} \right]$$

[from (66]

(70)    $\quad = - \left[ \dfrac{\theta}{1 - \theta} \right] \left[ \dfrac{\theta}{-\Sigma \dfrac{1}{p_i} \gamma K_i} \right] \left\{ \left[ \dfrac{p_j Y_j}{Y} \right] \left[ \left[ \dfrac{\sigma_j}{1 - \theta_j} \right] \dfrac{\theta_j}{\theta} - 1 \right] \right.$

$$\left. + \theta \left[ \varepsilon_e^{wj} - \varepsilon_e^{rj} \right] \right\}$$

The welfare implications of the tariff are summarized by (68) and (70). The signs of those expressions are not clear. Let us revert therefore to the special assumptions (28)–(30). From (61') and (68), we see that if (30) is satisfied, so that $\varepsilon_e^{wj} = \varepsilon_e^{rj}$, then

(71)    $\quad \text{sign} \left[ \dfrac{1}{U^0} \dfrac{dU^0}{d\tau} \bigg|_{\tau=0} \right] = \text{sign} \left[ \dfrac{1}{w^0} \dfrac{dw^0}{d\tau} \bigg|_{\tau=0} \right]$

$$= \text{sign} \left[ \dfrac{\sigma_j}{1 - \theta_j} \dfrac{\theta_j}{\theta} - 1 \right]$$

and that if the jth industry is unbiased in the sense of (28) and (29) then

$$(72) \quad \text{sign} \left[ \frac{1}{U^0} \frac{dU^0}{d\tau} \bigg|_{\tau=0} \right] = - \text{sign} \left[ \frac{1}{w^0} \frac{dw^0}{d\tau} \bigg|_{\tau=0} \right]$$

$$= \text{sign} \, (\varepsilon_e^{rj} - \varepsilon_e^{wj})$$

Equation (71) tells us that if workers and capitalists spend the same proportion of their incomes on the jth good then the greater is the elasticity of labour's marginal product in the jth industry and the more labour-intensive is the jth industry, the more likely is it that the tariff will raise the level of workers' well-being. And equation (72) tells us that if the jth industry is typical in the sense of (28) and (29) then the tariff will improve the lot of workers if the latter spend on the jth good a greater proportion of their incomes than capitalists.

Similarly, from (70) we see that if (29) and (30) are satisfied then

$$(73) \quad \text{sign} \left[ \frac{1}{u_r^0} \frac{du_r^0}{d\tau} \bigg|_{\tau=0} \right] = \text{sign} \left[ 1 - \frac{\sigma_j}{1 - \theta_j} \right]$$

and that if (28) and (30) are imposed then

$$(74) \quad \text{sign} \left[ \frac{1}{u_r^0} \frac{du_r^0}{d\tau} \bigg|_{\tau=0} \right] = \text{sign} \, (\theta - \theta_j)$$

## 5.   UNION-RIDDEN WORLD EQUILIBRIUM

We now dispense with the small-country assumption and re-examine our conclusions on the alternative assumption that each country (the home and the foreign) has some market power. For simplicity it will be assumed henceforth that all households have the same homothetic preferences, so that $e_w(p) = e_r(p) = e(p)$, and that the two countries share a common technology. Finally, it will be assumed that $n = 2$; accordingly we revert to the practice, familiar from Chapter II, of treating the first good as numeraire and writing $p \equiv p_2/p_1$.

### The union-distorted excess-demand curve

As in Section II.3, we begin by characterizing the union-distorted import or excess-demand function for the second good. This function can be written, quite generally, as

(75)  $ED_2 = \beta(p)Y(p, N, K_1, K_2) - Y_p(p, N, K_1, K_2)$

where $\beta(p) \equiv e'(p)/e(p)$ and Y is the revenue function, introduced in Section 2.

Suppose that the union sets a minimum wage $\bar{w}$. Then we can consider that function $p(\bar{w})$ which validates $\bar{w}$, in the sense of rendering it compatible with full employment; it is easy to see that $p(\bar{w})$ is the solution to the equation

(76)  $\bar{N} = \dfrac{c_w^1(\omega_1(\bar{w}), 1)}{c_r^1(\omega_1(\bar{w}), 1)} K_1 + \dfrac{c_w^2(\omega_2(\bar{w}/p), 1)}{c_r^2(\omega_2(\bar{w}/p), 1)} K_2$

In the pre-union situation,

(77)  $0 < \dfrac{pY_{Np}}{Y_N} = \dfrac{p}{w}\dfrac{dw}{dp} = \dfrac{\dfrac{N_2}{\bar{N}}\left[\dfrac{\sigma_2}{1 - \theta_2}\right]}{\dfrac{N_1}{\bar{N}}\left[\dfrac{\sigma_1}{1 - \theta_1}\right] + \dfrac{N_2}{\bar{N}}\left[\dfrac{\sigma_2}{1 - \theta_2}\right]} < 1$

so that, for $p > p(\bar{w})$, the minimum wage is ineffective. For $p > p(\bar{w})$, then, the price-slope of the excess-demand function is

(78)  $\dfrac{d}{dp} ED_2\Big|_{N=\bar{N}} = \beta'Y + \beta Y_p - Y_{pp}$

For $p < p(\bar{w})$, however, the minimum wage "binds" and employment settles at a level below $\bar{N}$. Excess demand is then described by (75), with N and p linked by the equation $\bar{w} = Y_N(p, N, K_1, K_2)$ and the slope of the excess-demand curve is

(79)  $\dfrac{d}{dp} ED_2\Big|_{w=\bar{w}} = \beta'Y + \beta\left[Y_p + Y_N\dfrac{dN}{dp}\Big|_{\bar{w}=Y_N}\right]$

$- \left[Y_{pp} + Y_{pN}\dfrac{dN}{dp}\Big|_{w=Y_N}\right]$

However,

$\dfrac{dN}{dp}\Big|_{\bar{w}=Y_N} = -\dfrac{Y_{Np}}{Y_{NN}}$

hence (79) can be re-written as

$$(79') \quad \frac{d}{dp} \, ED_2 \bigg|_{w=\bar{w}} = \beta'Y + \beta Y_p - Y_{pp} + \left[ \frac{Y_N Y_{Np}}{p Y_{NN}} \right] \left[ p\beta - \frac{p Y_{Np}}{Y_N} \right]$$

where, in view of (62a,b), $-(Y_N Y_{Np})/(p Y_{NN}) > 0$.  Thus, at $p = p(\bar{w})$,

$$\text{sign} \left[ \frac{d}{dp} \, ED_2 \bigg|_{w=\bar{w}} - \frac{d}{dp} \, ED_2 \bigg|_{N=\bar{N}} \right]$$

$$= \text{sign} \, (p\beta - p Y_{Np}/Y_N)$$

$$= \text{sign} \left[ p\beta - \frac{p}{w} \frac{dw}{dp} \bigg|_{N=\bar{N}} \right]$$

$$(80) \qquad = \text{sign} \left[ p\beta - \frac{\dfrac{N_2}{\bar{N}} \left[ \dfrac{\sigma_2}{1 - \theta_2} \right]}{\dfrac{N_1}{\bar{N}} \left[ \dfrac{\sigma_1}{1 - \theta_1} \right] + \dfrac{N_2}{\bar{N}} \left[ \dfrac{\sigma_2}{1 - \theta_2} \right]} \right]$$

Figures 1 and 2 display two alternative excess-demand curves, one for the case in which $p\beta > \dfrac{p}{w} \dfrac{dw}{dp} \bigg|_{N=\bar{N}}$ and one for the case in which the the inequality is reversed.

To understand these findings one must return to (77).  If $p$ declines, with $w$ held constant, the level of employment must decline; for $N$ and $w/p$ are negatively related.  The reduction in the level of employment causes the national income to decline by $Y_N \dfrac{dN}{dp} \bigg|_{\bar{w}=Y_N}$ which in turn causes the demand for the second good to decline by $\beta Y_N \dfrac{dN}{dp} \bigg|_{\bar{w}=Y_N}$.  On the other hand, the decline in employment entails a reduction in the output of the second good of $Y_{pN} \dfrac{dN}{dp} \bigg|_{\bar{w}=Y_N}$ Thus the position of the excess-demand curve $ED_2 \big|_{w=\bar{w}}$ is determined by the relative values of $\beta Y_N$ and $Y_{pN}$, that is, in view of (77), by

## Figure 1

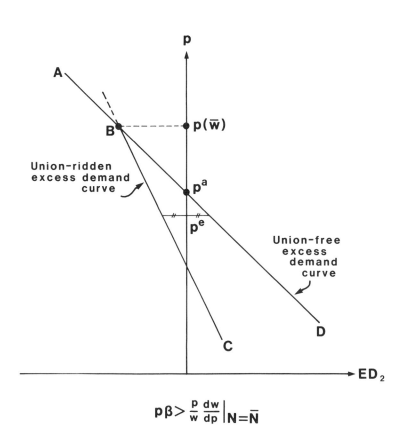

$$p\beta > \frac{p}{w}\frac{dw}{dp}\Big|_{N=\bar{N}}$$

## Figure 2

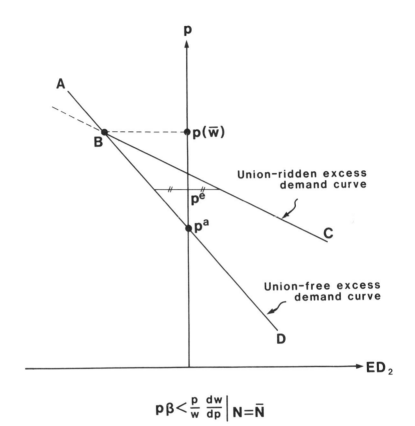

$$p\beta < \frac{p}{w}\frac{dw}{dp}\bigg|\, N=\bar{N}$$

the relative values of $\varepsilon_e$ and $\dfrac{p}{w}\dfrac{dw}{dp}\bigg|_{N=\bar{N}}$.

## World equilibrium with an arbitrary minimum wage

Suppose for the time being that the two countries are alike not only in tastes and technology but also in endowments. Then, in the absence of a home labour union, the home and foreign excess-demand curves will coincide and there will be no international trade; the world price ratio will settle at the pre-union autarkic level $p^a$. The same will be true if the union chooses a non-binding minimum wage, that is, a minimum wage not greater than its autarkic value $p^{-1}(p^a)$, for then $p(\bar{w}) \le p^a$. Trade can occur only if the union chooses a binding minimum wage, that is, a minimum wage greater than $p^{-1}(p^a)$, so that $p(\bar{w}) > p^a$. Let us assume that the condition is satisfied. Then we can distinguish two cases. If $p\beta > \dfrac{p}{w}\dfrac{dw}{dp}\bigg|_{N=\bar{N}}$ for $p \in [p^a, p(\bar{w})]$, the equilibrium world price $p^e$ is smaller than $p^a$, as in Figure 1; and, if the inequality goes the other way, $p^e$ is greater than $p^a$ and the home country exports the first good, as in Figure 2.

Now suppose that the union gradually raises the minimum wage above the critical level $p^{-1}(p^a)$. How do the union-distorted excess-demand curve and the equilibrium world price ratio respond? From (3), if $\bar{w} > p^{-1}(p^a)$ then

$$N = \frac{c_w^1(\omega_1(\bar{w}), 1)}{c_r^1(\omega_1(\bar{w}), 1)} K_1 + \frac{c_w^2(\omega_2(\bar{w}/p), 1)}{c_r^2(\omega_2(\bar{w}/p), 1)} K_2$$

On the other hand, for any given positive $p$, $\dfrac{d\omega_i}{\omega_i} \Big/ \dfrac{d\bar{w}}{\bar{w}} = \dfrac{1}{1 - \theta_i} > 1$,

implying that $\lim\limits_{\bar{w} \to \infty} \omega_i = \infty$. Hence, recalling the properties of the unit-cost functions (as described by [c.6] of Chapter II),

$$\lim_{\bar{w} \to \infty} = \frac{c_w^1(\omega_1(\bar{w}), 1)}{c_r^1(\omega_1(\bar{w}), 1)} = 0$$

$$\lim_{\bar{w} \to \infty} = \frac{c_w^2(\omega_2(\bar{w}/p), 1)}{c_r^2(\omega_2(\bar{w}/p), 1)} = 0 \quad \text{for any given } p > 0$$

and

(81)  $\lim_{\bar{w} \to \infty} N = 0$

Given (81) and [c.6], and recalling the definition of the revenue function in Section 2, we may verify that, for any given $p > 0$,

(82)  $\lim_{\bar{w} \to \infty} Y = \lim_{\bar{w} \to \infty} Y_p = 0$

This implies that the world equilibrium price, which is determined by the market-clearing and marginal productivity conditions

(83a)  $\beta(p) \left[ Y(p, N, K_1, K_2) + Y(p, \bar{N}, K_1, K_2) \right]$

$$= Y_p(p, N, K_1, K_2) + Y_p(p, \bar{N}, K_1, K_2)$$

and

(83b)  $\bar{w} = Y_N(p, N, K_1, K_2)$

must converge to $p^a$ as $\bar{w}$ goes to infinity. Consider Figure 3. In that figure, the dashed line $p^aG$ and the lower portion $p^aD$ of the foreign excess demand curve are symmetrical with respect to the vertical or price axis. As $\bar{w}$ rises from $p^{-1}(p^a)$, and $p(\bar{w})$ rises from $p^a$, the equilibrium point H moves from $p^a$ towards G. As we have just shown, however, eventually the equilibrium point returns from G and converges to $p^a$. Thus $p^aG$ may be compared with $C_1B_3$ in Figure II.10.

The assumption that the factor endowment is the same in both countries has enabled us to isolate the *trade-creating* potential of a labour union. We now relax the assumption, allowing the specific-factor endowment to be larger in one country than in the other, and proceed to demonstrate the *trade-reversing* potential of a union. In particular, we now assume that the foreign endowment of the second specific factor grows slightly, with the endowments of all other factors (including the home endowment of the second specific factor) unchanged.

The increase in the foreign endowment causes the foreign excess-demand curve to shift to the left. (This has been formally proved by Amano (1977).) In terms of Figure 4, AD is the old foreign excess-

Figure 3

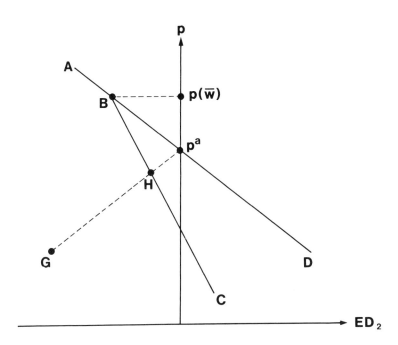

## Figure 4

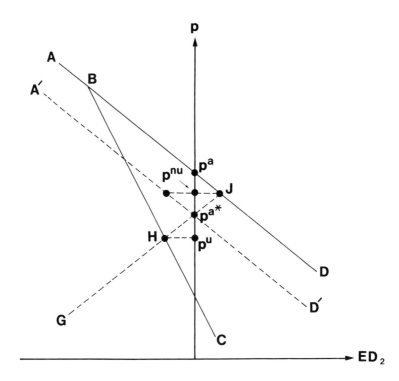

demand curve and A'D' is the new. In the absence of a labour union at home, the world equilibrium price ratio is $p^{nu}$, with the foreign country exporting the second good; but if there is a union which sets a minimum wage so far above the pre-union autarkic level $p^{-1}(p^a)$ that the union-distorted home excess demand is represented by ABHC then the world equilibrium price ratio is $p^u$, with the home country exporting the second commodity.

Of course, at this stage of our analysis we are merely drawing attention to the possibility of union-generated unemployment and trade reversal. Precise sufficient conditions for those outcomes will be provided in the next subsection.

### World equilibrium with an optimal minimum wage

We now require $\bar{w}$ to be optimal from the point of view of the union and proceed to examine the familiar but basic and therefore unavoidable questions concerning the existence of a world equilibrium and concerning the properties of an equilibrium if one exists.

The question of existence must be considered under more general assumptions than those so far imposed in this section. In particular, we now abandon the assumption that factor endowments are identical or closely similar across countries; throughout our discussion of existence it will be assumed only that all factor endowments are positive. Instead of (83), then, we must write

(84a)  $\beta(p)\left[Y(p, N, K_1, K_2) + Y(p, \bar{N}^*, K_1^*, K_2^*)\right]$

$$= Y_p(p, N, K_1, K_2) + Y_p(p, \bar{N}^*, K_1^*, K_2^*)$$

and

(84b)  $\bar{w} = Y_N(p, N, K_1, K_2)$

where the asterisks indicate variables relating to the foreign country.

Equations (84a) and (84b) are the materials from which we can formulate the problem confronting the union. Differentiating (84) with respect to $\bar{w}$, we obtain

$$(85a) \quad -\left[\frac{1-\varepsilon_e}{\sigma_e} + \frac{p(Y_{pp} + Y^*_{pp})}{Y_p + Y^*_p}\right]\frac{dp}{p}$$

$$+ \frac{NY_N}{p(Y_p + Y^*_p)}\left[\varepsilon_e - \frac{pY_{Np}}{Y_N}\right]\frac{dN}{N} = 0$$

$$(85b) \quad \frac{pY_{Np}}{Y_N}\frac{dp}{p} + \frac{NY_{NN}}{Y_N}\frac{dN}{N} = \frac{d\bar{w}}{\bar{w}}$$

where $Y^*_p \equiv Y_p(p, \bar{N}^*, K^*_1, K^*_2)$ and $Y^*_{pp} = Y_{pp}(p, \bar{N}^*, K^*_1, K^*_2)$ and where definitions of $\sigma_e$ and $\varepsilon_e$ may be found in Section II.5. Solving (85), we find that

$$(86a) \quad \frac{\bar{w}}{p}\frac{dp}{d\bar{w}} = \frac{(-1)}{\delta}\frac{NY_N}{p(Y_p + Y^*_p)}\left[\varepsilon_e - \frac{pY_{Np}}{Y_N}\right]$$

$$(86b) \quad \frac{\bar{w}}{N}\frac{dN}{d\bar{w}} = \frac{(-1)}{\delta}\left[\frac{1-\varepsilon_e}{\sigma_e} + \frac{p(Y_{pp} + Y^*_{pp})}{Y_p + Y^*_p}\right]$$

where

$$(87) \quad \delta \equiv -\left\{\left[\frac{NY_{NN}}{Y_N}\right]\left[\frac{1-\varepsilon_e}{\sigma_e} + \frac{p(Y_{pp} + Y^*_{pp})}{Y_p + Y^*_p}\right]\right.$$

$$\left. + \frac{NY_{Np}}{Y_p + Y^*_p}\left[\varepsilon_e - \frac{pY_{Np}}{Y_N}\right]\right\}$$

Holding $\bar{w}$ constant, and using (84b) to relate N to p, we can calculate that

$$(88) \quad \frac{p}{\left[\dfrac{\beta(Y + Y^*)}{Y_p + Y^*_p}\right]}\frac{d}{dp}\left[\frac{\beta(Y + Y^*)}{Y_p + Y^*_p}\right]\Bigg|_{d\bar{w}=0} = \frac{\delta}{\left[\dfrac{NY_{NN}}{Y_N}\right]}$$

But the left-hand side of (88) must be negative as a necessary condition of local Walrasian stability. Hence $\delta > 0$ and, from (62d) and (86b),

$$(89) \quad \frac{\bar{w}}{N}\frac{dN}{d\bar{w}} < 0$$

Finally let us denote by $p^e$ the price which satisfies (84a) when $N = \bar{N}$ and by $p^{a*}$ the foreign autarkic price which satisfies

$$(90) \quad \beta(p)Y(p,\bar{N}^*,K_1^*,K_2^*) = Y_p(p,\bar{N}^*,K_1^*,K_2^*)$$

Then (89) assures us that the task of the union is to solve

$$(P_0) \quad \max_{\bar{w}} \ U = \frac{\bar{w}N}{\bar{N}e(p)}$$

$$\text{s.t. (84a) and } \bar{w} \geq w^e \equiv Y_N(p^e,\bar{N},K_1,K_2)$$

**PROPOSITION 3:** $(P_0)$ has a solution if

$$(91) \quad \bar{N}w^e \geq \frac{e(p^e)}{e(p^{a*})} \lim_{\bar{w}\to\infty} \bar{w}N$$

**PROOF** For any given p, (81) holds. Hence $\lim_{\bar{w}\to\infty} p = p^{a*}$ and we can follow the proof of Proposition II.1. ◊

**Remark** In this chapter it has been assumed that the equation

$$1 - \theta_i(\omega_i) - \sigma_i(\omega_i) = 0$$

has a unique solution and that

$$\theta_i'(\omega_i) + \sigma_i'(\omega_i) > 0$$

These conditions guarantee the existence of a union-ridden world equilibrium, just as they did in Chapter II; see the corollary to Proposition II.1.

Existence ensured, we can return to the questions posed at the end of the preceding subsection. Under what sufficient condition is the union-ridden world equilibrium characterized by unemployment? by trade reversal? For the sake of clarity we revert to the special case in which the home and foreign endowment vectors differ only in the entry for the second specific factor, which is slightly more plentiful in the foreign country.

From (II.2), or from $(P_0)$,

$$(92) \quad \frac{\bar{w}}{U}\frac{dU}{d\bar{w}} = 1 + \frac{\bar{w}}{N}\frac{dN}{d\bar{w}} - \varepsilon_e\frac{\bar{w}}{p}\frac{dp}{d\bar{w}}$$

Substituting from (86) into (92),[1]

$$(93) \quad \frac{\bar{w}}{U} \frac{dU}{d\bar{w}} = \frac{(-1)}{\delta} \left\{ \left[ 1 + \frac{NY_{NN}}{Y_N} \right] \left[ \frac{1 - \varepsilon_e}{\sigma_e} + \frac{p(Y_{pp} + Y^*_{pp})}{Y_p + Y^*_p} \right] \right.$$

$$\left. - \frac{NY_N}{p(Y_p + Y^*_p)} \left[ \varepsilon_e - \frac{pY_{Np}}{Y_N} \right]^2 \right\}$$

This expression is positive if

$$(94) \quad 1 + \frac{NY_{NN}}{Y_N} < 0$$

or, recalling (62a, e), if

$$(95) \quad \gamma_1(\bar{w})K_1 + \gamma_2(\bar{w}/p)K_2 > 0$$

Thus we arrive at the required sufficient condition. Let $w^{nu}$ denote the home wage rate in the union-free world equilibrium and let $w^*$ denote the home wage rate when $p = p^{a^*}$.

**PROPOSITION 4**: If $\gamma_1(w^{nu})K_1 + \gamma_2(w^{nu}/p)K_2 > 0$ then the union-ridden world equilibrium involves some unemployment. If $\gamma_1(w^*)K_1 + \gamma_2(w^*/p)K_2 > 0$ then the union-ridden world equilibrium involves trade reversal.

**Remark**   Since

$$\gamma_1 K_1 + \gamma_2 K_2 = N - N_1\sigma_1/(1 - \theta_1) - N_2\sigma_2/(1 - \theta_2)$$

$$(96) \qquad\qquad = N\left[ 1 - \left[ \frac{N_1}{N} \frac{\sigma_1}{1 - \theta_1} + \frac{N_2}{N} \frac{\sigma_2}{1 - \theta_2} \right] \right]$$

we can re-state Proposition 4: If the economy-wide average of the elasticities of the marginal productivity of labour at home is smaller than one at $w^{nu}$ (respectively, $w^*$) then the union-ridden world equilibrium is characterized by some unemployment (trade reversal). The larger is $\bar{N} = \bar{N}^*$, the more likely is it that the condition will be satisfied.

## 6. WORLD EQUILIBRIUM: COMPARATIVE STATICS

That completes our discussion of existence. We now consider, quite briefly, the response of the equilibrium to small changes in the factor endowments of the two countries. In general, with factor endowments restricted only to be positive, the union-ridden world equilibrium is defined by (84) and

$$\left[ 1 + \frac{N Y_{NN}(p, N, K_1, K_2)}{Y_N(p, N, K_1, K_2)} \right] \cdot$$

$$\left[ \frac{1 - \varepsilon_e(p)}{\sigma_e(p)} + \frac{p(Y_{pp}(p, N, K_1, K_2) + Y_{pp}(p, \bar{N}^*, K_1^*, K_2^*))}{Y_p(p, N, K_1, K_2) + Y_p(p, \bar{N}^*, K_1^*, K_2^*)} \right]$$

$$- \left[ \frac{N Y_{NN}(p, N, K_1, K_2)}{p(Y_p(p, N, K_1, K_2) + Y_p(p, \bar{N}^*, K_1^*, K_2^*))} \right] \cdot$$

$$\left[ \varepsilon_e(p) \frac{p Y_{pN}(p, N, K_1, K_2)}{Y_N(p, N, K_1, K_2)} \right]^2$$

(93')      $= 0$

The following properties of the revenue function $Y(p, N, K_1, K_2)$ will be needed.

[r.1]   $Y$, $Y_p$ and $Y_{pp}$ are homogeneous of degree one in $N$, $K_1$ and $K_2$.

[r.2]   $Y_N$ and $Y_{Np}$ are homogeneous of degree zero in $N$, $K_1$ and $K_2$.

[r.3]   $Y_{NN}$ is homogeneous of degree minus one in $N$, $K_1$ and $K_2$.

**PROPOSITION 5:** (a) If $K_1$, $K_2$, $K_1^*$, $K_2^*$ and $\bar{N}^*$ all increase in the same proportion $\lambda$ then $N$ and $U$ also increase in the proportion $\lambda$ while $p$, $w$, $r_i$ and $u_r$ remain at their initial levels. (b) If $\bar{N}$ increases then $p$, $w$, $r_i$, $u_r$ and $N$ remain at their initial levels while $dU/U = -d\bar{N}/\bar{N}$.

**PROOF** Part (a) follows from (84), (93') and properties [r.1]–[r.3] of the revenue function. Part (b) follows from the fact that (84) and (93') are independent of $\bar{N}$.                                                  ◊

## 7.    INTERNATIONALLY-MOBILE SPECIFIC FACTORS

It has been assumed that neither the specific factors nor labour can move from one country to another. In the present section, which is companion to Section II.7, we allow for the possibility that the specific factors can freely and costlessly move between countries (but, of course, not between industries). Throughout the present section it is assumed that the same technology and the same homothetic preferences prevail everywhere.

At one extreme we have the pre-union world equilibrium with all factors fully employed. With both specific factors internationally mobile, and with a common constant-returns technology, the two economies behave like one. The equilibrium price ratio $p^{nu}$ is given by the market-clearing condition

$$(97a) \quad \beta(p)Y(p, \bar{N}+\bar{N}^*, \bar{K}_1, \bar{K}_2) = Y_p(p, \bar{N}+\bar{N}^*, \bar{K}_1, \bar{K}_2)$$

where $\bar{K}_i \equiv K_i + K_i^*$, and the associated home wage rate is given by the marginal productivity condition

$$(97b) \quad w^{nu} = Y_N(p^{nu}, \bar{N}+\bar{N}^*, \bar{K}_1, \bar{K}_2)$$

At the other extreme, we have a world economy from which the entire home work force has been withdrawn or, equivalently, a foreign economy to which the entire world stock of specific factors has been attracted. In such an economy there prevails the (price, wage)-pair $(p^{0*}, w^{0*})$ obtained as the solution to the market-clearance and marginal-productivity conditions

$$(98a) \quad \beta(p)Y(p, \bar{N}^*, \bar{K}_1, \bar{K}_2) = Y_p(p, \bar{N}^*, \bar{K}_1, \bar{K}_2)$$

$$(98b) \quad w = Y_N(p, \bar{N}^*, \bar{K}_1, \bar{K}_2)$$

respectively. Clearly, $w^{0*} > w^{nu}$. We proceed to show that the union will choose a minimum wage rate in the interval $[w^{nu}, w^{0*}]$.

The union will never choose a minimum wage rate below the pre-union level $w^{nu}$. Suppose that $\bar{w}$ is set between $w^{nu}$ and $w^{0*}$. (i) If the foreign wage rate $w^*$ were greater than $\bar{w}$ then each specific factor would receive a higher reward in the home country and the entire foreign stock would emigrate; excess supply would appear in the foreign labour market and $w^*$ would be forced down. (ii) If the foreign wage rate were lower than $\bar{w}$, the process would work in reverse: specific factors would receive a greater reward in the foreign country and the entire world stock of each factor would settle there; since $w^* < \bar{w} < w^{0*}$ excess demand would occur in the foreign labour market and $w^*$ would be forced up. Thus, whenever $w^{nu} < \bar{w} < w^{0*}$, $w^*$ and $\bar{w}$ must be equal. The level of world employment, $N^{\bar{w}}$ say, is then determined by the equations

(99a)  $\beta(p)Y(p, N^{\bar{w}}, \bar{K}_1, \bar{K}_2) = Y_p(p, N^{\bar{w}}, \bar{K}_1, \bar{K}_2)$

and

(99b)  $\bar{w} = Y_N(p, N^{\bar{w}}, \bar{K}_1, \bar{K}_2)$

Differentiating (99) with respect to $\bar{w}$ and solving for $dN^{\bar{w}}/d\bar{w}$, we find that

(100)  $\dfrac{\bar{w}}{N^{\bar{w}}} \dfrac{dN^{\bar{w}}}{d\bar{w}} = \dfrac{(-1)}{\delta'} \left[ \dfrac{1 - \varepsilon_e}{\sigma_e} + \dfrac{pY_{pp}}{Y_p} \right]$

where

$$\delta' \equiv - \left[ \left[ \dfrac{N^{\bar{w}}Y_{NN}}{Y_N} \right] \left[ \dfrac{1 - \varepsilon_e}{\sigma_e} + \dfrac{pY_{pp}}{Y_p} \right] \right.$$
$$\left. + \left[ \dfrac{N^{\bar{w}}Y_{pN}}{Y_p} \right] \left[ \varepsilon_e - \dfrac{pY_{pN}}{Y_N} \right] \right]$$

and is positive as a necessary condition of stability in the commodity market when $\bar{w}$ is given. Hence $dN^{\bar{w}}/d\bar{w}$ is negative and, since $\bar{w} > w^{nu}$, there is some unemployment at home. In fact, the level of home employment is $N = N^{\bar{w}} - \bar{N}^* < \bar{N}$. Since $\bar{w} < w^{0*}$ the level of home employment is positive.

Suppose, alternatively, that the union chooses a minimum wage above $w^{0*}$. If $w^*$ were greater than $\bar{w}$ then the entire stock of each specific factor would migrate to the home country, excess supply would develop in the foreign labour market, and $w^*$ would be forced down. If $w^*$ were between $w^{0*}$ and $\bar{w}$ then (since $w^* > w^{0*}$) the foreign labour market would suffer from excess supply, and $w^*$ would be forced down to the level of $w^{0*}$; at that point, the foreign work force would be fully employed and the home work force would be completely unemployed.

Effectively, then, the union must choose $\bar{w}$ from the interval

$[w^{nu}, w^{0*}]$. In view of (100), it faces a negatively-sloped trade-off curve from which it must choose a point which maximizes U; see Figure 5. Since the trade-off curve AB is compact, a union-ridden world equilibrium exists.

Formally, the union seeks

$$(P_1) \quad \max_{p, N} U = \frac{1}{e(p)\bar{N}} NY_N(p, N + \bar{N}^*, \bar{K}_1, \bar{K}_2)$$

$$\text{s.t.} \quad \beta(p)Y(p, N + \bar{N}^*, \bar{K}_1, \bar{K}_2) = Y_p(p, N + \bar{N}^*, \bar{K}_1, \bar{K}_2)$$

$$\bar{N} + \bar{N}^* \geq N + \bar{N}^* \geq \bar{N}^*$$

Since the wage rate must lie in the interval $[w^{nu}, w^{0*}]$, however, the inequality constraint is necessarily satisfied and so can be ignored. The Lagrangean for the problem is, therefore,

$$L = \frac{1}{e(p)\bar{N}} NY_N(p, N + \bar{N}^*, \bar{K}_1, \bar{K}_2) + \mu \left[ \beta(p)Y(p, N + \bar{N}^*, \bar{K}_1, \bar{K}_2) \right.$$

$$\left. - Y_p(p, N + \bar{N}^*, \bar{K}_1, \bar{K}_2) \right]$$

and the first-order conditions for an internal optimum are

$$(101a) \quad \frac{\partial L}{\partial N} = \frac{1}{e(p)\bar{N}} (Y_N + NY_{NN}) + \mu(\beta Y_N - Y_{pN}) = 0$$

$$(101b) \quad \frac{\partial L}{\partial p} = - \frac{N}{e(p)\bar{N}} (\beta Y_N - Y_{Np}) + \mu(\beta'Y + \beta Y_p - Y_{pp}) = 0$$

$$(101c) \quad \frac{\partial L}{\partial \mu} = \beta Y - Y_p = 0$$

However, the properties [r.1]–[r.3] of the revenue function enable us to rewrite the conditions as

$$\frac{1}{e(p)} \left[ Y_N(p, n, k, l) + nY_{NN}(p, n, k, l) \right]$$

$$(102a) \qquad + z \left[ \beta(p)Y_N(p, n, k, l) - Y_{pN}(p, n, k, l) \right] = 0$$

# Figure 5

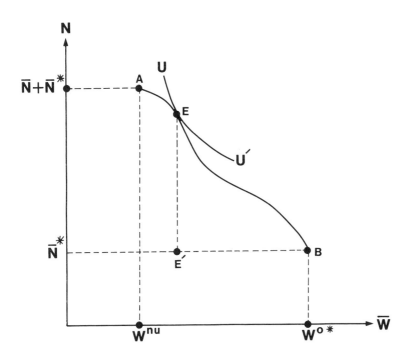

$$\frac{n}{e(p)} \left[ \beta(p) Y_N(p, n, k, l) - Y_{Np}(p, n, k, l) \right]$$

(102b)        $+ z\left[ \beta'(p)Y(p, n, k, l) + \beta(p)Y_p(p, n, k, l) - Y_{pp}(p, n, k, l) \right] = 0$

(102c)   $\beta(p)Y(p, n, k, l) - Y_p(p, n, k, l) = 0$

where $n \equiv N + \bar{N}^*/\bar{K}_2$, $k \equiv \bar{K}_1/\bar{K}_2$ and $z \equiv \mu\bar{N}$. By inspection, the solution to (102) depends on k only:

$n = n(k)$

$p = p(k)$

$z = z(k)$

Hence the solution to (101) can be expressed as

(103a)   $N = n(k)K_2$

(103b)   $p = p(k)$

(103c)   $\mu = z(k)/\bar{N}$

From (103) one can deduce the response of the equilibrium values to changes in home endowments. The results of the calculation are collected in Table 1.

**Table 1**

|  | dp/p | dw/w | $dr_i/r_i$ | dU/U | $du_r/u_r$ |
|---|---|---|---|---|---|
| $dK_1/K_1 = dK_2/K_2$ | 0 | 0 | 0 | + | 0 |
| $d\bar{N}/\bar{N}$ | 0 | 0 | 0 | − | 0 |

## 8.    SHORT-RUN SPECIFICITY: AN ADJUSTMENT PROCESS

Our treatment of specific factors has been completely static. Time
has had no place in the analysis. Hence we could not consider the
possibility that factors are specific in the short-run but not in the
long-run. In the present section we fill the gap, allowing the allocation of specific factors to gradually adjust to intersectoral differences
in earnings. This is most easily done when the specific factors are
physically identical; otherwise, it would be necessary to allow for $n + 1$
factors in each industry. The physically-homogeneous specific factors
will henceforth be called capital.

To keep complications to a minimum, we revert to the small-
country assumption of Sections 2–4; this time, however, the economy
is restricted to two sectors, each sector employing perfectly mobile
labour and the physically homogeneous specific factor capital.

Of course the objective function of the union must be reformulated
so that it makes sense in a dynamic context. Thus, in the present
section, it is assumed that the union seeks to maximize the time-
separable functional

$$\int_0^\infty \exp(-\delta t) \, \frac{w(t)N(t)}{e_w(p)\bar{N}} \, dt = \int_0^\infty \exp(-\delta t)U(t) \, dt$$

where $\delta$ is the union's constant rate of time preference and t denotes
time, a continuous variable. The assumption that the union maximizes
over an infinite horizon may be thought to be extravagant. However
it can be justified by assigning a collective "bequest motive" to each
generation of union members (Pazner and Razin (1980), Kemp and
Long (1982)); and the alternative assumption raises the well-known
and insoluble problem of valuing end-of-period stocks. The particular
functional displayed above was first proposed as a basis for the dynamic
analysis of union-ridden economies by Kemp and Long (1986, 1987).

We already know how a competitive two-sector economy behaves
when factor allocations adjust only slowly to intersectoral differences
in rewards; see Herberg and Kemp (1972), Okuguchi (1976), Kemp,
Kimura and Okuguchi (1977) and Kemp and Kimura (1978, pp. 209–216).
What is novel in the present analysis is the interaction of a maximizing labour union with the competitive components of the system.

It will be shown that there are three distinct types of long-run or
steady-state equilibrium and that the economy asymptotically proceeds

to one of them. Which steady state is chosen depends on the initial allocation of capital to the two industries. In the *first* of these equilibria the economy is completely specialized in producing the relatively capital-intensive second commodity and there is some unemployment. Evidently this is the static union-ridden equilibrium of Chapter II. However it does not emerge from the present higher-dimensional analysis as the only possible steady state. For the optimal dynamic path to converge on the static equilibrium it is necessary that the initial allocation of capital to the first industry be sufficiently small. In the *second* of the three types of long-run equilibrium production is incompletely specialized and there is some unemployment. For the optimal path to converge on a steady state of this kind, it is necessary that the initial allocation of capital favour neither industry unduly. In the *third* and last type of equilibrium production is incompletely specialized and there is full employment, that is, the union voluntarily refrains from exercising its market power. Evidently this is the familiar pre-union Heckscher-Ohlin equilibrium.

What is novel in these conclusions is the possibility of a steady-state equilibrium of the second type. Capital is free to drift from one industry to another, but it suits the union to choose a wage rate such that $r_1 = r_2$ and capital has no incentive to move.

### Assumptions and formulation of the union's problem

The migration of capital from sector to sector is governed by the dynamic adjustment equation

(104a)  $\dot{k}_1 = \dfrac{dk_1}{dt} = \psi(k_1, r_1 - r_2)$

$$\equiv \phi(k_1, r_1 - r_2)(r_1 - r_2)$$

where $k_1 \equiv K_1/\bar{K}$ is the proportion of the total capital stock allocated to the first or relatively labour-intensive industry and

(104b)  $\phi(k_1, r_1 - r_2) = \left\{ \begin{array}{c} 1 - k_1 \\ 0 \\ k_1 \end{array} \right\}$ according as $r_1 \left\{ \begin{array}{c} > \\ = \\ < \end{array} \right\} r_2$

Evidently the function $\psi(k_1, r_1 - r_2)$ is continuous on $Q \equiv \{(k_1, r_1 - r_2): 0 \le k_1 \le 1, (r_1 - r_2) \in R^1\}$ and has the following properties:

[$\psi$.1] $\psi(k_1, r_1 - r_2) > 0$ if $0 \le k_1 < 1$ and $r_1 - r_2 > 0$ ;

[$\psi$.2] $\psi(k_1, r_1 - r_2) < 0$ if $0 < k_1 \le 1$ and $r_1 - r_2 < 0$ ;

[$\psi$.3] $\psi(k_1, r_1 - r_2) = 0$ if $r_1 - r_2 = 0$, or if $k_1 = 1$ and $r_1 - r_2 > 0$, or if $k_1 = 0$ and $r_1 - r_2 < 0$ ;

[$\psi$.4] $\psi(k_1, r_1 - r_2)$ is differentiable with respect to $k_1$ if $0 < k_1 < 1$ and with respect to $r_1 - r_2$ if $r_1 - r_2 \neq 0$ ; moreover

[$\psi$.5] if $\psi$ is differentiable then

[$\psi$.5$\alpha$]
$$\frac{\partial \psi}{\partial k_1} \equiv \psi_k \begin{Bmatrix} < \\ = \end{Bmatrix} \text{ if and only if } r_1 - r_2 \begin{Bmatrix} \neq \\ = \end{Bmatrix} 0 ;$$

[$\psi$.5$\beta$]
$$\frac{\partial \psi}{\partial (r_1 - r_2)} \equiv \psi_r > 0 ;$$

[$\psi$.5$\gamma$]
$$\lim_{r_1 - r_2 \to 0^+} \frac{\partial \psi}{\partial (r_1 - r_2)} > 0 \text{ if } k_1 \in [0, 1)$$

[$\psi$.5$\delta$]
$$\lim_{r_1 - r_2 \to 0^-} \frac{\partial \psi}{\partial (r_1 - r_2)} > 0 \text{ if } k_1 \in (0, 1]$$

[$\psi$.5$\varepsilon$]
$$\lim_{r_1 - r_2 \to 0^+} \frac{\partial \psi(k_1, r_1 - r_2)}{\partial (r_1 - r_2)} \gtreqless \lim_{r_1 - r_2 \to 0^-} \frac{\partial \psi(k_1, r_1 - r_2)}{\partial (r_1 - r_2)} \text{ if } k_1 \lesseqgtr \frac{1}{2}$$

[$\psi$.5$\zeta$]
$$\frac{\partial^2 \psi(k_1, r_1 - r_2)}{\partial (r_1 - r_2) \partial k_1} \gtreqless 0 \text{ if and only if } r_1 - r_2 \lesseqgtr 0$$

We emphasize properties [$\psi$.5$\gamma$] and [$\psi$.5$\delta$]. In the analysis of market adjustment it is customary to assume that, when $r_1 - r_2 = 0$, $\psi_r$ exists and is equal to zero. The assumption is a great simplifier; in particular, it eliminates the possibility of hysteresis of long-run equilibrium. But the assumption is implausible; see Kemp and Wan (1974). We prefer to get along without it. Figure 6 enables one to take in the foregoing properties of $\psi$ at a glance. It also makes clear that $\psi$ is quasi-concave if $r_1 - r_2 > 0$ and quasi-convex if $r_1 - r_2 < 0$.

We can now formulate the union's problem as

## Figure 6

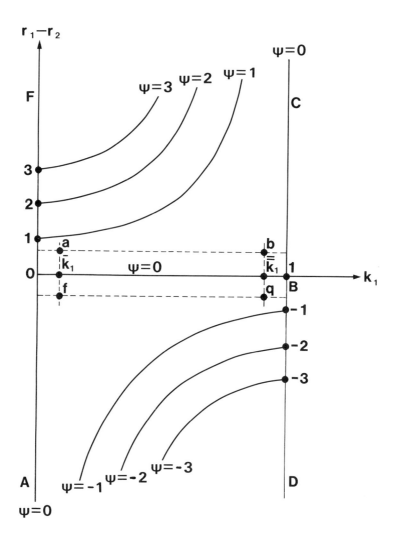

$(P_2)$ $\quad \max_{<w(t)>} \int_0^\infty \exp(-\delta t) \, \dfrac{w}{e_w z} \, [x_1(w)k_1 + x_2(w/p)(1 - k_1)] \, dt$

subject to

(104) $\dot{k}_1 = \psi(k_1, r_1 - r_2)$

(105) $x_1(w)k_1 + x_2(w/p)(1 - k_1) \le \bar{N}/\bar{K} \equiv z$

(106) $1 = c^1(w, r_1)$

(107) $p = c^2(w, r_2)$

(108) $k_1(0) \in (0, 1)$, given

In this formulation, p, $\delta$ and z are given, positive constants and

$$x_1(w) = \frac{c_w^1(w, r_1(w))}{c_r^1(w, r_1(w))}$$

$$x_2(w/p) = \frac{c_w^2(w/p, r_2(w/p, 1))}{c_r^2(w/p, r_2(w/p, 1))}$$

where $r_1(w)$ and $r_2(w,p)$ are the solutions to

$$1 = c^1(w, r_1)$$

and

$$p = c^2(w, r_2)$$

respectively.

Associated with $(P_2)$ are the current-value Hamiltonian

(109) $H(w, \mu, k_1) \equiv \dfrac{w}{e_w z} \, [x_1 k_1 + x_2(1 - k_1)] + \mu\psi(k_1, r_1(w) - r_2(w, p))$

and the Lagrangean

(110) $L \equiv H + \lambda\{z - [x_1 k_1 + x_2(1 - k_1)]\}$

Any solution to $(P_2)$ must satisfy the following equations and inequalities:

(111) $H(w, \mu, k_1) \ge H(\tilde{w}, \mu, k_1)$ for all $\tilde{w} \ge 0$ satisfying (105)

$$(112) \quad \begin{aligned} &z - [x_1 k_1 + x_2(1 - k_1)] \geq 0 \\ &\lambda \geq 0 \, , \, \lambda\{z - [x_1 k_1 + x_2(1 - k_1)]\} = 0 \end{aligned}$$

$$(113) \quad \begin{aligned} \dot{\mu} &= \delta\mu - \partial L/\partial k_1 \\ &= \delta\mu + \left[ \lambda - \frac{w}{e_w z} \right] (x_1 - x_2) - \mu\psi_k(k_1, r_1(w) - r_2(w, p)) \end{aligned}$$

$$(114) \quad \dot{k}_1 = \psi(k_1, r_1(w) - r_2(w, p))$$

where $\psi_k \equiv \partial\psi/\partial k_1$ .

Making sense of these conditions is not easy. To ease the way we now introduce several additional assumptions. Let us denote by $w_1$ and $w_2(p)$ the solutions to

$$\frac{d}{dw} (wx_1(w)) \equiv \gamma_1(w) = 0$$

and

$$\frac{\partial}{\partial w} (wx_2(w/p)) \equiv \gamma_2(w) = 0$$

respectively, and by $w(p)$ the solution to $r_1(w) = r_2(w, p)$.

[γ.1]   $w_1$ and $w_2(p)$ uniquely exist for any given and positive p.

[γ.2]   $w(p)$ uniquely exists for any given and positive p.

[γ.3]   For any $w > 0$ and $p > 0$,

$$\gamma_1'(w) \equiv d\gamma_1/dw < 0$$

$$\gamma_2'(w) \equiv d\gamma_2/dw < 0$$

[γ.4]   $\sigma_1(w(p)) = \sigma_2(w(p)/p) < 1$

To confine $\sigma_1$ and $\sigma_2$ below one might seem unreasonable. However in the small-country equilibria of Sections 2 and II.2 at least one of the elasticities must be less than one; and the same is true of any steady state of the present dynamic system. Moreover [γ.4] is a great simplifier. Thus it follows from [γ.4] that if $w(p)$ lies between $w_1$ and $w_2(p)$ then the following are equivalent statements:

$\theta_1(w(p)) \gtrless \theta_2(w(p)/p)$

$\gamma_1(w(p)) \lessgtr 0$ and $\gamma_2(w(p)/p) \gtrless 0$

$w_1 \lessgtr w(p) \lessgtr w_2(p)$

It also follows from [$\gamma$.4] that if $w(p)$ lies outside the interval $[\min(w_1, w_2(p)), \max(w_1, w_2(p))]$ but sufficiently close to one of its endpoints then the following statements are equivalent:

$\theta_1(w(p)) \gtrless \theta_2(w(p)/p)$

$\gamma_1(w(p)) \lessgtr \gamma_2(w(p)/p)$

$w_1 \gtrless w_2(p)$

We shall concentrate on the case in which $w(p)$ lies between $w_1$ and $w_2(p)$. Of course,

(115) $x_1(w(p)) > x_2(w(p)/p)$

We now introduce the stricter assumption that

[$\gamma$.5] $x_1(w) > x_2(w/p)$ for any $w \in [w_1, w_2(p)]$

Finally, we note that, if $w \neq w(p)$,

(116) $\dfrac{\partial H}{\partial w} = \dfrac{1}{e_w z} [\gamma_1 k_1 + \gamma_2(1 - k_1)]$

$\qquad\qquad - \mu \psi_r(k_1, r_1(w) - r_2(w, p))(x_1 - x_2)$

and assume that

[$\gamma$.6] $\dfrac{\partial^2 H}{\partial w^2} < 0$ for $w \neq w(p)$

### The optimal solution

The tedious task of piecing together a phase diagram from the first-order conditions (111)–(114) has been relegated to an appendix. Figure A.19, here reproduced as Figure 7, is the typical phase diagram — typical, in the sense that it displays the full variety of possible trajectories. The remaining task is that of choosing from the family of Pontryagin paths one that is optimal.

Two preliminary propositions are needed. Let $k_1^0$ be the initial

## Figure 7

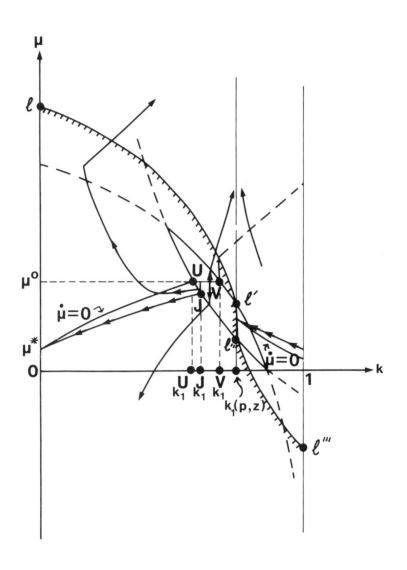

value of $k_1$, $k_1 \in [0, 1]$, and let

$$R(k_1^0) \equiv \{ <w(t), k_1(t)> : \dot{k}_1 t) = \psi(k_1(t), r_1(w(t)) - r_2(w(t), p)),$$
$$t \geq 0, \ k_1(0) = k_1^0, \ w(t) \text{ a non-negative piecewise}$$
continuous function of $t \}$

**LEMMA 1:** For all $<w(t), k(t)> \in R(k_1^0)$,

$$V(k_1^0) \equiv \int_0^\infty \exp(-\delta t) \ \frac{w(t)}{e_w z} \ [x_1(w(t))k_1(t) + x_2(w(t)/p)(1 - k_1(t))] \, dt$$

is bounded above.

**PROOF** From the definition of $\psi$ and from the fact that $k_1^0 \in [0, 1]$, $k_1(t) \in [0, 1]$ for all $t \geq 0$. Hence

$$\int_0^\infty \exp(-\delta t)w[x_1 k_1 + x_2(1 - k_1)] \, dt$$

$$\leq \int_0^\infty \exp(-\delta t) \max\{wx_1, wx_2\} \, dt$$

$$\leq \int_0^\infty \exp(-\delta t) \max\{w_1 x_1(w_1), w_2(p)x_2(w_2(p)/p)\} \, dt$$

$$= \max \{w_1 x_1(w_1), w_2(p)x_2(w_2(p)/p)\} \int_0^\infty \exp(-\delta t) \, dt$$

$$= \frac{1}{\delta} \max \{w_1 x_1(w_1), w_2(p)x_2(w_2(p)/p)\}$$

$$< \infty$$

**LEMMA 2:** Any Pontryagin path along which $\lim_{t \to \infty} \mu(t) < 0$ is suboptimal.

**PROOF** Consider Figure 8, in which *lml'* is a Pontryagin path which satisfies the condition of the lemma; and consider also the comparison path $l'mm_0m_1m_2 \ldots$ which jumps to the $k_1$-axis whenever it reaches the horizontal line Hm. Since the Pontryagin path approaches but never reaches the vertical axis, the jump is repeated indefinitely. After m, therefore, $\mu(t)$ is always greater on the comparison path than on the Pontryagin path. Setting $\partial H/\partial w = 0$, we then see from (116) and [γ.6] that, after m, w(t)x(t) is always larger on the comparison path. Hence the Pontryagin path is suboptimal.                    ◊

## Figure 8

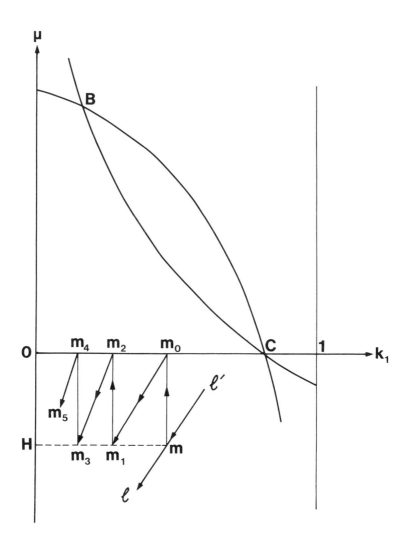

Now let us return to Figure 7. If $k_1(0) > k_1^V$ then, from Lemma 2, it is optimal for the union to do nothing, thus ensuring that labour is fully employed and that the wage rate monotonely rises or falls according as $k_1^0$ is below or above the steady-state value $k_1(p,z)$.

If $k_1^J < k_1(0) \le k_1^V$ there are two candidates for optimality, (a) the stationary path ($\mu(t) = \mu^0$, $k_1(t) = k_1^0$) and (b) the full-employment path with $(\mu(0), k_1(0))$ on or above the boundary line $l'l''l'''$ of Figure 7 and with $(k_1(t), w(t))$ determined by (A.23) and (A.25) alone.

**LEMMA 3:** Suppose that $k_1^J < k_1(0) \le k_1^V$ . Then the stationary path dominates the full employment path if and only if the rate of time preference $\delta$ is sufficiently large. The critical value of $\delta$ increases with increases in $k_1^0$.

**PROOF** Let $w_b(t)$ be the wage rate along the full-employment path and let $w(k_1^0)$ be the wage rate that maximizes $wx$ when $k_1 = k_1^0$. Then $w(k_1^0) > w(p) > w_b(0)$. Hence

$$w(k_1^0)\left[x_1(w(k_1^0))k_1^0 + x_2(w(k_1^0)/p)(1 - k_1^0)\right]$$

$$> w(p)\left[x_1(w(p))k_1^0 + x_2(w(p)/p)(1 - k_1^0)\right] > w_b(0)z$$

Along the full-employment path, however, $k_1(t)$ and, therefore, $w_b(t)$ are steadily increasing. Eventually, at $t = \tilde{t}$, say, $w_b(t)z$ overtakes $w(p)x$.

Since $\dot{w}_b(t) > 0$ for all $t \ge 0$,

$$\int_0^\infty \exp(-\delta t)[w(p)x - w_b(t)z]\, dt$$

$$(117) \quad = \left[\left[ -\frac{1}{\delta}\exp(-\delta t)[w(p)x - w_b(t)z]\right]\right]_0^\infty$$

$$- \int_0^\infty [-\dot{w}_b(t)z]\left[ -\frac{1}{\delta}\exp(-\delta t)\right] dt$$

$$= \frac{1}{\delta}[w(p)x - w_b(t)z] - \frac{1}{\delta}\int_0^\infty \dot{w}_b(t)z\exp(-\delta t)\, dt$$

$$= \frac{1}{\delta}\left\{[w(p)x - w_b(t)z] - \int_0^\infty \exp(-\delta t)\dot{w}_b(t)z\, dt\right\}$$

Now $w_b(t)$ is determined by the equations

$$z = x_1(w)k_1 + x_2(w/p)(1 - k_1)$$

$$\dot{k}_1 = \psi$$

Thus it does not depend on $\delta$. Moreover we can easily verify that $\dot{w}(t)$ is bounded. Since $w(p)x - w_b(t)z$ is positive, therefore, $\int_0^\infty \exp(-\delta t)[w(p)x - w_b(t)z]\,dt$ becomes positive for sufficiently large $\delta$.

Since $dw_b(0)/dk_1^0 > 0$ , the greater is $k_1^0$ the lower the critical value of $\delta$.                                                                                    ◊

If $k_1^U \le k_1^0 \le k_1^J$ then there is an additional candidate for optimality, viz. the stable arm $\mu^*J$. In Lemma 3 the stationary and full-employment paths are compared. In the next lemma the stationary and stable-arm paths are compared.

**LEMMA 4:** *Either* the stationary path is superior to the stable-arm path for all $k_1^0 \in [k_1^U, k_1^J]$ *or* the stable-arm path is superior for all $k_1^0 \in [k_1^U, k_1^J]$ *or* the stable-arm path is superior for all $k_1^0 \in [k_1^U, \tilde{k}_1]$ and the stationary path is superior for all $k_1 \in (\tilde{k}_1, k_1^J]$, where $\tilde{k}_1$ is between $k_1^U$ and $k_1^J$.

**PROOF** Let

$$V(k_1^0)\Big|_{UJ'} = \int_0^\infty \exp(-\delta t)\,\frac{wx}{e_w z}\,dt$$

$$= \frac{w(p)}{\delta e_w z}\left[x_1(w(p))k_1^0 + x_2(w(p)/p)(1 - k_1^0)\right]$$

be the value of the functional along the stationary path. Since $x_1(w(p)) > x_2(w(p)/p)$, $V(k_1^0)\Big|_{UJ'}$ increases with increases in $k_1^0$. This relationship is represented in Figure 9 by the curve mm'.

Let $V(k_1^0)\Big|_{\mu^*J}$ be the value of the functional along the stable arm. $V(k_1^0)\Big|_{\mu^*J}$ also varies with $k_1^0$. A candidate relationship is depicted in Figure 9 by the curve ff'. It will be shown that ff' intersects mm' once at most, and then from above.

Suppose the contrary, that ff' intersects mm' twice, as in Figure 9. If $k_1^0 - \tilde{k}_1$ then it is optimal to choose the stable-arm path. But then

Figure 9

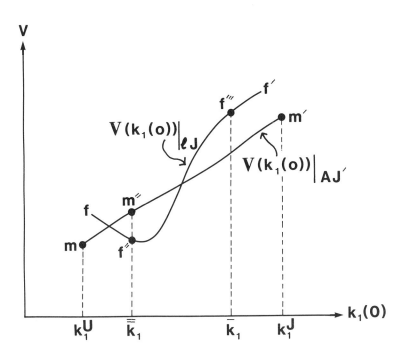

in finite time $k_1(t)$ will reach $\bar{\bar{k}}_1$, which implies that the value of the functional can be increased by jumping from f″ to m″, a contradiction. By a similar argument, the possibility that ff′ intersects mm′ once only, from below, can be excluded.                                      ◊

Finally, it is possible that $0 \le k_1(0) \le k_1^U$. Then the candidates for optimality are the stable-arm path and the full-employment path. Not surprisingly, given Lemmas 3 and 4, *either* the stable-arm path is optimal for all $k_1^0 \in [0, k_1^U)$ *or* the full-employment path is optimal for all $k_1^0 \in [0, k_1^U)$ *or* the stable-arm path is optimal for all sufficiently small $k_1^0$ in the interval $[0, k_1^U)$ and the full-employment path is optimal for all sufficiently large $k_1^0$ in the interval. Excluded are repeated switching from one regime to the other and switching from full-employment to unemployment as $k_1^0$ increases.

Summarizing, there are three types of optimal path. First, there are the paths which lie in the stable arm $\mu^*J$. Along paths of this type there is always some unemployment and the economy asymptotically approaches a state of complete specialization in the second or relatively capital-intensive commodity. Second, there are the stationary paths with initial points on UV. Along such paths there is always some unemployment and production is incompletely specialized. The hysteresis of equilibria on UV can be traced to the (realistic) lack of smoothness of the adjustment function $\psi$. Finally, there are the full-employment paths along which the union is completely passive and there is incomplete specialization at all points of time.

Let the economy be specified in all respects but the initial value of $k_1$; and let $k_1^0$ increase through all values from 0 to 1. Then, as demonstrated in the appendix, for sufficiently low values of $k_1^0$ the optimal path lies in the stable arm, for intermediate values of $k_1^0$ the optimal path is stationary, and for high values of $k_1^0$ it is optimal to choose full employment. However the $k_1^0$-intervals over which the optimal policy is of the first or second type may be degenerate. In particular, full employment may be optimal for all values of $k_1^0$.

Given $k_1^0$, the union may have to choose between a policy involving relatively high but declining wages and some unemployment (a stable-arm policy) and a policy of initially low but possibly growing wages and full employment; or it may have to choose between a policy of stable wages and some unemployment and a policy of initially low wages and full employment; or it may have to choose between all three policies. Not surprisingly, the union's choice of policy depends on its rate of time preference $\delta$.

## Comparative statics

To conclude this very long section, we briefly report on some comparative statics calculations. These are confined to the novel incompletely-specialized stationary equilibria represented by points on the segment UV of Figure 7.

We know that in any such equilibrium the wage rate is $w(p)$. Hence the effect of a small change in $p$ on wage and rental rates is exactly as predicted by the Stolper-Samuelson Theorem. However the typical worker's well-being, after the wage bill has been shared, may increase or decrease. Thus

$$(118) \quad V = \int_0^\infty \exp(-\delta t) \, \frac{w(p)}{e_w z} \left[ x_1(w(p)) k_1^0 + x_2(w(p)/p)(1 - k_1^0) \right] dt$$

$$= \frac{1}{\delta} \, \frac{w(p)}{e_w(p) z} \left[ x_1(w(p)) k_1^0 + x_2(w(p)/p)(1 - k_1^0) \right]$$

so that, differentiating with respect to $p$,

$$(119) \quad \frac{\partial V}{\partial p} = - \frac{e'_w w}{z \delta e_w} [x_1 k_1^0 + x_2(1 - k_1^0)] + \frac{1}{\delta e_w z} \, w'(p) \, \frac{\partial}{\partial w} (wx)$$

$$- \frac{w^2 x'_2}{\delta e_w z p^2} (1 - k_1^0)$$

where $x \equiv x_1 k_1^0 + x_2(1 - k_1^0)$. The second and third terms of (119) are positive. Thus $w'(p) < 0$ and, since $w(p)$ is greater than the wage rate which maximizes $wx$ when $k_1 = k_1^0$, $\partial(wx)/\partial x$ must be negative at $w(p)$; moreover $x'_2 < 0$. However the first term is negative and may outweigh the other terms. Thus while the discounted total wage bill increases when $p$ rises, the level of welfare of each worker may decline.

Let us now consider the response of outputs to price changes. Here some surprises await us. Thus, noting that

$$\frac{d}{dp} x_1(w(p)) = x_1' \frac{dw}{dp} > 0$$

$$\frac{d}{dp} x_2(w(p)/p) = x_2' \frac{d}{dp} (w/p) > 0$$

and that $k_1^0$ is a given constant, we see that total employment and the output of each commodity increase with increases in p, the price of the relatively capital-intensive good.

Inspection of (118) reveals that any small change in $k_1^0$ leaves factor rewards unchanged but causes the supply side of the economy to change, an increase in $k_1^0$ reducing the output of the relatively labour-intensive first industry and increasing the output of the capital-intensive second industry. In other words, the Rybczynski Theorem continues to apply. One sees also that small changes in z and $\delta$ leave unchanged all endogenous variables except $V$ itself, which is a decreasing function of both parameters.

# APPENDIX TO SECTION 8:
## CONSTRUCTION OF PHASE DIAGRAM

In this appendix we construct the phase diagram associated with $(P_2)$. At the outset we draw attention to the technical difficulty that $\partial H/\partial w$ is generally discontinuous at $w = w(p)$. (The discontinuity of $\partial H/\partial w$ is, of course, related to the discontinuity of $\psi_r$.) Let

$$\gamma_1(w(p)) \equiv \bar{\gamma}_1 , \qquad\qquad \gamma_2(w(p)/p) \equiv \bar{\gamma}_2$$

$$x_1(w(p)) \equiv \bar{x}_1 , \qquad\qquad x_2(w(p)/p) \equiv \bar{x}_2$$

where, from (115),

$$\bar{\gamma}_1 < 0 < \bar{\gamma}_2$$

$$\bar{x}_1 > \bar{x}_2$$

Then, from (116),

$$\lim_{w \to w(p)^+} \frac{\partial H}{\partial w} = \frac{1}{e_w z} [\bar{\gamma}_1 k_1 + \bar{\gamma}_2(1 - k_1)]$$

$$- \mu(\bar{x}_1 - \bar{x}_2) \lim_{w \to w(p)^+} \psi_r(k_1, r_1 - r_2)$$

(A1)
$$= \frac{1}{e_w z} [\bar{\gamma}_1 k_1 + \bar{\gamma}_2(1 - k_1)]$$

$$- \mu(\bar{x}_1 - \bar{x}_2) \lim_{(r_1 - r_2) \to 0^-} \psi_r(k_1, r_1 - r_2)$$

and

$$\lim_{w \to w(p)^-} \frac{\partial H}{\partial w} = \frac{1}{e_w z} [\bar{\gamma}_1 k_1 + \bar{\gamma}_2(1 - k_1)]$$

$$- \mu(\bar{x}_1 - \bar{x}_2) \lim_{w \to w(p)^-} \psi_r(k_1, r_1 - r_2)$$

(A2)
$$= \frac{1}{e_w z} \, [\overline{\gamma}_1 k_1 + \overline{\gamma}_2 (1 - k_1)] - \mu(\overline{x}_1 - \overline{x}_2)\psi_r(k_1,0^+)$$

where $\psi_r(k_1,0^+) \equiv \lim_{(r_1 - r_2) \to 0} \psi_r(k_1, r_1 - r_2)$. Hence

(A3)  $\lim_{w \to w(p)^+} \dfrac{\partial H}{\partial w} - \lim_{w \to w(p)^-} \dfrac{\partial H}{\partial w} = \mu(\overline{x}_1 - \overline{x}_2)[\psi_r(k_1,0^+) - \psi_r(k_1,0^-)]$

which, in view of [ψ.vε] in Section 8, implies that, if $k_1 \neq \frac{1}{2}$ and $\mu \neq 0$, $\partial H/\partial w$ is discontinuous at $w = w(p)$.

How this difficulty can be overcome will be revealed later. At this stage we merely introduce two loci in the $(k_1, \mu)$-plane: the locus $\mu = \mu_+(k_1)$ on which $\lim\limits_{w \to w(p)^+} (\partial H/\partial w) = 0$, and the locus $\mu = \mu_-(k_1)$ on which $\lim\limits_{w \to w(p)^-} (\partial H/\partial w) = 0$. From (116), the required loci are

$$\mu_+(k_1) = \frac{1}{e_w z} \cdot \frac{\overline{\gamma}_1 k_1 + \overline{\gamma}_2 (1 - k_1)}{(\overline{x}_1 - \overline{x}_2)\psi_r(k_1,0^-)}$$

and

$$\mu_-(k_1) = \frac{1}{e_w z} \cdot \frac{\overline{\gamma}_1 k_1 + \overline{\gamma}_2 (1 - k_1)}{(\overline{x}_1 - \overline{x}_2)\psi_r(k_1,0^+)}$$

Recalling [γ.1]–[γ.6] of Section 8 and the properties of ψ, we can depict the two loci graphically, as in Figures A1 and A2.

We now take up in earnest the task of constructing the phase diagram for $(P_2)$.


## Trajectories with less-than-full employment

For the time being we proceed on the assumption that along any Pontryagin path there is some unemployment, so that $\lambda = 0$ in (112).

**The locus $\dot{k} = 0$**  Consider the dashed line SQQ′T in Figure A1. At any point on SQ, other than Q itself, $\mu > \mu_-(k_1) > \mu_+(k_1)$, which implies that

$$\lim_{w \to w(p)^+} \frac{\partial H}{\partial w} < 0$$

## Figure A1

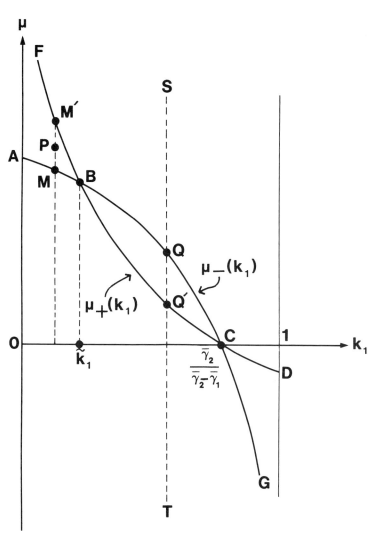

$$\overline{\gamma}_1 \tilde{k}_1 + \overline{\gamma}_2 (1-\tilde{k}_1) > 0$$

## Figure A2

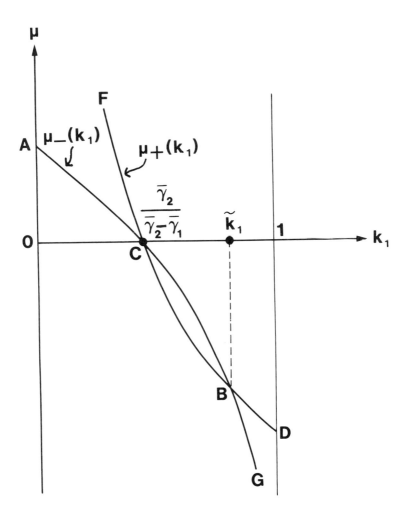

$$\bar{\gamma}_1\tilde{k}_1+\bar{\gamma}(1-\tilde{k}_1)<0$$

$$\lim_{w \to w(p)^-} \frac{\partial H}{\partial w} < 0$$

(Figure A3 depicts $H(w)$ in a neighbourhood of $w = w(p)$.) It follows that $w(p)$ does not maximize $H(w)$ at that point. Hence $\dot{k}_1 \neq 0$ at that point, for $\dot{k}_1 = 0$ only if $w = w(p)$. Moreover, from [γ.6], any $w$ that maximizes $H$ on the open interval SQ must be less than $w(p)$. From [γ.5], therefore, $\omega_1 < \omega_2$; see Figure A4, in which $\underline{w}$ is any $w$ less than $w(p)$ and $\bar{w}$ is any $w$ greater than $w(p)$. Hence $\dot{k}_1 > 0$. By a similar argument, $\dot{k}_1 < 0$ at any point on Q'T except Q'. Finally, at any point on QQ', $H(w)$ is as depicted in Figure A5; hence $w(p)$ maximizes $H$ and $\dot{k}_1 = 0$. Generalizing, $\dot{k}_1 = 0$ everywhere in the compact set BQ'CQB of Figure A1.

Consider next the points M and M' in Figure A1. At M, the wage rate which maximizes $H(w)$ is greater than $w(p)$; hence $\dot{k}_1 < 0$. At M', on the other hand, the maximizing $w$ is less than $w(p)$; hence $\dot{k}_1 > 0$. It follows that between M and M' there is a point P at which $H(w)$ reaches its maximum twice, at $w^* < w(p)$ and at $w^{**} > w(p)$; see Figure A6. At $w^*$, $\dot{k}_1 > 0$; at $w^{**}$, $\dot{k}_1 < 0$. Generalizing, there is a locus which lies between FB and AB and which passes through P such that, at any point on the locus, the sign of $\dot{k}_1$ is indeterminate; moreover it can be shown that the locus is asymptotic to the vertical axis. Between CD and CG there is a second locus CE with properties analogous to those of BP.

Finally, pooling the above information, we arrive at Figure A7, which shows how $k_1$ moves in the several regions of the $(k_1, \mu)$-plane. Above and to the right of the curve HBQCE, $\dot{k}_1 > 0$; below and to the left of the curve HBQ'CE, $\dot{k}_1 < 0$; and, in the compact set BQCQ'B, $\dot{k}_1 = 0$. On the dashed curves HB and CE, the sign of $\dot{k}_1$ is indeterminate. After we have examined the behaviour of $\mu$, however, it will become clear that the indeterminacy is inconsequential; that is, it does not prevent us from describing the motion of $(k_1, \mu)$.

**The locus $\dot{\mu} = 0$** From the first-order conditions (111)–(114), the locus $\dot{\mu} = 0$ is described by the equations

## Figure A3

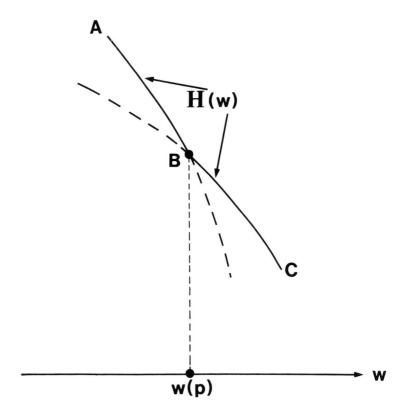

## Figure A4

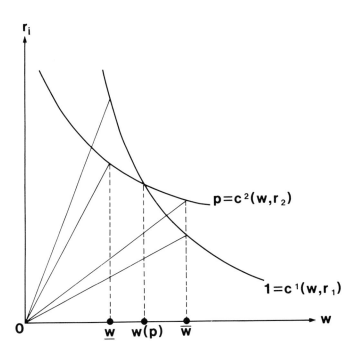

Notice that $\omega_1(\underline{w}) < \omega_2(\underline{w}/p)$ and $\omega_1(\overline{w}) > \omega_2(\overline{w}/p)$

## Figure A5

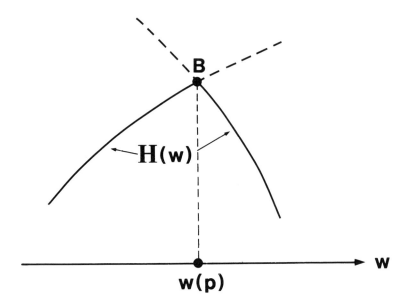

## Figure A6

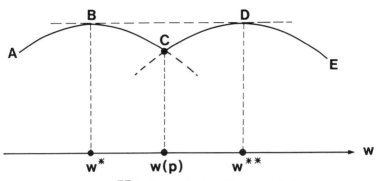

**ABCDE: H(w) at P in Figure A1**

## Figure A7

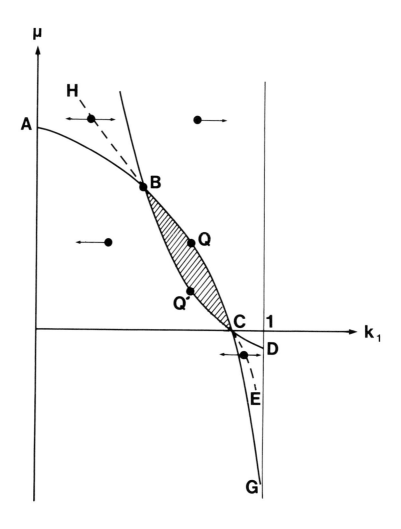

$$\frac{\partial H}{\partial w} = \frac{1}{e_w z} [\gamma_1(w)k_1 + \gamma_2(w/p)(1 - k_1)]$$

$$- \mu[x_1(w) - x_2(w/p)]\psi_r(k_1, r_1(w) - r_2(w,p))$$

(A4)      $= 0$

$$\dot{\mu} = \delta\mu - \frac{w}{e_w z} [x_1(w) - x_2(w/p)] - \mu\psi_k(k_1, r_1(w) - r_2(w/p)) = 0$$

or recalling (104), by the equations

$$\frac{1}{e_w z} [\gamma_1(w)k_1 + \gamma_2(w/p)(1-k_1)] - \mu[x_1(w) - x_2(w/p)][1-k_1] = 0$$

(A5a)

$$\delta\mu - \frac{w}{e_w z} [x_1(w) - x_2(w/p)] + \mu[r_1(w) - r_2(w,p)] = 0$$

$\left. \begin{array}{l} \\ \\ \\ \\ \end{array} \right\}$ if $r_1 > r_2$, i.e. if $w_1 \le w < w(p)$

and

$$\frac{1}{e_w z} [\gamma_1(w)k_1 + \gamma_2(w/p)(1-k_1)] - \mu[x_1(w) - x_2(w/p)]k_1 = 0$$

(A5b)

$$\delta\mu - \frac{w}{e_w z} [x_1(w) - x_2(w/p)] + \mu[r_1(w) - r_2(w,p)] = 0$$

$\left. \begin{array}{l} \\ \\ \\ \\ \end{array} \right\}$ if $r_1 < r_2$, i.e. if $w(p) \le w < w_2(p)$

Solving first (A5a) and then (A5b) for $\mu$ and $k_1$, we obtain

$$\mu = \frac{\dfrac{w}{e_w z} [x_1(w) - x_2(w/p)]}{\delta + [r_1(w) - r_2(w,p)]}$$

(A6a)

$$k_1 = \frac{\mu[x_1(w) - x_2(w/p)] \dfrac{1}{e_w z} \gamma_2(w/p)}{\mu[x_1(w) - x_2(w/p)] + \dfrac{1}{e_w z} [\gamma_1(w) - \gamma_2(w/p)]}$$

$\left. \begin{array}{l} \\ \\ \\ \\ \\ \end{array} \right\}$ if $r_1 > r_2$, i.e. if $w_1 \le w < w(p)$

and

$$\mu = \frac{\dfrac{w}{e_w z}\,[x_1(w) - x_2(w/p)]}{\delta + [r_1(w) - r_2(w, p)]}$$

(A6b)

$$k_1 = \frac{\dfrac{1}{e_w z}\,\gamma_2(w/p)}{\mu[x_1(w) - x_2(w/p)] + \dfrac{1}{e_w z}\,[\gamma_1(w) - \gamma_2(w/p)]}$$

$$\left.\begin{array}{l} \text{if}\\ r_1 < r_2,\\[4pt] \text{i.e. if}\\[4pt] w(p) < w \le w_2(p) \end{array}\right\}$$

It is easy to verify that, on the locus $\dot\mu = 0$ ,

$$\mu = \mu^* \equiv \frac{\dfrac{w_2(p)}{e_w z}\,[x_1(w_2(p)) - x_2(w_2(p)/p)]}{\delta - \psi_k(0, r_1(w_2(p)) - r_2(w_2(p)/p))} > 0$$

$$\left.\begin{array}{l} \text{if}\\[4pt] k_1 = 0 \end{array}\right\}$$

(A7a)

$$w = w_2(p)$$

and

$$\mu = \mu^{**} \equiv \frac{\dfrac{w_1}{e_w z}\,[x_1(w_1) - x_2(w_1/p)]}{\delta - \psi_k(1, r_1(w_1) - r_2(w_1, p))} > 0$$

$$\left.\begin{array}{l} \text{if}\\[4pt] k_1 = 1 \end{array}\right\}$$

(A7b)

$$w = w_1$$

Let us now define

$$A(w) \equiv \frac{\dfrac{w}{e_w z}\,[x_1(w) - x_2(w/p)]^2}{\delta + [r_1(w) - r_2(w/p)]} - \frac{1}{e_w z}\,\gamma_2(w/p)$$

so that, from (A6a),

(A8)   $$k_1 = \frac{A(w)}{A(w) + \dfrac{1}{e_w z}\,\gamma_1(w)}$$

**LEMMA A1:** $A(w_1) \neq 0$ .

**PROOF**   Suppose that $A(w_1) = 0$ .   Then, since $\gamma_1(w_1) = 0$ and recalling LHopital's rule,

(A9)        $1 = \lim\limits_{w \to w_1} k_1 = \dfrac{\lim\limits_{w \to w_1} A'(w)}{\lim\limits_{w \to w_1} A'(w) + \dfrac{1}{e_w z} \gamma_1'(w)}$

From the definition of $A(w)$, $\lim\limits_{w \to w_1} A'(w)$ is finite; and this, combined with the negativity of $\gamma_1'(w)$, implies that the right-hand side of (A9) is not equal to 1, a contradiction.                              ◊

There remain two possibilities: $A(w_1) > 0$ and $A(w_1) < 0$ .  Suppose that $A(w_1) > 0$ .

**LEMMA A2:** If $A(w_1) > 0$ then the locus $\dot{\mu} = 0$ has no point in common with the segment BQC of Figure A7.

**PROOF**  Since $A(w_1) > 0$ and since $\gamma_1(w_1) = 0$ and $\gamma_1'(w_1) < 0$ , it follows from (A8) that $k_1$ is greater than (less than) one if and only if w is greater than (less than) one.  Hence $k_1 < 1$ implies that $w < w_1$, so that $(\mu, k_1)$ is uniquely determined by (A6a).  On the other hand, $w = w(p)$ on BQC.  Hence the locus $\dot{\mu} = 0$ has no point in common with BQC.                                                            ◊

**LEMMA A3:** If $A(w_1) > 0$ then there is no point on the locus $\dot{\mu} = 0$ such that $\mu = 0$ and $w > 0$.

**PROOF**  Suppose that there is a point on the locus $\dot{\mu} = 0$ such that $\mu = 0$, $w > 0$ .  In view of Lemma A2 and the fact that $\mu^{**} > 0$, the locus must reach the axis $\mu = 0$ to the right of C or to the left of B in Figure A7.  Suppose that the locus reaches the axis to the right of C. From (A4), at the point of intersection,

$\gamma_1(w)k_1 + \gamma_2(w/p)(1 - k_1) = 0$

$w \in (0, w_1), \quad k_1 \in (0, 1)$

But if $w \in (0, w_1)$ then $\gamma_1(w)$ and $\gamma_2(w/p)$ are positive, a contradiction. Suppose alternatively that the locus $\dot{\mu} = 0$ reaches the axis $\mu = 0$ to the left of B.  From (A4), at the point of intersection,

$$\gamma_1(w)k_1 + \gamma_2(w/p)(1 - k_1) = 0$$

$$w > w_2(p), \quad k_1 \in (0,1)$$

But if $w > w_2(p)$ then $\gamma_1(w)$ and $\gamma_2(w/p)$ are negative, a further contradiction. ◊

**LEMMA A4:** If there exists $\sigma_1^* \in (0,1)$ such that $\sigma_1$ is always smaller than $\sigma_1^*$ then there exists $\tilde{w} \in (0,w_1)$ such that $k\big|_{(A8)} = 0$ at $\tilde{w}$.

**PROOF** Since $\gamma_2(w/p) > 0$ for $w \le w_1$,

$$\frac{\gamma_1(w)}{A(w)} > \frac{\gamma_1(w)e_wz[\delta + r_1(w) - r_2(w,p)]}{w[x_1(w) - x_2(w/p)]^2}$$

$$> \frac{\gamma_1(w)e_wz\delta}{w[x_1(w) - x_2(w/p)]^2} \qquad \text{[because } r_1 > r_2\text{]}$$

$$= \frac{x_1(w)[1 - \sigma_1/(1 - \theta_1)]e_wz\delta}{w[x_1(w) - x_2(w/p)]^2}$$

$$= \frac{[1 - \sigma_1/(1 - \theta_1)]e_wz\delta}{w[x_1(w) - x_2(w/p)][1 - x_2(w/p)/x_1(w)]}$$

$$> \frac{[1 - \sigma_1/(1 - \theta_1)]e_wz\delta}{wx_1(w)} \qquad \text{[because } x_1 > x_2\text{]}$$

Now we know that, since $\sigma_1 < \sigma_1^* < 1$, $\theta_1$ decreases as $w$ decreases, and that, for $w < w_1$, $1 - \sigma_1/(1 - \theta_1) > 0$ . Thus, denoting $\lim_{w \to 0} \theta_1 \equiv \theta_1^*$,

$$\lim_{w \to 0} \frac{\gamma_1(w)}{A(w)} > \frac{[1 - \sigma_1^*/(1 - \theta_1^*)]e_wz\delta}{\lim_{w \to 0} wx_1(w)}$$

Moreover, $\lim_{w \to 0} wx_1(w) = 0$ . Hence

$$\lim_{w \to 0} \frac{\gamma_1(w)}{A(w)} = \infty$$

From (A8), therefore,

$$\lim_{w \to 0} k_1\bigg|_{(A8)} = 0$$

It remains to note that if there exists $\tilde{w} \in 0, w_1)$ such that $A(\tilde{w}) = 0$ then $k_1 \big|_{(A8)} = 0$ at $w = \tilde{w}$ . $\lozenge$

In view of Lemmas (A2)–(A4), the locus $\dot{\mu} = 0$ must look like $\mu^* K \mu^{**}$ in Figure A8. For points on $K\mu^{**}$, the closer they are to K the higher the associated wage rate. At K the wage rate jumps up to some value $\bar{w}_G$, $\bar{w}_G \in (w(p), w_2(p))$. For $w \in [\bar{w}_G, w_2(p)]$, $(\mu, k_1)$ is uniquely determined by (A6b) and is represented by a point on the segment $\mu^* K$.

At this stage of our argument, Figure A8 is a possible phase diagram when $A(w_1) > 0$ . However several details of the figure remain to be justified. The justification is contained in the following four lemmas.

**LEMMA A5:** The locus $\dot{\mu} = 0$ never passes below $\mu = \mu^*$ or above $\mu = \mu^{**}$.

**PROOF** Below HBQ'CE the Pontryagin paths are described by the equations

$$\dot{k}_1 = \psi\left(k_1, w\left(\frac{1}{\omega_1} - \frac{1}{\omega_2}\right)\right)$$

(A10) $\quad \dot{\mu} = \delta\mu - \dfrac{\omega}{e_w z}(x_1 - x_2) - \mu\psi_k$

$$\frac{\partial H}{\partial w}\bigg|_{w > w(p)} = \frac{1}{e_w z}[\gamma_1 k_1 + \gamma_2(1 - k_1)] - \mu(x_1 - x_2)\psi_r = 0$$

Setting $\dot{\mu} = 0$ and differentiating the second and third equations with respect to $\mu$, $k_1$ and w, we obtain

$$0 = (\delta - \psi_k)\,d\mu - \mu\psi_{kk}\,dk_1 - \left[\frac{1}{e_w z}(\gamma_1 - \gamma_2) - \mu(x_1 - x_2)\psi_{kr}\right]dw$$

$$0 = \left[\frac{\partial^2 H}{\partial w^2}\bigg|_{w > w(p)}\right]dw + \left[\frac{1}{e_w z}(\gamma_1 - \gamma_2) - \mu(x_1 - x_2)\psi_{kr}\right]dk_1$$
$$- (x_1 - x_2)\psi_r\,d\mu$$

Eliminating dw,

## Figure A8

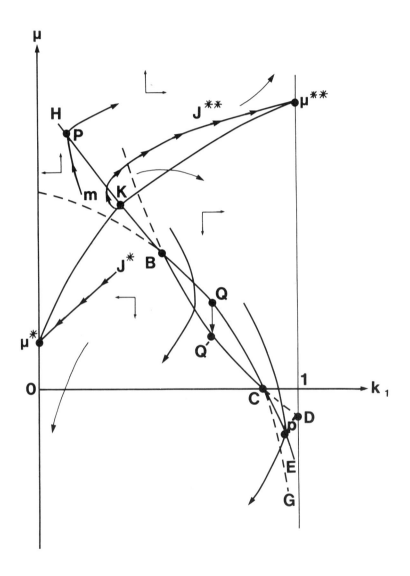

(A11) $0 = [\delta - \psi_k - \dfrac{\Sigma}{\Delta} \psi_r(x_1 - x_2)]d\mu + \left[\dfrac{\Sigma^2}{\Delta} - \mu\psi_{kk}\right]dk_1$

where

$$\Sigma \equiv \dfrac{1}{e_w z} (\gamma_1 - \gamma_2) - \mu(x_1 - x_2)\psi_{kr},$$

$$\Delta \equiv \dfrac{\partial^2 H}{\partial w^2}\bigg|_{w > w(p)}$$

From (A10), on the $k_1$-axis,

$$\gamma_1(w)k_1 + \gamma_2(w/p)(1 - k_1) = 0$$

Let $w(k_1)$ be the solution to this equation. Evidently $w_1 < w(k_1) < w(p) < w_2(p)$. From [$\gamma$.5], therefore,

$$\dfrac{w(k_1)}{e_w z} [x_1(w(k_1)) - x_2(w(k_1)/p)] > 0$$

It then follows from the second member of (A10) that, on the $k_1$-axis, $\dot{\mu} < 0$. Hence the locus $\dot{\mu} = 0$ must lie everywhere above the $k_1$-axis. On the other hand, $\psi_{kk} = 0$ and $\Sigma^2/\Delta < 0$. In view of (A11), then, the locus $\dot{\mu} = 0$ never drops below $\mu = \mu^*$.

By a similar argument, the locus $\dot{\mu} = 0$ never passes above $\mu = \mu^{**}$.                                                                  ◊

LEMMA A6: There is a unique path which asymptotically approaches $\mu^*$ and a unique path which asymptotically approaches $\mu^{**}$.

PROOF Lemma A5 assures us that, in a sufficiently small neighbourhood of $\mu^*$, the slope of the curve $\dot{\mu} = 0$ is positive. This implies that $\mu^*$ is a saddlepoint. Similarly, $\mu^{**}$ is a saddlepoint.                    ◊

Let $J^*\mu^*$ and $J^{**}\mu^{**}$ be the paths mentioned in Lemma A6.

LEMMA A7: Any Pontryagin path which passes below $J^*\mu^*$ must cross OC to the right of O, and any Pontryagin path which passes above $J^{**}\mu^{**}$ is asymptotic to the line $k_1 = 1$.

PROOF From Lemma A6, $\mu^*$ is a saddlepoint; and it can be verified that the vertical axis, on which $\dot{k}_1 = 0$, is the unstable locus of the saddle. Hence any path passing through a small neighbourhood of

$\mu^*$ must asymptotically approach the axis. In particular, any such path below $J^*\mu^*$ must cross OC at $k_1 > 0$ .

The second part of the lemma may be established by similar reasoning.                                                                   ◊

A final lemma concerns the behaviour of Pontryagin paths as they reach the lines HB and CE, on which $\dot{k}_1$ is of indeterminate sign.

**LEMMA A8:** Any Pontryagin path which reaches CE (or HB) in Figure A8 passes through CE (or HB).

**PROOF** Let us concentrate on the path mP. We have already shown that at P there are two optimal wage rates, $w^*$ and $w^{**}$; without loss, $w^* < w(p) < w^{**}$. Thus the line HB is determined by the system of equations

$$H(w^*, \mu, k_1) = H(w^{**}, \mu, k_1)$$

(A12)    $$\left. \frac{\partial}{\partial w} H(w^*, \mu, k_1) \right|_{w < w(p)} = 0$$

$$\left. \frac{\partial}{\partial w} H(w^{**}, \mu, k_1) \right|_{w > w(p)} = 0$$

Given $k_1$, (A12) determines $\mu$, $w^*$ and $w^{**}$; HB in Figure A8 is the graph of $\mu(k_1)$. Totally differentiating the first member of (A12), bearing in mind the second and third members, we obtain

$$\frac{\partial}{\partial \mu} H(w^*, \mu, k_1) d\mu + \frac{\partial}{\partial k_1} H(w^*, \mu, k_1) dk_1$$

(A13)          $$= \frac{\partial}{\partial \mu} H(w^{**}, \mu, k_1) + \frac{\partial}{\partial \mu} H(w^{**}, \mu, k_1)$$

Recalling the definition of $H$,

$$\partial H / \partial \mu = \dot{k}_1$$

$$\partial H / \partial k_1 = \delta\mu - \dot{\mu}$$

Hence, from (A13),

$$\dot{k}_1 \bigg|_{w^*} d\mu + (\delta\mu - \dot{\mu} \bigg|_{w^*}) dk_1 = \dot{k}_1 \bigg|_{w^{**}} d\mu + (\delta\mu - \dot{\mu} \bigg|_{w^{**}}) dk_1$$

or

$$\frac{du}{dk_1}\bigg|_{CG} = \frac{\dot{\mu}\big|_{w^{\cdot}} - \dot{\mu}\big|_{w^{\cdot\cdot}}}{\dot{k}_1\big|_{w^{\cdot}} - \dot{k}_1\big|_{w^{\cdot\cdot}}}$$

It follows that

$$\frac{du}{dk_1}\bigg|_{CG} - \frac{\dot{\mu}\big|_{w^{\cdot}}}{\dot{k}_1\big|_{w^{\cdot}}} = \left[\frac{\dot{k}_1\big|_{w^{\cdot\cdot}}}{\dot{k}_1\big|_{w^{\cdot}} - \dot{k}_1\big|_{w^{\cdot\cdot}}}\right]\left[\frac{\dot{\mu}_1\big|_{w^{\cdot}}}{\dot{k}_1\big|_{w^{\cdot}}} - \frac{\dot{\mu}_1\big|_{w^{\cdot\cdot}}}{\dot{k}_1\big|_{w^{\cdot\cdot}}}\right]$$

and that

$$\frac{du}{dk_1}\bigg|_{CG} - \frac{\dot{\mu}\big|_{w^{\cdot\cdot}}}{\dot{k}_1\big|_{w^{\cdot\cdot}}} = \left[\frac{\dot{k}_1\big|_{w^{\cdot}}}{\dot{k}_1\big|_{w^{\cdot}} - \dot{k}_1\big|_{w^{\cdot\cdot}}}\right]\left[\frac{\dot{\mu}_1\big|_{w^{\cdot}}}{\dot{k}_1\big|_{w^{\cdot}}} - \frac{\dot{\mu}_1\big|_{w^{\cdot\cdot}}}{\dot{k}_1\big|_{w^{\cdot\cdot}}}\right]$$

Now, at P,

$$\dot{\mu}\bigg|_{w^{\cdot}} < 0, \qquad \dot{\mu}\bigg|_{w^{\cdot\cdot}} < 0$$

and, since $w^* < w(p) < w^{**}$,

$$\dot{k}_1\bigg|_{w^{\cdot}} > 0, \qquad \dot{k}_1\bigg|_{w^{\cdot\cdot}} < 0$$

Hence

(A14a) $$\frac{\dot{\mu}\big|_{w^{\cdot}}}{\dot{k}_1\big|_{w^{\cdot}}} < \frac{du}{dk_1}\bigg|_{CG} < \frac{\dot{\mu}\big|_{w^{\cdot\cdot}}}{\dot{k}_1\big|_{w^{\cdot\cdot}}}$$

where

$$\frac{\dot{\mu}\big|_{w^{\cdot}}}{\dot{k}_1\big|_{w^{\cdot}}} < 0 < \frac{\dot{\mu}\big|_{w^{\cdot\cdot}}}{\dot{k}_1\big|_{w^{\cdot\cdot}}}$$

It follows from (A14) that, whether $w^*$ or $w^{**}$ is selected at P, the Pontryagin path must enter the region above HB.

By similar reasoning, the Pontryagin path through P' must enter the region below CE.                                                                    ◊

That completes our discussion of the case $A(w_1) > 0$. Suppose now that $A(w_1) < 0$. Since $\gamma_1(w_1) = 0$ and $\gamma_1'(w_1) < 0$, we deduce from (A8) that $k_1 < 1$ if and only if $w > w_1$, so that $(\mu, k_1)$ is uniquely determined by (A6a). In the present case we cannot rule out the possibility that the locus $\dot{\mu} = 0$ intersects the segment BQC of Figure A7. This possibility complicates the phase diagram and, as is shown in Section 8, enriches the set of long-run equilibria. Let us suppose, then, that the locus $\dot{\mu} = 0$ contains interior points of the compact set BQCQ'B of Figure A7.

Consider one such point $(k_1, \mu)$. At that point, $w = w(p)$; hence, recalling (113) and our tentative assumption that $\lambda = 0$,

$$\dot{\mu} = \delta\mu - \frac{w(p)}{e_w z} [x_1(w(p)) - x_2(w(p)/p)]$$

It follows that

$$\dot{\mu} \gtreqless 0 \text{ if and only if } \mu \gtreqless \mu^0$$

where

$$\mu^0 \equiv \frac{w(p)}{\delta e_w z} [x_1(w(p)) - x_2(w(p)/p)]$$

and, from [γ.5], $\mu^0 > 0$. Let the line $\mu = \mu^0$ intersect the $\mu_+$–curve FBUCD at U and the $\mu_-$–curve ABVCG at V; see Figure A9.

Suppose next that $(k_1, \mu)$ lies above the curve BVC in a neighbourhood of V. Above BVC the motion of $(k_1, \mu)$ is described by

$$\dot{k}_1 = \psi(k_1, w(\frac{1}{\omega_1} - \frac{1}{\omega_2}))$$

$$(A15) \quad \dot{\mu} = \delta\mu - \frac{w}{e_w z} (x_1 - x_2) - \mu\psi_k(k_1, w(\frac{1}{\omega_1} - \frac{1}{\omega_2}))$$

$$\frac{\partial H}{\partial w}\bigg|_{w < w(p)} = \frac{1}{e_w z} [\gamma_1 k_1 + \gamma_2(1 - k_1)] - \mu\psi_r(x_1 - x_2) = 0$$

(Recall that $\dfrac{\partial}{\partial w} [w(\dfrac{1}{\omega_1} - \dfrac{1}{\omega_2})] = \dfrac{\partial}{\partial w} (r_1 - r_2) = -(x_1 - x_2)$.)

Figure A9

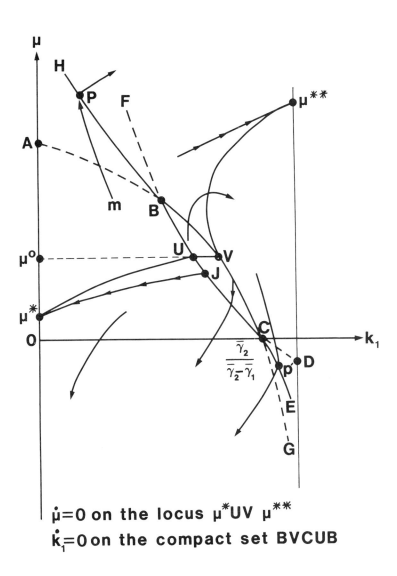

$\dot{\mu}=0$ on the locus $\mu^{*}UV\ \mu^{**}$

$\dot{k}_{1}=0$ on the compact set BVCUB

Linearizing (A15) at $(k_1^V, \mu^V)$, the coordinates of V, we obtain

(A16)
$$\zeta_k^V = \frac{\bar{\psi}_r}{\Delta_V} (\bar{x}_1 - \bar{x}_2)\bar{\eta}\,\zeta_k^V - \frac{1}{\Delta_V} [\bar{\psi}(\bar{x}_1 - \bar{x}_2)]^2 \zeta_\mu^V$$

$$\zeta_\mu^V = \frac{1}{\Delta_V} \bar{\eta}^2 \zeta_k^V + [\delta - \frac{\bar{\eta}}{\Delta_V} \bar{\psi}_r(\bar{x}_1 - \bar{x}_2)]\zeta_\mu^V$$

where

$$\zeta_k^V \equiv k_1 - k_1^V$$

$$\zeta_\mu^V \equiv \mu - \mu^V$$

$$\Delta_V = \left.\frac{\partial^2 H}{\partial w^2}\right|_{V, w < w(p)} < 0$$

$$\bar{\psi}_r = \lim_{(r_1 - r_2) \to 0^+} \psi_r(k_1^V, r_1 - r_2)$$

$$\bar{\eta} \equiv \frac{1}{e_w z} (\bar{\gamma}_1 - \bar{\gamma}_2) - \mu^V(\bar{x}_1 - \bar{x}_2) \lim_{(r_1 - r_2) \to 0^+} \psi_{kr}(k_1^V, r_1 - r_2)$$

It follows that the slope of the locus $\dot{\mu} = 0$ at V is

(A17)
$$\left.\frac{du}{dk_1}\right|_{V, \dot{\mu}=0} = \left.\frac{\zeta_\mu^V}{\zeta_k^V}\right|_{\zeta_\mu^V=0} = \frac{\bar{\eta}^2}{\delta\Delta_V - \bar{\eta}\bar{\psi}_r(\bar{x}_1 - \bar{x}_2)}$$

while the slope of BVC at V is

(A18)
$$\left.\frac{du}{dk_1}\right|_{V, BDC} = \left.\frac{du}{dk_1}\right|_{V, \dot{k}_1=0} = \left.\frac{\zeta_\mu^V}{\zeta_k^V}\right|_{\dot{\zeta}_\mu^V=0} = \frac{\bar{\eta}}{\bar{\psi}_r(\bar{x}_1 - \bar{x}_2)}$$

From (A17) and (A18),

$$\text{sign}\left[\left.\frac{du}{dk_1}\right|_{V, \dot{\mu}=0}\right] = \text{sign}\left[\left.\frac{du}{dk_1}\right|_{V, \dot{\mu}=0} - \left.\frac{du}{dk_1}\right|_{V, \dot{k}_1=0}\right]$$

(A19)
$$= \text{sign}\,(\delta - \bar{\eta}\bar{\psi}_r(\bar{x}_1 - \bar{x}_2)/\Delta_V)$$

Thus we have two cases, depending on the sign of $\delta - \bar{\eta}\bar{\psi}_r(\bar{x}_1 - \bar{x}_2)/\Delta_V$. These are illustrated by Figures A10 and A11, which display the motion of $(k_1, \mu)$ in a neighbourhood of V.

Suppose next that $(k_1, \mu)$ lies below BUC in a neighbourhood of U. By means of an argument very like that of the preceding paragraph,

**Figure A10**

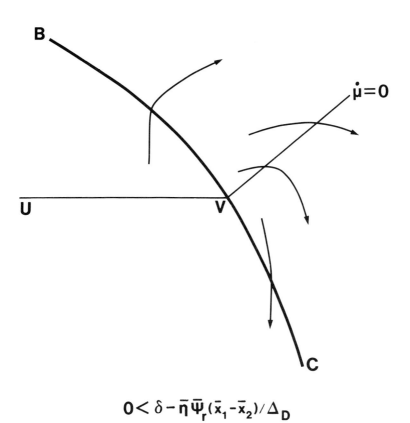

$$0 < \delta - \bar{\eta}\,\bar{\Psi}_r(\bar{x}_1 - \bar{x}_2)/\Delta_D$$

## Figure A11

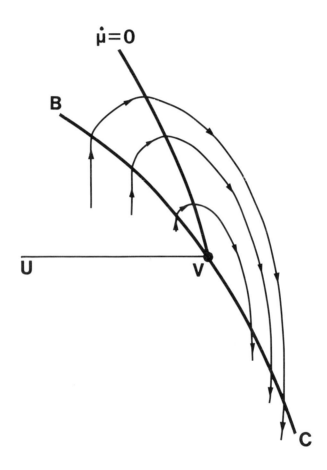

$$0 > \delta - \bar{\eta}\bar{\psi}_r(\bar{x}_1 - \bar{x}_2)/\triangle_D$$

we arrive at

$$\text{sign}\left[\left.\frac{d\mu}{dk_1}\right|_{U,\dot\mu=0}\right] = \text{sign}\left[\left.\frac{d\mu}{dk_1}\right|_{U,\dot\mu=0} - \left.\frac{d\mu}{dk_1}\right|_{U,\dot k_1=0}\right]$$

(A20)          $$= \text{sign}\,(\delta - \bar{\bar{\eta}}\bar{\bar{\psi}}_r(\bar x_1 - \bar x_2)/\Delta_U)$$

where

$$\bar{\bar{\psi}}_r \equiv \lim_{(r_1-r_2)\to 0^-}\psi_r(k_1^U, r_1 - r_2)$$

and

$$\bar{\bar{\eta}} \equiv \frac{1}{e_w z}\,(\gamma_1 - \gamma_2) - \mu^U(\bar x_1 - \bar x_2)\lim_{(r_1-r_2)\to 0^-}\psi_{kr}(k_1^U, r_1 - r_2)$$

Thus, again, we have two cases, depending on the sign of $\delta - \bar{\bar{\eta}}\bar{\bar{\psi}}_r(\bar x_1 - \bar x_2)/\Delta_U$. These are illustrated by Figures A12 and A13.

Let us now examine the behaviour of $\mu$ outside the compact set BQCQ′B and beyond the immediate neighbourhoods of U and V in Figure A9. From (A15), above BVC the locus $\dot\mu = 0$ is described by the equations

$$\dot\mu = \delta\mu - \frac{w}{e_w z}\,(x_1 - x_2) - \mu\psi_k = 0$$

(A21)

$$\left.\frac{\partial H}{\partial w}\right|_{w<w(p)} = \frac{1}{e_w z}\,[\gamma_1 k_1 - \gamma_2(1 - k_1)] - \mu(x_1 - x_2)\psi_r = 0$$

where, since $w < w(p)$, $r_1 - r_2 > 0$ and, from [ψ.iv], $\psi_k < 0$ . Now let $\mu$ increase without bound, with $k_1$ held constant. From [γ.6] and the second equation of (A21), w monotonely declines as $\mu$ increases. If, for some sufficiently large value of $\mu$, $w < w_1$ then $(wx_1)/(e_w z)$, which is greater than $[(wx_1)/(e_w z)][x_1 - x_2]$, is an increasing function of w and, from the first equation of (A21), $\dot\mu > 0$. It follows that the locus $\dot\mu = 0$ eventually (for sufficiently large $\mu$) is positively sloped. If near V it is negatively sloped (as in Figure A11) then it must eventually bend back. In any case, the locus reaches the line $k_1 = 1$ at $\mu = \mu^{**}$. To see that this is so, recall the properties of $\psi$ and consider (A21). If $k_1 = 1$ then $\psi_r = 0$ when $w < w(p)$. Hence $\left.(\partial H/\partial w)\right|_{w<w(p)} = \gamma_1(w)/(e_w z)$ which, from the definition of $w_1$, is equal to zero when $w = w_1$. The first equation of (A21) then reduces to (A7(b)). By similar reasoning,

**Figure A12**

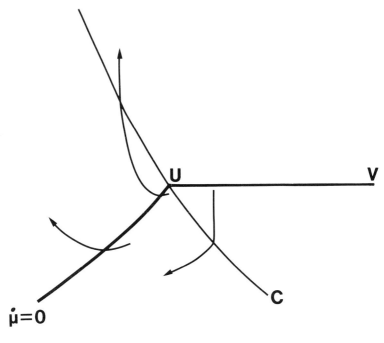

$$\delta > \bar{\bar{\eta}}\,\bar{\bar{\psi}}_r(\bar{x}_1 - \bar{x}_2)/\triangle_U$$

## Figure A13

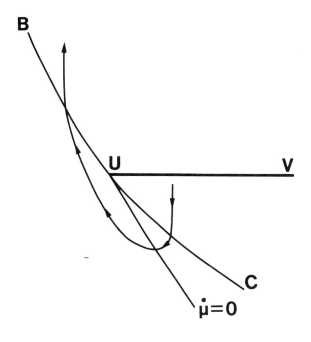

$$\delta < \bar{\bar{\eta}}\,\bar{\bar{\psi}}_r(\bar{x}_1 - \bar{x}_2)/\Delta_U$$

below BUC the locus $\dot{\mu} = 0$ eventually (for sufficiently small $\mu$) is positively sloped. If near U it is negatively sloped, as in Figure A13, then it must eventually bend back. In any case, the locus reaches the $\mu$-axis at $\mu = \mu^*$.

Pulling together the above information, and recalling Lemmas (A5)–(A8), we can complete Figure A9, the less-than-full-employment phase diagram when $A(w_1) < 0$.

### Full-employment trajectories

To this point we have ignored the employment constraint (105), assuming in effect that along each Pontryagin path there is some unemployment. Suppose now that the constraint holds with equality, so that the Pontryagin paths are described by the system

$$\frac{\partial L}{\partial w} = \frac{1}{e_w z} [\gamma_1(w)k_1 + \gamma_2(\frac{w}{p})(1 - k_1)]$$

$$- \mu[x_1(w) - x_2(\frac{w}{p})]\psi_r(k_1, r_1(w) - r_2(w,p))$$

(A22)        $$- \lambda[x_1'(w)k_1 + x_2'(\frac{w}{p})(1 - k_1)] = 0$$

(A23)   $z = x_1(w)k_1 + x_2(w/p)(1 - k_1)$

(A24)   $\dot{\mu} = \delta\mu - \psi_k(k_1, r_1(w) - r_2(w,p))\mu - [\frac{w}{e_w z}\lambda][x_1(w) - x_2(w/p)]$

(A25)   $\dot{k}_1 = \psi(k_1, r_1(w) - r_2(w,p))$

(A26)   $\lambda \geq 0$

Before examining this system in detail we introduce some additional definitions and a preliminary proposition. First, let us define $\bar{w}_1(z)$ and $\bar{w}_2(p,z)$ to be the solutions to the equations $z = x_1(w)$ and $z = x_2(w/p)$, respectively. It is easy to see that $\bar{w}_1(z) > \bar{w}_2(p,z)$ and that there exists $k_1(p,z) \in (0,1)$ such that

(A27)   $z = x_1(w/p)k_1(p,z) + x_2(w(p)/p)[1 - k_1(p,z)]$

if and only if

(A28)   $\bar{w}_1(z) > w(p) > \bar{w}_2(p,z)$

Henceforth it will be assumed that (A.28) is satisfied. Proceeding, let us next define

(A29)   $Q(k_1; p) \equiv \gamma_1(w)k_1 + \gamma_2(w/p)(1 - k_1)$

where w is linked with $k_1$ by (A23). Differentiating (A29) with respect to $k_1$, we obtain

(A30)   $\dfrac{dQ}{dk_1} = (\gamma_1 - \gamma_2) + [\gamma_1' k_1 + (1/p)\gamma_2'(1 - k_1)]\left. \dfrac{dw}{dk_1} \right|_{(A18)}$

where

(A31)   $\left. \dfrac{dw}{dk_1} \right|_{(A18)} = - \dfrac{(x_1 - x_2)}{[x_1' k_1 + (1/p)x_2'(1 - k_1)]} > 0$

Evidently $dQ/dk_1 < 0$ . Since, in addition,

$$Q(0; p) = \gamma_2(\bar{w}_2(p,z)/p) > \gamma_2(w(p)/p) > 0$$

and

$$Q(1; p) = \gamma_1(\bar{w}_1(z)) < \gamma_1(w(p)) < 0$$

there exists a unique $k_1$, say $k_1^*(p,z)$, such that $Q(k_1^*(p,z); p) = 0$ and such that $Q(k_1; p)$ is positive or negative as $k_1 \in [0, k_1^*(p, z))$ or $k_1 \in (k_1^*(p,z), 1]$, respectively. Finally, let us recall that $\bar{\gamma}_1 \equiv \gamma_1(\bar{w}(p))$ and $\bar{\gamma}_2 \equiv \gamma_2(\bar{w}(p)/p)$ and let us define $w^*(p,z)$ as the solution to the equation

$$z = x_1(w)k_1^*(p, z) + x_2(w/p)[1 - k_1^*(p, z)]$$

**LEMMA A9:** The following statements are equivalent:

(A32)   $k_1^*(p,z) \gtreqless \bar{\gamma}_2/(\bar{\gamma}_2 - \bar{\gamma}_1)$

(A33)   $w(p) \gtreqless w^*(p,z)$

(A34)   $k_1(p,z) \gtreqless k_1^*(p,z)$

**Proof** From (A31), (A33) and (A34) are equivalent. On the other hand,

$$\frac{\partial}{\partial w} \left[ \frac{\gamma_2(w/p)}{\gamma_2(w/p) - \gamma_1(w)} \right] = \frac{\gamma_2 \gamma_1' - (1/p)\gamma_1 \gamma_2'}{[\gamma_2(w/p) - \gamma_1(w)]^2}$$

which, since $\gamma_1' < 0$, $\gamma_1 < 0$ and $\gamma_2 > 0$ , is negative; and, since

$$Q(k_1^*(p,z); p) = \gamma_1(w^*(p, z)k_1^*(p, z) + \gamma_2(w^*(p, z)/p)[1 - k_1^*(p,z)]$$

$$= 0,$$

$$k_1^*(p, z) = \gamma_2(w^*(p, z)/p)/[\gamma_2(w^*(p, z)/p) - \gamma_1(w^*(p, z))]$$

Hence (A32) and (A33) are equivalent.

Let us now return to the system (A22)–(A26). For the time being, however, we shall ignore (A26).

**The locus $\dot{k}_1 = 0$** Inspection of the above system reveals that (A23) and (A25) completely determine the motion of $k_1$ and $w$ and that, on the $(k_1, w)$-plane, the locus $\dot{k}_1 = 0$ is the vertical line $k_1 = k_1(p, z)$.

**The locus $\dot{\mu} = 0$** From (A22) and (A24), with $\dot{\mu} = 0$, we obtain

$$(A35) \quad \lambda = \frac{\dfrac{1}{e_w z} Q(k_1; p) - [x_1(w) - x_2(w/p)]\psi_r \mu}{x_1'(w)k_1 + (1/p)x_2'(w/p)(1 - k_1)}$$

and

$$(A36) \quad \lambda = \frac{w}{e_w z} - \left[ \frac{\delta - \psi_k(k_1, r_1(w) - r_2(w, p))}{x_1(w) - x_2(w/p)} \right] \mu$$

respectively. However, from (A23), $w$ is uniquely associated with $k_1$. For each $k_1 \in [0,1]$, therefore, the graphs of (A35) and (A36) are straight lines in the $(\lambda, \mu)$-plane, with a positive slope for (A35), a negative slope for (A36), and a unique intersection. It follows that the locus $\dot{\mu} = 0$ exists and expresses $\mu$ as a function of $k_1$, $k_1 \in [0,1]$; Figure A14 illustrates. However, from (A35), bearing in mind that $\psi_r$ is discontinuous at $r_1 - r_2 = 0$, that is, at $w = w(p)$, the locus lacks continuity; in fact, there is a jump in (A35) at $k_1 = k_1(p, z)$. Let us assume that

$$(A37) \quad k_1(p, z) > \frac{1}{2}$$

so that, from [ψ.5ε],

## Figure A14

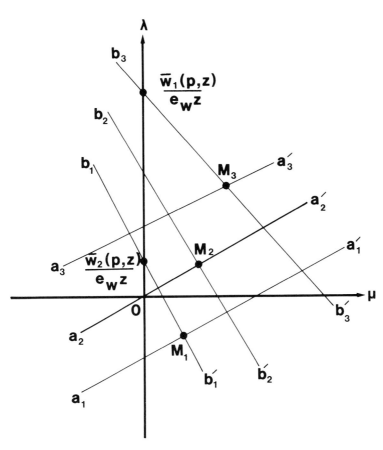

$a_1 a_1'$: eq.(A35) with $k_1 = 0$            $b_1 b_1'$: eq.(A36) with $k_1 = 0$

$a_2 a_2'$: eq.(A35) with $k_1 = k_1^*(p,z)$      $b_2 b_2'$: eq.(A36) with $k_1 = k_1^*(p,z)$

$a_3 a_3'$: eq.(A35) with $k_1 = 1$            $b_3 b_3'$: eq.(A36) with $k_1 = 1$

$$\lim_{w \to w(p)^-} \psi_r(k_1(p,z), r_1(w) - r_2(w,p))$$

$$< \lim_{w \to w(p)^+} \psi_r(k_1(p,z), r_1(w) - r_2(w,p))$$

It can then be seen that (A35) jumps in the manner indicated by the thick arrows of Figure A15. In Figure A15(a), either bb' or $\tilde{b}\tilde{b}'$ is the graph of (A36) at $w = w(p)$ and $\mu$ jumps either from F to G or from F' to G', respectively. In Figure A15(b), the jump is from F to G.

Pulling together the foregoing results we arrive at the "full-employment" phase diagram, of which Figures A16(a) and A16(b) are two examples. In that figure, each point of the segment BC represents a steady state and the dashed lines $l_1B$ and $l_2C$ are stable loci. (It will be clear that B and C have saddlepoint properties.)

## The complete phase diagram

It remains to combine the phase diagrams associated with the regimes of full employment and less-than-full employment, and for that it is necessary that we be able to draw, on the $(k_1, \mu)$-plane, the boundary line separating the region of full employment from the region of less-than-full employment. The boundary line is obtained by setting $\lambda = 0$ in (A22) and (A23):

$$0 = \frac{1}{e_w z} Q(k_1; p) - \mu[x_1(w) - x_2(w/p)]\psi_r(k_1, r_1(w) - r_2(w/p))$$

(A38)

$$z = x_1(w)k_1 + x_2(w/p)(1 - k_1)$$

Equation (A38) can be solved for $w$ and $\mu$ in terms of $k_1$. The relationship between $\mu$ and $k_1$ marks the boundary.

Suppose that $k_1(p, z)$ is between $k_1^y$ and $\bar{\gamma}_2/(\bar{\gamma}_2 - \bar{\gamma}_1)$, as in Figure A17. Recalling the definitions of $\mu_+(k_1)$ (represented by B$l''$C in Figure A17) and $\mu_-(k_1)$ (represented by BV$l'$C), it is clear that one portion of the boundary line, $ll'$, must lie above FBV$l'$, and that another portion, $l''l'''$, must lie below $l''$CM. In that case, $k_1^*(p, z)$ is the point of intersection of $l''l'''$ and the horizontal axis. The boundary is therefore marked by the jointed curve $ll'l''l'''$ of Figure A17. Above the boundary, full employment prevails and the motion of $(k_1, \mu)$ is described by Figure A16. Below the boundary, there is unemployment

# Figure A15

(a)

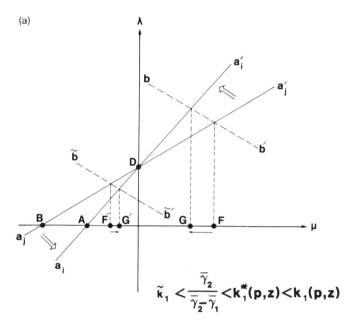

$$\tilde{k}_1 < \frac{\overline{\gamma}_2}{\overline{\gamma}_2 - \overline{\gamma}_1} < k_1^*(p,z) < k_1(p,z)$$

(b)

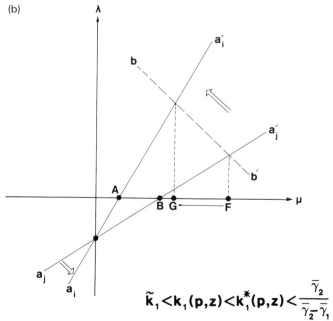

$$\tilde{k}_1 < k_1(p,z) < k_1^*(p,z) < \frac{\overline{\gamma}_2}{\overline{\gamma}_2 - \overline{\gamma}_1}$$

# Figure A16

(a)

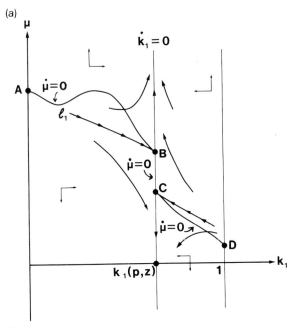

(b)

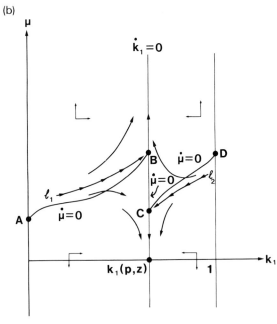

## Figure A17

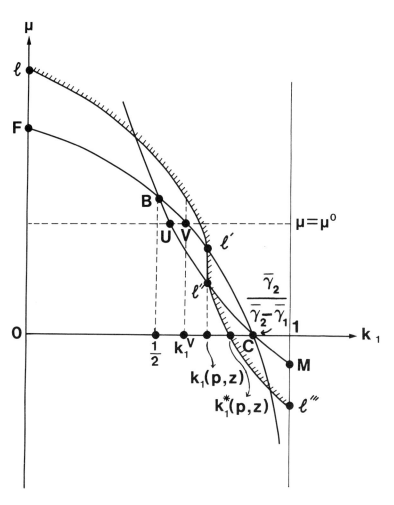

$$\tfrac{1}{2} < k_1(p,z) < k_1^*(p,z) < \overline{\gamma}_2 / (\overline{\gamma}_2 - \overline{\gamma}_1)$$

and the motion is described by Figure A8 or Figure A9. Figures A18 and A19 are the complete phase diagrams, Figure A18 being a composite of Figures A8 and A16, Figure A19 a composite of Figures A9 and A16.

Other cases might be considered; for example, the case in which $k_1(p,z)$ is greater than $\bar{\gamma}_2/(\bar{\gamma}_2 - \bar{\gamma}_1)$ and the case in which $k_1(p, z) < \frac{1}{2}$. However, in those cases, no new possibilities emerge. Indeed, in the further analysis of Section 8 we shall focus on Figure A19 which displays the richest variety of possible paths.

**Figure A18**

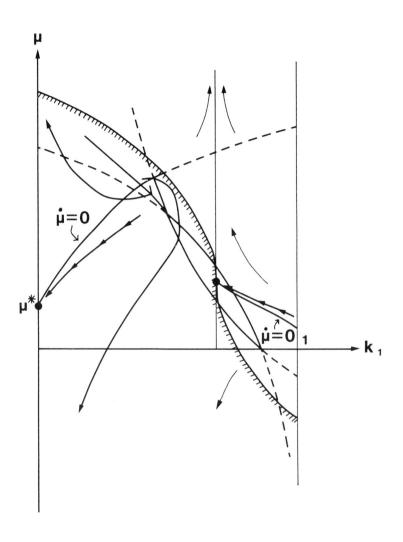

## Figure A19

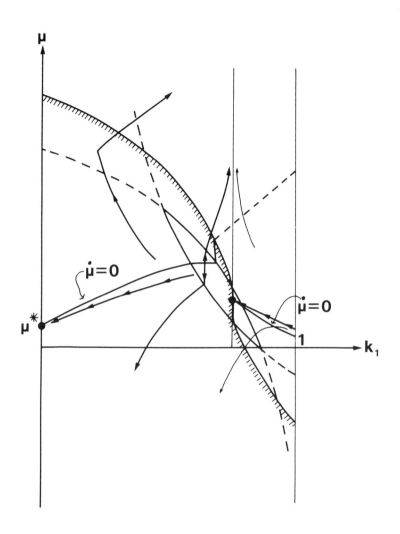

# FOOTNOTES

(1)  Recalling (62a),

$$1 + \frac{NY_{NN}}{Y_N} = \frac{-N}{H}\left[\left[1 - \frac{\sigma_1}{1-\theta_1}\right]\frac{N_1}{N} + \left[1 - \frac{\sigma_2}{1-\theta_1}\right]\frac{N_2}{N}\right]$$

$$= \frac{\dfrac{NY_N}{p(Y_p + Y_p^*)}\left[\varepsilon_e - \dfrac{pY_{Np}}{Y_N}\right]^2}{\left[\dfrac{1-\varepsilon_e}{\sigma_e} + \dfrac{p(Y_{pp} + Y_{pp}^*)}{Y_p + Y_p^*}\right]}$$

which goes to zero as $Y_{pp}^*$ goes to infinity.  Thus the first-order condition obtained by equating (93) to zero reduces to (9) in the small-country case.

CHAPTER FOUR

A LABOUR UNION IN EVERY COUNTRY

In Chapters II and III we have examined some of the consequences
of the formation in a single trading country of a rational and well-
informed economy-wide labour union. However, if workers can organize themselves in one trading country, they can organize themselves
in all trading countries. Accordingly, we now allow for the possibility
that there is such a union in each trading country.

Putting aside the uninteresting case in which all countries are small,
at least some national unions will perceive that they stand in strategic
relationships to other unions. Thus we are led to an explicitly game-
theoretical analysis. This contrasts sharply with the discussion of
Chaps. II and III but resembles the familiar Scitovsky (1942)-Johnson
(1954)-Gorman (1958) treatment of the reciprocal tariff game of the
theory of international trade. Indeed we shall seek to answer questions most of which have parallels in that corner of trade theory: Is
it possible for the workers of all countries to be worse off [better off]
in a union-ridden world than in a union-free world? Is it possible for
the pattern of world trade to be upset by the formation of a union in
each trading country? How does the world wage-employment equilibrium respond to changes in national factor endowments and other
parameters of the game?

1. ASSUMPTIONS, DEFINITIONS, AND OTHER PRELIM-
   INARIES

To make way for the complication of a strategic relationship between
unions, we retreat to the model of Chapter II. Thus, throughout the
present chapter, it is assumed that there are two trading countries (the
home country and the foreign country), two factors of production
(capital and labour) and two produced and tradeable consumption

goods. There is a no-joint-products, constant-returns technology, the same for each country; the first commodity is relatively labour-intensive. Moreover, it is now assumed that all households (capitalist or worker, home or foreign) have the same homothetic preferences. Finally, it is assumed that in each country there is a strong labour union. Following the discussion of Section II.1, the objective function of the home union is

$$(1) \quad U = \frac{N}{\bar{N}} \frac{w}{e(p)} = \frac{x}{z} \frac{w}{e(p)}$$

and, distinguishing foreign variables by asterisks, the objective function of the foreign union is

$$(2) \quad U^* = \frac{N^*}{\bar{N}^*} \frac{w^*}{e(p)} = \frac{x^*}{z^*} \frac{w^*}{e(p)}$$

Our assumptions about technology and preferences laid out, we proceed to define the GNP or revenue function of the home country:

$$Y(P,N,K) = \max_{N_i, K_i} \left\{ Y_1 + pY_2 : Y_i = F_i(N_i,K_i), N \geq \Sigma N_i, K \geq \Sigma K_i \right\}$$

Evidently the function is homogeneous of degree one in $N$ and $\bar{K}$; hence

$$Y(p,N,K) = KY(p,N/K,1) \equiv Ky(p,x)$$

where $y$ is the maximum value of output (in terms of the numeraire) per unit of capital. It is well known that

$$Y_p(p,N,K) = Ky_p(p,x) = Y_2$$

Moreover, if factor markets are competitive,

$$(3) \quad w = Y_N(p,N,K) = y_x(p,x)$$

and

$$(4) \quad r = Y_K(p,N,K) = y(p,x) - xy_x(p,x)$$

so that (1) can be rewritten as

$$(1') \quad U = \frac{x}{z} \frac{y_x(p,x)}{e(p)}$$

Similarly, (2) can be rewritten as

$$(2') \quad U^* = \frac{x^*}{z^*} \frac{y_x(p,x^*)}{e(p)}$$

Drawing on the properties of the revenue function, and recalling from Section II.3 that $pe'(p)/e(p)$ is the proportion of each household's budget devoted to the second commodity, we can now set down the market-clearing equation

$$(5) \quad ED_2 + ED_2^* = \frac{e'(p)}{e(p)} y(p,x) - y_p(p,x)$$

$$+ h\left[ \frac{e'(p)}{e(p)} y(p,x^*) - y_p(p,x^*) \right] = 0$$

(Walras' Law ensures that if one market clears then so does the other market.)

Equation (5) describes a world economy in which $x$ and $x^*$ are given numbers; in particular, it models the pre-union economy in which $x = \bar{N}/K \equiv z$ and $x^* = \bar{N}^*/K^* \equiv z^*$. Suppose that $(x,x^*) \geq 0$ is given, with not both $x$ and $x^*$ zero. Since there are just two commodities and since the excess-demand functions are continuous, (5) has a solution; see Arrow and Hahn (1971, pp. 24–25). We may go further. At any positive and finite equilibrium price ratio $\bar{p}$,

$$\frac{\partial}{\partial p} (ED_2 + ED_2^*) = \frac{e''(\bar{p})}{e(\bar{p})} y(\bar{p},x) - y_{pp}(\bar{p},x)$$

$$+ h\left[ \frac{e''(\bar{p})}{e(\bar{p})} y(\bar{p},x^*) - y_{pp}(\bar{p},x^*) \right] < 0$$

Hence the equilibrium price is unique and the system globally stable. Of course, the unique equilibrium price need not be positive and finite. However that additional property is secured if the unit expenditure function is subjected to the mild requirement that

$$(6) \quad \sup_{p \geq 0} \frac{pe'(p)}{e(p)} < 1 \quad \text{for any } (x,x^*) \geq 0, (x,x^*) \neq 0$$

Thus suppose, without loss, that $x > 0$ and consider expression (5).

Let p converge to zero. Then, given the assumed properties of $y(p,x)$ and $e(p)$, for given x

$$e'(p)/e(p) \to \infty, \quad y(p,x) \to y(0,x) > 0, \quad y_p(p,x) \to 0,$$

implying that $(ED_2 + ED_2^*)$ diverges to infinity. Let p diverge to infinity. Then

$$\frac{e'(p)}{e(p)} y(p,x) - y_p(p,x) \to -\left[ 1 - \lim_{p \to \infty} \frac{pe'(p)}{e(p)} \right] \lim_{p \to \infty} y_p(p,x)$$

where $\lim_{p \to \infty} y_p(p,x)$ is positive and finite. In view of (6), therefore, $(ED_2 + ED_2^*)$ converges to some negative value. That completes the proof that the equilibrium price is positive and finite. Our findings to this point are summarized by the following lemma.

**LEMMA:** For any non-negative x and $x^*$ with not both x and $x^*$ zero, equation (5) has a unique and globally stable equilibrium; if in addition

$$\sup_{p \geq 0} \frac{pe'(p)}{e(p)} < 1$$

then the equilibrium price ratio is positive and finite.

In a union-ridden world, x and $x^*$ are not given but are the outcome of a game played by the two national labour unions. Consider Figure 1. Since the available technical information is everywhere the same and since all households have the same homothetic preferences, any outcome $(x, x^*)$ on or sufficiently close to the 45 degree line must be associated with incomplete specialization in each country. Let AB and A'B' mark the boundary of the region in which neither country specializes. For the sake of brevity we shall concentrate on Nash equilibria which lie in that region.

In Chapter II it was assumed that the union sets the wage rate, firms then deciding how many workers to hire in the light of that wage. It might have been assumed, instead, that the union sets the level of aggregate employment, leaving to the market wage rate the task of rationing the available supply. In the pure-monopoly context of Chapter II the union's choice of instrument has no bearing on the set of equilibria. In the present context of imperfect duopoly, that is

**Figure 1**

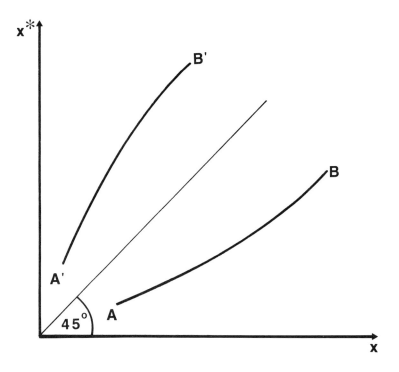

not so. We therefore must distinguish Cournot-Nash equilibria, in which each union adjusts employment, from Bertrand-Nash equilibria, in which each union adjusts the wage rate. In general the two sets of equilibria are different. In particular, the Cournot-Nash equilibrium exists uniquely under mild assumptions whereas a multiplicity of Bertrand-Nash equilibria can be ruled out only by imposing severe restrictions on preferences and technology. Since it is proposed to perform several comparative statics calculations, attention is focused on Cournot-Nash equilibria; however a brief discussion of Bertrand-Nash equilibria may be found in the appendix to this chapter.

## 2.    COURNOT-NASH EQUILIBRIUM: CAPITAL INTERNATIONALLY IMMOBILE

Let us denote a Cournot-Nash equilibrium by the triplet $(\hat{x}, \hat{x}^*, \hat{p})$ and let us call an equilibrium internal if $0 < \hat{x} < z$, $0 < \hat{x}^* < z^*$ and $0 < \hat{p} < \infty$. In the present section we provide an interesting sufficient condition for the existence of an internal Cournot-Nash equilibrium with incomplete specialization everywhere and demonstrate that, in any such equilibrium and whatever the value of $h \equiv K^*/K$, home and foreign employment levels must be equal. In Section 3 we consider some comparative statics of internal Cournot-Nash equilibria with incomplete specialization.

PROPOSITION 1: Suppose that there exists an internal Cournot-Nash equilibrium with incomplete specialization everywhere. In such an equilibrium the same level of employment prevails in each country.

The proposition is extremely plausible. Since production is everywhere incompletely specialized, the same wage rate prevails in each country (factor price equalization). In view of (1) and (2), therefore, each union maximizes the product of the level of employment and $w/e(p)$.

PROOF Differentiating (1'), (2') and (5) on the region of incomplete specialization, we obtain

$$(7) \quad \frac{dp}{p} = \phi(p) \left[ \frac{x}{x+hx^*} \frac{dx}{x} + \frac{hx^*}{x+hx^*} \frac{dx^*}{x^*} \right]$$

$$(8) \quad \frac{dU}{U} = \frac{dx}{x} - \left[ \varepsilon_e + \frac{1 - \theta_1}{\theta_1 - \theta_2} \right] \frac{dp}{p}$$

$$(9) \quad \frac{dU^*}{U^*} = \frac{dx^*}{x^*} - \left[ \varepsilon_e + \frac{1 - \theta_1}{\theta_1 - \theta_2} \right] \frac{dp}{p}$$

where

$$(10) \quad \phi(p) \equiv \frac{1}{\Lambda} (\theta_1 - \theta_2)[\theta_1 - \varepsilon_e(\theta_1 - \theta_2)][\varepsilon_e(\theta_1 - \theta_2) + (1 - \theta_1)] > 0$$

$$\Lambda \equiv (1/\sigma_e)\varepsilon_e(1 - \varepsilon_e)(\theta_1 - \theta_2)^2 + \sigma_1(1 - \varepsilon_e)\theta_1(1 - \theta_1)$$

$$+ \sigma_2\varepsilon_e\theta_2(1 - \theta_2)$$

and, from Chapter II, $\sigma_e \equiv -(1 - \varepsilon_e)e'/(pe'')$, $\varepsilon_e \equiv pe'/e$, $\sigma_i \equiv (c^i c^i_{wr})$ $/(c^i_w/c^i_r)$ and $\theta_i \equiv wc^i_w/c^i$, $i = 1, 2$. Substituting (7) into (8) and (9), we obtain

$$(8') \quad \frac{dU}{U} = \left[ 1 - \left[ \varepsilon_e + \frac{1 - \theta_1}{\theta_1 - \theta_2} \right] \left[ \frac{x}{x + hx^*} \right] \phi(p) \right] \frac{dx}{x}$$

$$- \left[ \varepsilon_e + \frac{1 - \theta_1}{\theta_1 - \theta_2} \right] \left[ \frac{hx}{x + hx^*} \right] \phi(p) \frac{dx^*}{x^*}$$

and

$$(9') \quad \frac{dU^*}{U^*} = \left[ 1 - \left[ \varepsilon_e + \frac{1 - \theta_1}{\theta_1 - \theta_2} \right] \left[ \frac{x^*}{x + hx^*} \right] \phi(p) \right] \frac{dx^*}{x^*}$$

$$- \left[ \varepsilon_e + \frac{1 - \theta_1}{\theta_1 - \theta_2} \right] \left[ \frac{hx}{x + hx^*} \right] \phi(p) \frac{dx}{x}$$

Suppose that there is an internal Cournot-Nash equilibrium in the region of incomplete specialization. Then $(\hat{x}, \hat{x}^*, \hat{p})$ satisfies

$$(11) \quad 1 - \left[ \varepsilon_e(p) + \frac{1 - \theta_1(p)}{\theta_1(p) - \theta_2(p)} \right] \left[ \frac{x}{x + hx^*} \right] \phi(p) = 0$$

$$1 - \left[ \varepsilon_e(p) + \frac{1 - \theta_1(p)}{\theta_1(p) - \theta_2(p)} \right] \left[ \frac{hx^*}{x + hx^*} \right] \phi(p) = 0$$

and (5), which can be rewritten as

$$(5') \quad \frac{x + hx^*}{1 + h} = \frac{r(p)}{w(p)} \frac{\theta_1(p) - \varepsilon_e(p)[\theta_1(p) - \theta_2(p)]}{\varepsilon_e(p)[\theta_1(p) - \theta_2(p)] + 1 - \theta_1(p)}$$

It follows from (11) that for the existence of $(\hat{x}, \hat{x}^*, \hat{p})$ it is necessary that

$$(12) \quad x = hx^*$$

and, therefore, that $\hat{N} = \hat{N}^*$. ◊

**COROLLARY 1:** Suppose that there exists an internal Cournot-Nash equilibrium with incomplete specialization everywhere. Then (i) the level and rate of unemployment at home are greater than [less than, equal to] the level and rate of unemployment abroad if and only if the home work force is greater than [less than, equal to] the foreign work force. Moreover (ii) the pattern of international trade depends on the ratio $h \equiv K^*/K$, with the home country exporting the first [the second, neither] commodity if and only if h is greater than [less than, equal to] one; that is, the pattern of trade is determined not by international differences in factor endowment *ratios* but simply by international differences in capital endowments.

**PROOF** Part (ii) of the Corollary follows from (12) and the Heckscher-Ohlin Theorem. ◊

In Proposition 1 it is taken for granted that there exists an interior Cournot-Nash equilibrium with incomplete specialization in both countries. We now provide conditions which, if satisfied, ensure the existence of such an equilibrium. Let us define

$$\bar{p} \equiv \sup \{p \in A\}$$

and

$$\underline{p} \equiv \inf \{p \in A\}$$

where

$$A \equiv \{p \mid 1 = c^1(w,r) \text{ and } p = c^2(w,r) \text{ have a solution } (w,r) \geq 0\}$$

**PROPOSITION 2:** There exists a unique internal Cournot-Nash equilibrium with incomplete specialization in both countries if

(i) $z \equiv \bar{N}/K$ and $z^* \equiv \bar{N}^*/K^*$ are sufficiently great,

(ii) $\eta(p) \equiv \left[ \varepsilon_e(p) + \dfrac{1 - \theta_1(p)}{\theta_1(p) - \theta_2(p)} \right] \phi(p)$ is an increasing function

of p over $(\underline{p},\bar{p})$,

(iii) $\lim\limits_{p \to \bar{p}} \varepsilon_e(p) = 1$ and $\lim\limits_{p \to \underline{p}} \varepsilon_e(p) = 0$, and

(iv) $\lim\limits_{p \to \bar{p}} \dfrac{1 - \theta_2(p)}{\sigma_2(p)} > 2 > \lim\limits_{p \to \underline{p}} \dfrac{1 - \theta_1(p)}{\sigma_1(p)}$

**PROOF** If an internal Cournot-Nash equilibrium exists, it must satisfy

(13) $2 - \eta(p) = 0$

Hence (ii) ensures uniqueness of the equilibrium.

Now suppose that (13) has a solution, say $\hat{p}$. It will be shown that, given (i), $(\hat{x},\hat{x}^*,\hat{p})$ is an internal Cournot-Nash equilibrium, with

(14) $\hat{x} = h\hat{x}^* = (1 + h) \dfrac{r(\hat{p})}{w(\hat{p})} \dfrac{\{\theta_1(\hat{p}) - \varepsilon_e(\hat{p})[\theta_1(\hat{p}) - \theta_2(\hat{p})]\}}{\{\varepsilon_e(\hat{p})[\theta_1(\hat{p}) - \theta_2(\hat{p})] + 1 - \theta_1(\hat{p})\}}$

Recalling (7) and (9), p is an increasing function of x. Since $x/(x+hx^*)$ $[hx^*/(x+hx^*)]$ is also an increasing function of x $[x^*]$, $(1-\eta(p)(x/(x+hx^*)))$ $[1-\eta(p)(hx^*/(x+hx^*))]$ must be a decreasing function of x $[x^*]$ for any given $x^*$ $[x]$. Hence $\hat{x}$ $[\hat{x}^*]$ uniquely maximizes U $[U^*]$ for any given $x^*$ $[x]$.

It remains to show that (13) has a solution. In view of (iii), one can easily verify that

$$\lim\limits_{p \to \underline{p}} \eta(p) = \lim\limits_{p \to \underline{p}} \dfrac{1 - \theta_1(p)}{\sigma_1(p)}$$

and

$$\lim\limits_{p \to \bar{p}} \eta(p) = \lim\limits_{p \to \bar{p}} \dfrac{1 - \theta_2(p)}{\sigma_2(p)}$$

Hence (iv) ensures that (13) has a solution. ◊

**PROPOSITION 3:** Conditions (ii)–(iv) of Proposition 2 are satisfied if $1/\sigma_e(p) = \sigma_1(p) = \sigma_2(p) \equiv \sigma$ is constant and lies in the open interval $(0, 1)$.

**PROOF** If $1/\sigma_e = \sigma_1 = \sigma_2 \equiv \sigma$,

$$1 - \eta(p)[x/(x + hx^*)] = 1 - \frac{(1/\sigma)\{1 - [\theta_1(1 - \varepsilon_e) + \theta_2\varepsilon_e]\}x}{x + hx^*}$$

By calculation,

$$\frac{d}{dp}[\theta_1(1 - \varepsilon_e) + \theta_2\varepsilon_e]p = - \left\{ \frac{1 - \sigma}{\theta_1 - \theta_2}[\theta_1(1 - \theta_1)(1 - \varepsilon_e) \right.$$

$$\left. + \theta_2(1 - \theta_2)\varepsilon_e] + \varepsilon_e(1 - \varepsilon_e)(\theta_1 - \theta_2) \right\} < 0$$

Hence $1 - [\theta_1(1 - \varepsilon_e) + \theta_2\varepsilon_e]$ is an increasing function of $x$, which implies that Proposition 2(ii) is satisfied. Moreover, since $\sigma < \frac{1}{2}$, $\theta_i(p)$, $i = 1, 2$, and $\varepsilon_e(p)$ converge to zero [one] as $p$ goes to $\bar{p}$ [$\underline{p}$]. Hence (iii) and (iv) also are satisfied.                                                    ◊

Propositions 2 and 3 offer sufficient conditions for factor price equalization. Indeed the conditions may be satisfied even when the factor endowment ratios of the trading countries fail to both lie in the cone of diversification defined by the competitive equilibrium prices or in the cone defined by the Cournot-Nash prices. It is ironical, perhaps, that factor price equalization may prevail not merely *when* the assumption of perfect competition is put aside but precisely *because* it is put aside.

Finally it is possible to answer two of the questions posed at the beginning of this chapter: Might the pattern of world trade be upset by the formation of a labour union in each trading country? Might the workers of all countries be better off [worse off] in a union-ridden world than in a world free of unions?

The answer to the first question is quite straightforward. Suppose that $\bar{N} > \bar{N}^*$, $K > K^*$, $z > z^*$. In the absence of unions, the home country exports the first or relatively labour-intensive good. If the sufficient conditions of Proposition 2 are satisfied, however, after the appearance of unions $N = N^*$ and $x < x^*$, implying that the first country exports the second or relatively capital-intensive good. Thus unionization may reverse the direction of trade.

The second question is more difficult. Let us return to equations (1'), (2') and (5). After the elimination of p with the aid of (5), (1') and (2') yield U and $U^*$ as functions of x and $x^*$:

$$U = \tilde{U}(x,x^*)$$

$$U^* = \tilde{U}^*(x,x^*)$$

It can be verified that

$$\frac{\partial}{\partial x^*} \tilde{U}(x,x^*)$$

(15a)

$$= \frac{hxy_x(p,x)y_x(p,x^*)}{zp^2e(p)\Delta} \left[ \frac{py_{xp}(p,x)}{y_x(p,x)} - \frac{pe'(p)}{e(p)} \right]$$

$$\left[ \frac{py_{xp}(p,x^*)}{y_x(p,x^*)} - \frac{pe'(p)}{e(p)} \right]$$

and that

$$\frac{\partial}{\partial x} \tilde{U}(x,x^*)$$

(15b)

$$= \frac{x^*y_x(p,x)y_x(p,x^*)}{z^*p^2e(p)\Delta} \left[ \frac{py_{xp}(p,x^*)}{y_x(p,x^*)} - \frac{pe'(p)}{e(p)} \right]$$

$$\left[ \frac{py_{xp}(p,x)}{y_x(p,x)} - \frac{pe'(p)}{e(p)} \right]$$

where

(16)   $\Delta < 0$

is the partial derivative with respect to p of the expression on the left-hand side of (5).

Now consider Figure 2. The loci AB and A'B' bear the same interpretations as in Figure 1. The union-ridden equilibrium is represented by point E and the union-free equilibrium by point F, both points lying in the region of incomplete specialization bounded by AB and A'B'. Suppose that E and F are sufficiently close in the sense that

# Figure 2

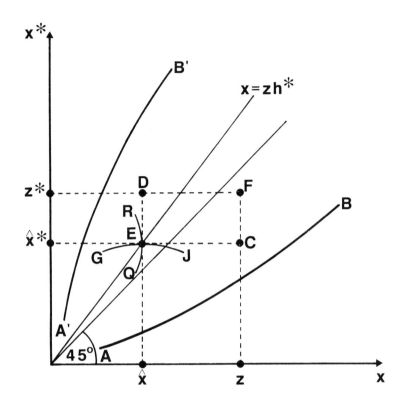

**GEJ: An indifference curve of $U(x,x^*)$**

**REQ: An indifference curve of $U^*(x,x^*)$**

points $C(z,\hat{x}^*)$ and $D(\hat{x},z^*)$ both lie within the region of incomplete specialization. For points in that region,

$$\left[ \frac{py_{xp}(p,x^*)}{y_x(p,x^*)} - \frac{pe'(p)}{e(p)} \right]\left[ \frac{py_{xp}(p,x)}{y_x(p,x)} - \frac{pe'(p)}{e(p)} \right]$$

$$(17) \quad = \left[ \frac{py_{xp}(p,x)}{y_x(p,x)} - \frac{pe'(p)}{e(p)} \right]^2 > 0$$

Hence, applying (16) and (17) to (15),

$$(18a) \quad \frac{\partial}{\partial x^*} \tilde{U}(x,x^*) < 0$$

and

$$(18b) \quad \frac{\partial}{\partial x} \tilde{U}(x,x^*) < 0$$

everywhere in the region of incomplete specialization. It follows that

$$(19a) \quad \tilde{U}(z,z^*) < \tilde{U}(z,\hat{x}^*)$$

and

$$(19b) \quad \tilde{U}^*(z,z^*) < \tilde{U}^*(\hat{x},z^*)$$

On the other hand, by definition of the Cournot-Nash equilibrium,

$$\hat{x} \equiv \arg \max_x \; \tilde{U}(x,\hat{x}^*) \qquad \text{s.t. } 0 \le x \le z$$

and

$$\hat{x}^* \equiv \arg \max_{x^*} \; \tilde{U}^*(\hat{x},x^*) \qquad \text{s.t. } 0 \le x^* \le z^*$$

Hence

$$(20a) \quad \tilde{U}(z,\hat{x}^*) \le \tilde{U}(\hat{x},\hat{x}^*)$$

and

$$(20b) \quad \tilde{U}^*(\hat{x},z^*) \le \tilde{U}^*(\hat{x},\hat{x}^*)$$

Finally, from (19) and (20),

$$\tilde{U}(z,z^*) < \tilde{U}(\hat{x},\hat{x}^*)$$

and

$$\tilde{U}^*(z,z^*) < \tilde{U}^*(\hat{x},\hat{x}^*)$$

thus establishing that if the pre-union and cum-union equilibria are sufficiently near each other then all workers, whatever their country of residence, are better off in the cum-union equilibrium. Roughly, under the stated conditions, the joint monopoly power of the unions is only partly dissipated by their duopolistic competition.

**Remark** We have required that the pre-union and cum-union equilibria be "sufficiently close" without specifying the restrictions on the basic data of the economy (preferences, technology, endowments) implied by that requirement. We now draw attention to the fact that $(\hat{x},\hat{x}^*)$ is determined by (11) and (5′) and therefore is independent of $(z,z^*)$. Evidently it is always possible, whatever the preferences and technologies of the two countries, to choose $(z,z^*)$ sufficiently close to the *constant* $(\hat{x},\hat{x}^*)$.

It has been shown that there are circumstances in which all workers benefit from world-wide unionization. Are there other circumstances in which all workers suffer? It follows from our earlier analysis that for home [foreign] workers to suffer it is necessary that point C [point D] lie below [above] the locus AB [the locus A′B′]. Consider the extreme symmetrical case in which the same constant-coefficients production function prevails in each industry, so that the loci AB and A′B′ coincide and the region of incomplete specialization is one-dimensional; and in which z and z* are both equal to the constant ratio of inputs common to the two industries. (See Figure 3.) Then, from (15),

$$(21a) \quad \frac{\partial}{\partial x^*} \tilde{U}(z,x^*) = \frac{hf_1'(z)f_2'(x^*)}{pe(p)\Delta} \left[ -\frac{pe'(p)}{e(p)} \right]\left[ 1 - \frac{pe'(p)}{e(p)} \right]$$

Since $\Delta < 0$ and $0 < pe'(p)/e(p) < 1$ , expression (21a) is positive. In contrast to (19a), therefore,

$$(22a) \quad \tilde{U}(z,z^*) > \tilde{U}(z,\hat{x}^*)$$

Similarly,

## Figure 3

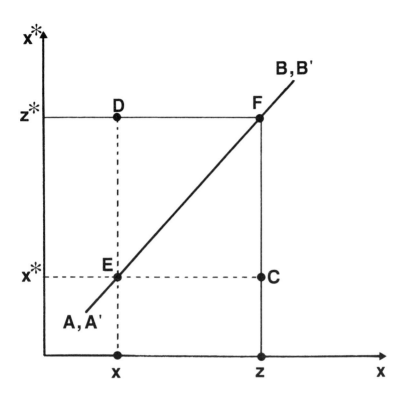

(21b) $\quad \dfrac{\partial}{\partial x} \tilde{U}^*(x,z^*) = \dfrac{hf_1'(z)f_2'(x)}{pe(p)\Delta}\left[ -\dfrac{pe'(p)}{e(p)} \right]\left[ 1 - \dfrac{pe'(p)}{e(p)} \right]$

and

(22b) $\quad \tilde{U}^*(z,z^*) > \tilde{U}^*(\hat{x},z^*)$

Next, we infer from the assumption of fixed coefficients that

(23a) $\quad \tilde{U}(z,\hat{x}^*) = \tilde{U}(\hat{x},\hat{x}^*)$

and that

(23b) $\quad \tilde{U}^*(\hat{x},z^*) = \tilde{U}^*(\hat{x},\hat{x}^*)$

Finally, from (22) and (23),

(24a) $\quad \tilde{U}(z,z^*) > \tilde{U}(\hat{x},\hat{x}^*)$

and

(24b) $\quad \tilde{U}^*(z,z^*) > \tilde{U}^*(\hat{x},\hat{x}^*)$

thus establishing that there are circumstances in which the joint monopoly power of the two labour unions is more than dissipated in duopolistic rivalry, so that all workers, whatever their country of residence, are impoverished by unionism. Of course, our example is very special; its extreme symmetry ensures that, both in the pre-union equilibrium and in its cum-union counterpart, there is no international trade. Almost needless to say, the example is unnecessarily special. The general impoverishment of workers is possible without a fixed-coefficients technology, with production functions which differ from industry to industry, and with endowment ratios which differ from country to country.

Attention has been drawn to the formal similarity between the reciprocal tariff game of the theory of international trade and the reciprocal employment game discussed in this chapter. We now see that the similarity is not perfect. In the reciprocal tariff game, at least one of the two players loses. In the reciprocal employment game, on the other hand, it is possible for both players to benefit; for in that game the players have the opportunity of jointly exploiting the capitalist bystanders.

## 3.    COMPARATIVE STATICS

Having established sufficient conditions for the existence of a unique internal Cournot-Nash equilibrium with incomplete specialization, we now consider the manner in which the equilibrium responds to small changes in the values of parameters. For brevity, attention is confined to changes in the endowment vector.

Since p is determined by (13), in which none of the endowments appears, the equilibrium value of p depends only on the common technology and preferences. Hence the comparative statics of changing endowments can be computed from [(5'), (11)] with p held constant.

Availing ourselves of this insight, we differentiate (11) with respect to x, $x^*$ and h to obtain

$$(25) \quad \frac{dx}{x} = \frac{h}{1 + h} \left[ \frac{dK^*}{K^*} - \frac{dK}{K} \right]$$

and

$$(26) \quad \frac{dx^*}{x^*} = \frac{-1}{1 + h} \left[ \frac{dK^*}{K^*} - \frac{dK}{K} \right]$$

On the other hand, from (1') and (2'),

$$(27) \quad \frac{dU}{U} = \frac{h}{1 + h} \frac{dK^*}{K^*} + \frac{1}{1 + h} \frac{dK}{K} - \frac{d\bar{N}}{\bar{N}}$$

and

$$(28) \quad \frac{dU^*}{U^*} = \frac{h}{1 + h} \frac{dK^*}{K^*} + \frac{1}{1 + h} \frac{dK}{K} - \frac{d\bar{N}^*}{\bar{N}^*}$$

Hence

$$(29) \quad \frac{K^*}{U} \frac{\partial U}{\partial K^*} = \frac{K^*}{U^*} \frac{\partial U^*}{\partial K^*} = \frac{h}{1 + h}$$

$$(30) \quad \frac{K}{U} \frac{\partial U}{\partial K} = \frac{K}{U^*} \frac{\partial U^*}{\partial K} = \frac{h}{1 + h}$$

(31) $\dfrac{\bar{N}}{U}\dfrac{\partial U}{\partial \bar{N}^*} = \dfrac{\bar{N}^*}{U^*}\dfrac{\partial U^*}{\partial \bar{N}^*} = -1$

Since p is independent of the factor endowments, so are the factor rewards w(p) and r(p) and the well-being of each capitalist, r(p)/e(p).

Finally, we consider the implications of changes in endowments for levels of output and employment. Suppose that K and $K^*$ change slightly. From Proposition 1, $N = N^*$, and, from (5'), $N + N^* = J(p)(K + K^*)$, where J(p) is the expression on the right-hand side of (5') and is positive. Hence

(32)   $N = N^* = \dfrac{1}{2}J(p)(K + K^*)$

and

(33)   $dN = dN^* = \dfrac{1}{2}J(p)(dK + dK^*)$

On the other hand, from the properties of unit-cost functions and from (32),

$$K = c_r^1 Y_1 + c_r^2 Y_2$$

(34)   $$J(p)(K + K^*) = c_w^1 Y_1^* + c_w^2 Y_2^*$$

$$K^* = c_r^1 Y_1^* + c_r^2 Y_2^*$$

$$J(p)(K + K^*) = c_w^1 Y_1^* + c_w^2 Y_2^*$$

so that, solving for $Y_i$ and $Y_i^*$,

$$Y_1 = [(c_w^2 - Jc_r^2)K - Jc_r^2 K^*] / |Q|$$

$$Y_2 = [(c_r^1 J - c_w^1)K - Jc_r^1 K^*] / |Q|$$

$$Y_1^* = [(c_w^2 - Jc_r^2)K^* - Jc_r^1 K] / |Q|$$

$$Y_2^* = [(c_r^1 J - Jc_w^1)K^* - Jc_r^1 K] / |Q|$$

where

$$|Q| = \begin{bmatrix} c_r^1 & c_r^2 \\ c_w^1 & c_w^2 \end{bmatrix} = c_r^1 c_r^2 (c_w^2/c_r^2 - c_w^1/c_r^1) < 0$$

Recalling the definition of J(p), we find that

$$c_w^2 - Jc_r^2 = c_w^2 \left\{ 1 - \frac{rc_r^2}{wc_w^2} \left[ \frac{\theta_1 - \varepsilon_e(\theta_1 - \theta_2)}{\varepsilon_e(\theta_1 - \theta_2) + 1 - \theta_1} \right] \right\}$$

$$= c_w^2 \left\{ 1 - \frac{(1 - \theta_2)[\theta_1 - \varepsilon_e(\theta_1 - \theta_2)]}{\theta_2[\varepsilon_e(\theta_1 - \theta_2) + 1 - \theta_1]} \right\}$$

$$= \frac{c_w^2(\theta_1 - \theta_2)(1 - \varepsilon_e)}{\theta_2[\varepsilon_e(\theta_1 - \theta_2) + 1 - \theta_1]}$$

$$< 0$$

and that

$$c_r^1 J - c_w^1 = c_w^1 \left\{ \frac{rc_r^1}{wc_w^1} \left[ \frac{\theta_1 - \varepsilon_e(\theta_1 - \theta_2)}{\varepsilon_e(\theta_1 - \theta_2) + 1 - \theta_1} \right] - 1 \right\}$$

$$= c_w^1 \left\{ \frac{(1 - \theta_2)[\theta_1 - \varepsilon_e(\theta_1 - \theta_2)]}{\theta_1[\varepsilon_e(\theta_1 - \theta_2) + 1 - \theta_1]} - 1 \right\}$$

$$= - \frac{c_w^1 \varepsilon_e(\theta_1 - \theta_2)}{\theta_1[\varepsilon_e(\theta_1 - \theta_2) + 1 - \theta_1]}$$

$$< 0$$

Hence

$$\frac{\partial Y_1}{\partial K} = \frac{\partial Y_1^*}{\partial K^*} > 0$$

$$\frac{\partial Y_1}{\partial K^*} = \frac{\partial Y_1^*}{\partial K} > 0$$

$$\frac{\partial Y_2}{\partial K} = \frac{\partial Y_2^*}{\partial K^*} > 0$$

$$\frac{\partial Y_2}{\partial K^*} = \frac{\partial Y_2^*}{\partial K} > 0$$

The above results are collected in Table 1.

## Table 1

| Variable<br>Parameter | U | U* | N | N* | $Y_1$ | $Y_2$ | $Y_1^*$ | $Y_2^*$ |
|---|---|---|---|---|---|---|---|---|
| K | + | + | + | + | + | + | + | + |
| K* | + | + | + | + | + | + | + | + |
| $\bar{N}$ | − | 0 | 0 | 0 | 0 | 0 | 0 | 0 |
| $\bar{N}^*$ | 0 | − | 0 | 0 | 0 | 0 | 0 | 0 |

## 4.    COURNOT-NASH EQUILIBRIUM: CAPITAL INTERNATION-ALLY MOBILE

When capital is perfectly mobile between countries, factor rewards must be everywhere equal and production everywhere incompletely specialized, at least incipiently.  Since in Sections 2 and 3 incomplete specialization is *imposed* as a simplifying assumption, one expects the conclusions of those sections to carry over with only minor and fairly obvious changes to a world in which capital is mobile.

The task of the home union is to find

$$\max_{N} \frac{N}{\bar{N}} \frac{w(p)}{e(p)}$$

subject to the restriction $N \leq \bar{N}$, where p is determined by the market-clearing condition

(35) $\dfrac{e'(p)}{e(p)} [(N + N^*)w(p) + (K + K^*)r(p)] = (N + N^*)w'(p) +$

$\qquad (K + K^*)r'(p)$

and $N^*$ is taken as given. Similarly, the foreign union seeks

$$\max_{N^*} \ \dfrac{N^*}{\bar{N}^*} \dfrac{w(p)}{e(p)}$$

subject to $N^* \leq \bar{N}^*$ and (25), with N taken as given.

Following the reasoning of Section 2, we obtain

(36) $\dfrac{dp}{p} = \phi(p)\left[ \dfrac{N}{N + N^*} \dfrac{dN}{N} + \dfrac{N^*}{N + N^*} \dfrac{dN^*}{N^*} \right]$

(37) $\dfrac{dU}{U} = \dfrac{dN}{N} - \left[ \varepsilon_e + \dfrac{1 - \theta_1}{\theta_1 - \theta_2} \right] \dfrac{dp}{p}$

(38) $\dfrac{dU^*}{U^*} = \dfrac{dN^*}{N^*} - \left[ \varepsilon_e + \dfrac{1 - \theta_1}{\theta_1 - \theta_2} \right] \dfrac{dp}{p}$

or, substituting from (26) into (27) and (28),

(39) $\dfrac{dU}{U} = \left[ 1 - \left[ \varepsilon_e + \dfrac{1 - \theta_1}{\theta_1 - \theta_2} \right]\left[ \dfrac{N}{N + N^*} \right] \phi(p) \right] \dfrac{dN}{N}$

$\qquad - \left[ \varepsilon_e + \dfrac{1 - \theta_1}{\theta_1 - \theta_2} \right]\left[ \dfrac{N^*}{N + N^*} \right] \phi(p) \dfrac{dN^*}{N^*}$

(40) $\dfrac{dU^*}{U^*} = - \left[ \varepsilon_e + \dfrac{1 - \theta_1}{\theta_1 - \theta_2} \right]\left[ \dfrac{N}{N + N^*} \right] \phi(p) \dfrac{dN}{N}$

$\qquad + \left[ 1 - \left[ \varepsilon_e + \dfrac{1 - \theta_1}{\theta_1 - \theta_2} \right]\left[ \dfrac{N}{N + N^*} \right] \phi(p) \right] \dfrac{dN}{N}$

It follows that, if there exists an internal Cournot-Nash equilibrium, it satisfies

$$(41) \quad 1 - \left[ \varepsilon_e(p) + \frac{1 - \theta_1(p)}{\theta_1(p) - \theta_2(p)} \right] \left[ \frac{N}{N + N^*} \right] \phi(p) = 0$$

$$(42) \quad 1 - \left[ \varepsilon_e(p) + \frac{1 - \theta_1(p)}{\theta_1(p) - \theta_2(p)} \right] \left[ \frac{N^*}{N + N^*} \right] \phi(p) = 0$$

$$(35') \quad \frac{N + N^*}{K + K^*} = \frac{r(p)}{w(p)} \frac{\{\theta_1(p) - \varepsilon_e(p) [\theta_1(p) - \theta_2(p)]\}}{\{\varepsilon_e(p)[\theta_1(p) - \theta_2(p)] + 1 - \theta_1(p)\}}$$

Evidently (41), (42) and (35') are virtually the same as (11) and (5'). Under conditions (i) and (ii) of Proposition 2, therefore, there is a unique Cournot-Nash equilibrium. Moreover, (12) continues to hold; that is, $x = hx^*$.

## 5. COURNOT-NASH EQUILIBRIUM: LABOUR INTERNATIONALLY MOBILE

Let us now reverse the assumptions of Section 4 by supposing that labour is internationally mobile, capital immobile.

Since we are confining our attention to equilibria with incomplete specialization in both countries, we may be sure that, before and after unionization, the same gross wage rate prevails in both countries. Moreover, since labour is mobile, the take-home wage (gross wage less the contribution of each employed worker to the relief of the unemployed) must also be the same everywhere. Thus we are dealing with a thoroughly integrated world economy.

It is reasonable to suppose that in such an economy the two national labour unions will learn to cooperate, that is, to behave like a single world-wide union. Then, clearly, the upshot of unionism is an increase in the well-being of all workers, a reduction in the effective global labour : capital endowment ratio and an increase in the relative price of the more labour-intensive commodity.

## APPENDIX:

## BERTRAND-NASH EQUILIBRIA

In Sections 2–4 it was assumed that each labour union controls one of the two national employment levels, with the corresponding wage rates determined by the competitive bidding of firms. We now briefly examine the alternative possibility, that each union controls one of the two real wage rates $u \equiv w/e(p)$ and $u^* \equiv w^*/e(p)$, with levels of employment determined by the profit-maximizing decisions of competitive firms. For simplicity, attention is confined to the case in which capital is internationally immobile, $h = 1$ and the possible production patterns are as depicted in Figure A1.

Consider the system of equations

$$y_p(p,x) + y_p(p,x^*) = \frac{e'(p)}{e(p)} [y(p,x) + y(p,x^*)]$$

(A1)  $\quad u = \dfrac{1}{e(p)} y_x(p,x)$

$$u^* = \frac{1}{e(p)} y_x(p,x^*)$$

in the variables $u$, $u^*$, $x$, $x^*$ and $p$. Given some arbitrary value of $u^*$, say $u_0^*$, (A1) defines the locus of points $\bar{a}'' \, \bar{a}'aa'a''a'''$ in the $(x,x^*)$-plane of Figure A1. For example, the segment $aa'$ is defined by

(5″)  $\quad \dfrac{x + x^*}{2} = \dfrac{r(p^*)\{\theta_1(p^*) - \varepsilon_e(p^*) [\theta_1(p^*) - \theta_2(p^*)]\}}{w(p^*)\{\varepsilon_e(p^*) [\theta_1(p^*) - \theta_2(p^*)] + 1 - \theta_1(p^*)\}}$

where $p^*$ is the solution to $u_0^* = w(p)/e(p)$. By simple but tedious calculation one can verify that, along the locus $\bar{a}''a'''$, $(dx/du)\big|_{u^*=u_0^*} < 0$, with a discontinuity at $u = u_0^*$. This information is contained in Figure A2. Evidently there is a similar relationship between $u^*$ and $x^*$ for

## Figure A1

$$\theta_1 > \theta_2$$

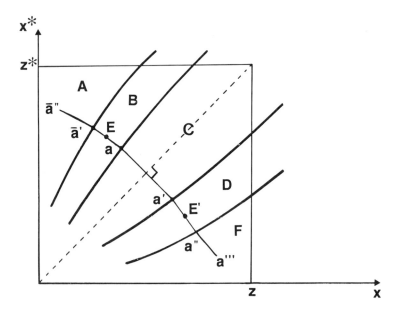

Region A: Both countries completely specialized (the home country in the second commodity, the foreign country in the first commodity.

Region B: The home country produces only the second commodity, the foreign country, both.

Region C: Both countries incompletely specialized

Region D: the home country produces both commodities, the foreign country only the second.

Region F: Both countries completely specialized (the home country in the first commodity, the foreign country in the second).

## Figure A2

(a)

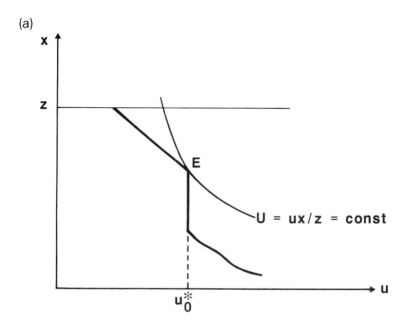

(b)

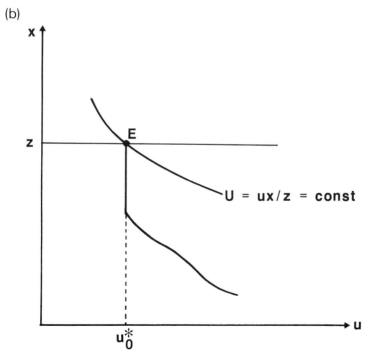

given u.

It is possible that there is an equilibrium represented by E in Figure A2(a) and by E and E′ in Figure A1. In that equilibrium, each country is completely specialized, one in the production of each commodity. By symmetry, then, there must be a second equilibrium in which specializations are reversed. That is, in general, the Bertrand-Nash equilibrium is not unique.

CHAPTER FIVE

## UNION POWER IN THE LONG RUN[1]

### 1.    INTRODUCTION

It is a serious shortcoming of Chapters II to IV that they lack a time dimension[2] and therefore either telescope or ignore phenomena which by their very nature unfold gradually.   In particular, in that earlier analysis we perforce ignored both the implications of the union's wages policy for the rate of capital accumulation and the feedback from accumulation to policy formulation.   This suggests that some of our earlier conclusions may evaporate when the suppressed dimension is restored.

In the present chapter we develop a model of a small, growing and union-ridden economy in which the union's wage policies and the processes of growth are allowed to interact.  Some of our conclusions are surprising, in the sense that they could not have been foreseen on the basis of our earlier timeless analysis.  In particular, it is shown that if workers do not save and if there exists a non-trivial steady state then eventually (after finite time) the union will find it to its advantage to refrain from exercising its market power; that is, under the stated sufficient conditions and in the long run, the union is effectively impotent.   Thus if workers do not save then either the union is eventually impotent or it drives the economy to the trivial steady state in which the capital : labour endowment ratio is zero. Whether there exists a non-trivial steady state depends on the union's rate of time preference.   Specifically, if the rate of time preference is higher than a certain level then there is no steady state.

One sees intuitively that the union's choice of policy at any moment depends critically on the elasticities of factor substitution in the active industries.   If all elasticities are equal to one (the Cobb-Douglas case), or greater, then any advance of real wages over the free-market level must both reduce the size of the national pie (by creating unemployment) and reduce or (in the Cobb-Douglas case) leave unchanged labour's share of the pie; moreover, by forcing down the return to capital and therefore the rate of saving, it will reduce the size of future pies. In these circumstances a rational union will do nothing. But if the union is passive at all times then, under standard assumptions about production and about saving, there is a stable and non-trivial steady state; hence our conclusions are obviously true. What is unexpected is that they are true even when all elasticities of substitution are less than one in magnitude.

## 2.    THE MODEL

As in earlier chapters, it is assumed that there is one big union to which all workers belong and which looks after its own unemployed; and, following Section III.8, it is assumed that the union maximizes over an infinite time horizon.

As in Chapter II, there are two concave constant-returns production functions

$$Y_i = F^i(K_i, N_i)$$

$$= K_i F^i(1, N_i/K_i)$$

$$= K_i f_i(x_i) \qquad i = 1, 2$$

where $Y_i$ is the output of the ith industry, $(K_i, N_i)$ is the vector of capital and labour inputs to the ith industry and $x_i \equiv N_i/K_i$ is the labour : capital ratio in the ith industry. Let $Y = F(K, N)$ be maximum total output, in terms of the first or numeraire good, given the available stock of capital K and the level of employment N, and given the commodity price ratio p. (Since p is held constant throughout the analysis, it is not listed as an argument of F.) From the assumption of constant returns,

$$Y = F(K, N)$$

$$= KF(1, N/K)$$

$$\equiv Kf(x)$$

where $x \equiv N/K$ is the aggregate (employed) labour : capital ratio. Suppose, as in earlier chapters, that the first industry is relatively labour-intensive. Then Figure 1 shows that the aggregate average-product function $f(x)$ may be derived from the sectoral average-product functions $f_i(x_i)$, $i = 1, 2$. If $x \in (0, \bar{x}_2]$, only the second or relatively capital-intensive good is produced and $f(x) \equiv pf_2(x)$ is strictly concave; if $x \in [\bar{x}_1, \infty)$, only the first or relatively labour-intensive good is produced and $f(x) \equiv f_1(x)$ is again strictly concave; and, finally, if $x \in (\bar{x}_2, \bar{x}_1)$, both goods are produced and $f(x)$ is linear in $x$, with $f'(x) = f'(\bar{x}_1) = pf'(\bar{x}_2)$. (It will be recalled from the Appendix to Section III.8 that $\bar{x}_1 \equiv x_1(w(p))$ and $\bar{x}_2 \equiv x_2(w(p)/p)$.) Let $\theta_i(x_i) \equiv x_i f_i'(x_i)/f_i(x_i)$ be the share of labour in the output of the ith industry and let

$$\sigma_i(x_i) \equiv -f_i'(x_i)[f_i(x_i) - x_i f_i'(x_i)]/[x_i f_i(x_i) f_i''(x_i)]$$

be the (positive) elasticity of factor substitution in the ith industry, i = 1, 2. (In Section II.2, $\theta_i$ and $\sigma_i$ were equivalently defined in terms of the ith unit cost function.) By analogy, let $\theta(x) \equiv xf'(x)/f(x)$ be the share of labour in total output and let

$$\sigma(x) \equiv -f'(x)[f(x) - xf'(x)]/[xf(x)f''(x)]$$

be the aggregate elasticity of factor substitution. In keeping with the assumptions of earlier chapters, it will be assumed that the equation

$$1 - \theta_i(x_i) - \sigma_i(x_i) = 0$$

has a positive and finite solution and that $[1 - \theta_i(x_i)]/\sigma_i(x_i)$ is an increasing function. Moreover, recalling Section III.8, it will be assumed that [γ.4] is satisfied and that $w(p)$ lies between $w_1$ and $w_2(p)$.

The total labour force is $\bar{N}$. Since $\bar{N} \geq N$, we have $x \leq z \equiv \bar{N}/K$. It is assumed that the stock of capital does not depreciate and that the labour force grows at the constant and positive rate n. (The latter assumption could be relaxed if capital depreciation were admitted.)

At least one of the two produced goods serves as a capital good, and at least one serves as a consumption good. Since relative prices are constant there is no need to be more specific about the nature of the two produced goods.

Since only capitalists save, the process of capital formation is described by

$$\dot{K} = sKF_K = sK[f(x) - xf'(x)]$$

where s, $0 < s \leq 1$, is the constant average propensity to save of capitalists and $F_K \equiv \partial F/\partial K$. It follows that

## Figure 1

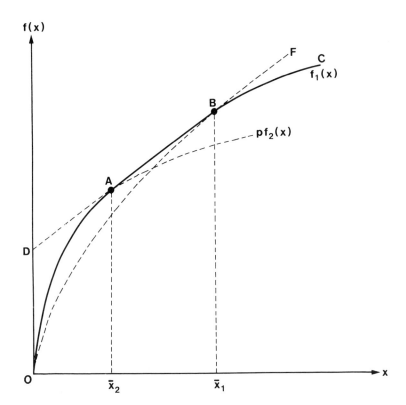

$$\dot{z}/z = \dot{N}/\bar{N} - \dot{K}/K = n - s[f(x) - xf'(x)]$$

The total wage bill is $NF_N(K,N) = Nf'(x)$ which, after sharing, provides an income of $Nf'(x)/\bar{N} = (x/z)f'(x)$ per worker. Thus, reverting to the time separable utility functional of Section III.8, the union's problem is to find

(P)    $\max\limits_{<x(t)>} \int_0^\infty \exp(-\delta t) \dfrac{xf'(x)}{ze_w(p)} \, dt$

s.t.   $z \geq x$

$\dot{z} = z\big\{n - s[f(x) - xf'(x)]\big\}$

$z(0) = z_0$, given

where the constant $\delta$ may be interpreted as the difference between the union's rate of time preference and the rate of growth of the labour force, and where $z_0$ is the labour:capital endowment ratio at $t = 0$. It is assumed that $\delta$ is positive; otherwise, (P) would have no solution. For convenience only, units are chosen so that $e_w(p) = 1$.

Associated with (P) are the Hamiltonian

$$H(x,z,\mu) \equiv (x/z)f'(x) + \mu z\big\{n - s[f(x) - xf'(x)]\big\}$$

and the Lagrangean

$$L = H + \lambda(z - x)$$

The Hamiltonian is the sum of two terms, representing current utility per worker and the union's valuation (in terms of utility) of an increase in the stock of capital per worker. Any solution to (P) must satisfy the conditions

(1)    $H(x^*,z,\mu) \geq H(x,z,\mu)$   for all $x \in [0,z]$

(2)    $L_x = H_x - \lambda = 0$

(3)    $\lambda \geq 0, \quad z - x \geq 0, \quad \lambda(z-x) = 0$

(4)    $\dot{\mu} = \delta\mu - L_z$

(5)    $\dot{z} = z\big\{n - s[f(x) - xf'(x)]\big\}$

where $L_x \equiv \partial L/\partial x$ and $H_x \equiv \partial H/\partial x$.

## 3.    PROPERTIES OF THE MODEL

Ignoring the constraint $x \leq z$ for the time being, we examine the shape of the function $H(x,z,\mu)$ for given u and z.    Differentiating $H$ with respect to the control x, we obtain

$$H_x = \frac{1}{z} [xf''(x) + f'(x)] + s\mu zxf''(x)$$

$$= [f'(x)/z]\{1 - (1 + s\mu z^2)[\frac{-xf''(x)}{f'(x)}]\}$$

(6)         $$= [f'(x)/z]\{1 - (1 + s\mu z^2)[\frac{1 - \theta(x)}{\sigma(x)}]\}$$

where, it will be recalled, $\theta(x)$ is the share of labour in total output and $\sigma(x)$ is the aggregate elasticity of factor substitution, so that

$$\frac{1 - \theta(x)}{\sigma(x)} = \begin{cases} \dfrac{1 - \theta_2(x)}{\sigma_2(x)} & \text{if } x \in (0, \bar{x}_2) \\[2ex] 0 & \text{if } x \in (\bar{x}_2, \bar{x}_1) \\[2ex] \dfrac{1 - \theta_1(x)}{\sigma_1(x)} & \text{if } x \in (\bar{x}_1, \infty) \end{cases}$$

and

$$\lim_{x \to \bar{x}_2^+} \frac{1 - \theta(x)}{\sigma(x)} = 0$$

$$\lim_{x \to \bar{x}_2^-} \frac{1 - \theta(\bar{x})}{\sigma(x)} = \frac{1 - \theta_2(\bar{x}_2)}{\sigma_2(\bar{x}_2)}$$

$$\lim_{x \to \bar{x}_1^+} \frac{1 - \theta(x)}{\sigma(x)} = \frac{1 - \theta_1(\bar{x}_1)}{\sigma_1(\bar{x}_1)}$$

$$\lim_{x \to \bar{x}_1^+} \frac{1 - \theta(x)}{\sigma(x)} = 0$$

As will be seen later, only the region defined by $s\mu z^2 > -1$ is relevant. Hence $1/(1 + s\mu z^2)$ is always finite and positive, and (6) can be rewritten as

(6)     $H_x = [f'(x)/z](1 + s\mu z^2)\phi_\zeta(x)$

where

$$\phi_\zeta(x) \equiv \frac{1}{1 + s\mu z^2} - \frac{1 - \theta(x)}{\sigma(x)}$$

$$\equiv \zeta - \frac{1 - \theta(x)}{\sigma(x)}$$

is the essential sign-changing term. The graph of $[1 - \theta(x)]/\sigma(x)$ is displayed in Figure 2. Notice that AF is drawn greater than one, GC less than one. Those inequalities are not the product of casual drafting; they are implications of assumptions made. Thus, from Section III.8, if the first industry is relatively labour-intensive then $w_1 < w(p) < w_2(p)$; hence

(7)     $x_1(w_1) > x_1(w(p)) > x_2(w(p)/p) > x_2(w_2(p)/p)$

The inequalities $AF > 1 > GC$ follow from (7).

  If $\zeta \geq OE$ in Figure 2 then $\phi_\zeta(x) > 0$ for all $x \in (0,\infty)$; if $OE > \zeta > AF$ then there exists a unique $x$, $x > x_1(w_1)$, such that $\phi_\zeta(x) = 0$ and at which $H$ reaches a maximum; and if $\zeta$ is sufficiently small, like $\zeta^*$ in Figure 3, then there exists a unique $x$, $x < x_2(w_2(p)/p)$, such that $\phi_\zeta(x) = 0$ and at which $H$ reaches a maximum. For other values of $\zeta$ matters are less straightforward. Let $\tilde{x}_i(\zeta)$ be the solution to $\zeta = [1 - \theta_i(x)]/\sigma_i(x)$. Then it is clear from (6) and Figure 3 that there is a unique $\zeta$, say $\tilde{\zeta}$, such that

$$\int_{\bar{x}_2(\tilde{\zeta})}^{\bar{x}_2} (-H_x)\,dx = \frac{1}{z}\,[f(\bar{x}_1) - (\bar{x}_2)] + \int_{\bar{x}_1}^{\tilde{x}_1(\tilde{\zeta})} H_x\,dx$$

where the expression on the left-hand side is the cumulative loss incurred by moving from the local maximum $\tilde{x}_2(\tilde{\zeta})$ to $\bar{x}_2$ and the expression on the right is the cumulative gain from moving from $\bar{x}_2$ to the second local maximum at $\tilde{x}_1(\tilde{\zeta})$. When the two sides balance, the two local maxima are equally attractive, that is, yield the same value of $H$ and it is a matter of indifference to the union which one

## Figure 2

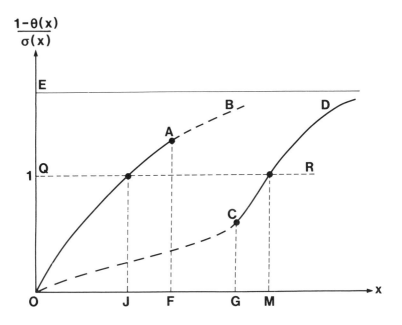

OAFGCD: the graph of $(1-\theta(x))/\sigma(x)$
OAB: the graph of $(1-\theta_2(x))/\sigma_2(x)$
OCD: the graph of $(1-\theta_1(x))/\sigma_1(x)$
$OJ = x_2(w_2(p)/p \equiv x_2^*$
$OF = x_2(w(p)/p) \equiv x_2$
$OG = x_1(w(p)) \equiv x_1$
$OM = x_1(w_1) \equiv x_1^*$

## Figure 3

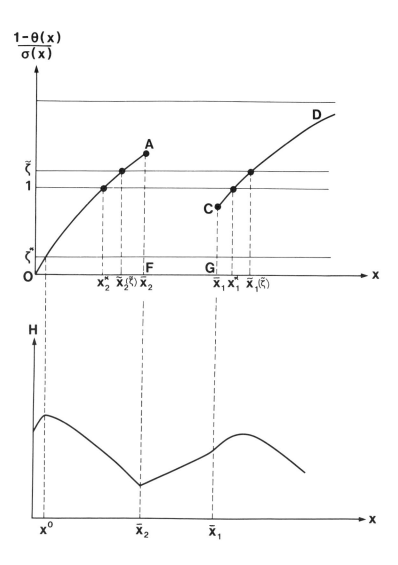

is chosen. It is clear also that (i) if $\tilde{\zeta} < (1 + s\mu z^2)^{-1}$ then $H$ is maximized by the value of x which lies at the intersection of GCD in Figure 3 and the horizontal line $\zeta = (1 + s\mu z^2)^{-1}$; that (ii) if $\tilde{\zeta} > (1 + s\mu z_2)^{-1}$ then $H$ is maximized by that value of x which lies at the intersection of OA and the horizontal line $\zeta = (1 + s\mu z^2)^{-1}$; and that (iii) if $\tilde{\zeta} = (1 + s\mu z^2)^{-1}$ then $H$ reaches its maximum at both $\tilde{x}_1$ and $\tilde{x}_2$ in Figure 3. The indeterminacy in case (iii) is momentary only and does not prevent us from constructing a phase diagram and isolating a unique optimal trajectory.

Suppose that $\tilde{\zeta}$ lies between 1 and $[1 - \theta_2(\bar{x}_2)]/\sigma_2(\bar{x}_2)$ $(= AF)$, as in Figure 3. Then, basing ourselves on the foregoing argument, we can determine the value of x which maximizes $H$ for given $\mu z^2$:

(a) if $s\mu z^2 \leq \eta \equiv \left[ \lim_{x \to \infty} \dfrac{1 - \theta_1(x)}{\sigma_1(x)} \right]^{-1} - 1$ then $\;x = \infty$ ;

(b) if $\eta < s\mu z^2 < (1/\tilde{\zeta}) - 1$ then $\;x = x_1(\mu z^2) \equiv \tilde{x}_1((1 + s\mu z^2)^{-1})$;

(c) if $s\mu z^2 = (1/\tilde{\zeta}) - 1$ then x is either $\tilde{x}_1(\tilde{\xi})$ or $\tilde{x}_2(\tilde{\xi})$; and

(d) if $s\mu z^2 > (1/\tilde{\zeta}) - 1$ then $\;x = x_2(\mu z^2) \equiv \tilde{x}_2((1 + s\mu z^2)^{-1})$.

(For the definitions of $\tilde{x}_1(\cdot)$ and $\tilde{x}_2(\cdot)$, see p. 187.) Let $\mu z^2$ be denoted by $\psi$; and let $x(\psi)$ denote the relationship between x and $\psi$ described by (a)–(d). The relationship is illustrated by the unbroken curves of Figure 4. (Notice that AB′B represents $x_2(\psi)$.)

To this point we have ignored the constraint $x \leq z$. If $x(\psi) \leq z$ the constraint either does not bind or just begins to bind; hence it is optimal to set $x = x(\psi)$. If, on the other hand, $x(\psi) > z$ then the constraint binds and we are left uncertain about the optimal x.

Let us return to Figure 4. By construction of the figure, the constraint begins to bind at all points on AB′ and C′D. Moreover, at all points to the left of AB′ or C′D, $\partial H/\partial x > 0$; at such points, therefore, it is optimal to set $x = z$. Now consider any $\psi$, say $\psi^*$, between $\tilde{\psi}$ $[\equiv ((1/\tilde{\xi}) - 1)/s]$ and $\psi_0$, where $\psi_0$ is defined by $x_2(\psi_0) = \bar{x}_2$. Figure 5 depicts the Hamiltonian as a function of x for the three alternative values of $\psi$, $viz$ $\tilde{\psi}$, $\psi^*$ and $\psi_0$. In drawing the figure use has been made of the fact that, as $\psi$ increases in magnitude between $\tilde{\psi}$ and $\psi_0$, the local maximum at $x_1(\psi)$ increases faster than the local maximum at $x_2(\psi)$. To verify the fact, suppose that $\psi = \psi^*$. Since $H(x, \psi^*)$ reaches a local maximum at $x_1(\psi^*)$ and $x_2(\psi^*)$, we can avail ourselves

## Figure 4

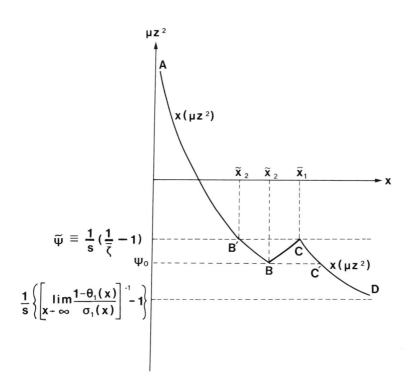

## Figure 5

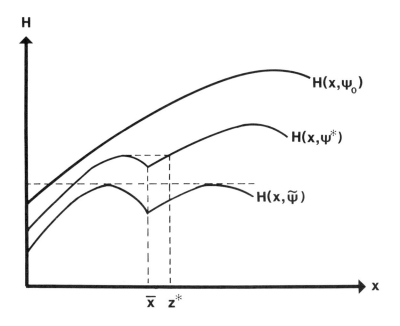

of the envelope theorem and write

$$\frac{d}{d(-\psi)}\, H(x_i(\psi^*),\psi^*) = \frac{\partial}{\partial(-\psi)}\, H(x_i(\psi^*),\psi^*)$$

$$= s\left[f(x_i(\psi^*)) - x_i(\psi^*)f'(x_i(\psi^*))\right] + n/z \quad i = 1,2$$

The verification is completed by noting that, since $x_1(\psi^*) > x_2(\psi^*)$, the rental of capital $f - xf'$ is greater at $x_1(\psi^*)$ than at $x_2(\psi^*)$. If now $z = z^*$, the union is indifferent between the local maximum at $x_2(\psi^*)$ and the constrained maximum at $x = z^*$. In fact, by allowing $\psi$ to vary between $\tilde{\psi}$ and $\psi_0$, one can generate similar constrained maxima for all values of $z$ between $\tilde{x}_2$ and $\tilde{x}_1$. The set of such constrained maxima is represented in Figure 4 by the curve BC; it is shown in an appendix that the curve is necessarily monotone. Thus, summarizing the conclusions of this paragraph, the set of all points at which the constraint $x \le z$ begins to bite is represented in Figure 4 by the locus AB'BCC'D.

At points above AB'BCC'D there is unemployment; for example, at any point on the horizontal segment B'C (other than B' and C), $x = x_2(\psi_0) < z$. At points below the locus, there is full employment, with the constraint fully engaged. To justify this assertion, consider any point $(z,\psi) = (\hat{z}, x_1^{-1}(\hat{z})) \equiv (\hat{z}, \hat{\psi})$ on CD of Figure 4. By construction of the figure, it is optimal to set $x = \hat{z}$. Now let $\psi$ decline from $\hat{\psi}$ to $\hat{\psi} + \Delta\psi$, where $\Delta\psi$ is negative. We need to show that the constrained maximum at $x = \hat{z}$ dominates the local maximum at $x_2(\hat{\psi} + \Delta\psi)$. Since $H$ reaches a local maximum at $x_2(\hat{\psi})$ we can again apply the envelope theorem to obtain

$$\frac{d}{d(-\psi)}\, H(x_2(\hat{\psi}),\hat{\psi}) = \frac{\partial}{\partial(-\psi)}\, H(x_2(\hat{\psi}),\hat{\psi})$$

$$= s\left[f(x_2(\hat{\psi})) - x_2(\hat{\psi})f'(x_2(\hat{\psi}))\right] + n/\hat{z}$$

In contrast,

$$\frac{\partial}{\partial(-\psi)} H(\hat{z},\hat{\psi}) = s\left[f(\hat{z}) - \hat{z}f'(\hat{z})\right] + n/\hat{z}$$

The demonstration is then completed by noting that $f(x) - xf'(x)$ is necessarily larger at $z$ than at $x_2(\hat{\psi}) < \hat{z}$.

The motion of $\psi$ is obtained from (4) and (5). Thus

$$\dot{\psi} = \frac{d}{dt} (\mu z^2) = \dot{\mu} z^2 + 2\mu z \dot{z}$$

$$= z^2 \{\delta\mu - [-(1/z^2)xf'(x) + \mu(n - s(f(x) - xf'(x)))] - \lambda\}$$
$$+ 2\mu z^2 \{n - s[f(x) - xf'(x)]\}$$

$$= xf'(x) + \psi\{(\delta + n) - s[f(x) - xf'(x)]\} - \lambda z^2$$

Pulling together what we have learned to this point, we obtain a complete description of the Pontryagin paths associated with (P). There are two regimes: in Regime I unemployment is possible; in Regime II there is full employment.

**REGIME 1:** $z \geq x(\psi)$

(8)     $\dot{z} = z\{n - s[f(x(\psi)) - x(\psi)f'(x(\psi))]\}$

(9)     $\dot{\psi} = x(\psi)f'(x(\psi)) + \psi\{(n + \delta) - s[f(x(\psi)) - x(\psi)f'(x(\psi))]\}$

       $\equiv M(\psi)$

**REGIME II:** $z < x(\psi)$

(10)    $\dot{z} = z\{n - s[f(z) - zf'(z)]\}$

(11)    $\dot{\psi} = zf'(z) + \psi\{(n + \delta) - s[f(z) - zf'(z)]\} - \lambda z^2$

       $= -z^2 f''(z) + \psi\{(n + \delta) - s[f(z) - zf'(z) + z^2 f''(z)]\}$

(In deriving (11) use has been made of (2).) In terms of Figure 6, Regime I operates in Region I, above and to the right of AB'BCC'D, and Regime II operates in Region II, below and to the left of AB'BCC'D.

**The locus $\dot{z} = 0$** Denote by $z^e$ the solution to the equation $s[f(z) - zf'(z)] = n$. The greater is $n/s$, the greater is $z^e$. Let us assume that $n/s$ is large enough to ensure that $z^e > \tilde{x}_1$. Then, bearing in mind (8) and (10), the locus $\dot{z} = 0$ must be as shown in Figure 6.

**The locus $\dot{\psi} = 0$** Consider first those points in Figure 6 which lie above ABB'CC'D, the graph of $x(\psi)$, and which therefore are associ-

## Figure 6

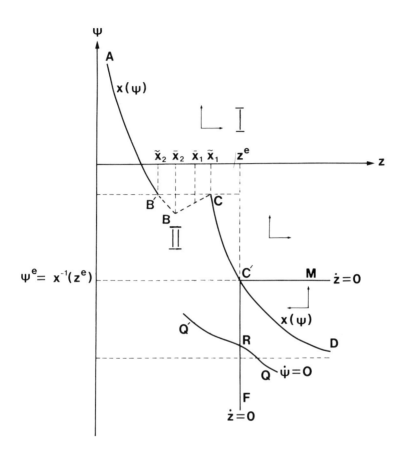

ated with less than full employment. From (9),

$$\frac{d\dot{\psi}}{d\psi} = M'(\psi)$$

$$= [xf'' + f' + \psi sxf''] \frac{dx}{d\psi} + [(n + \delta) - s(f - xf')]$$

(12a)      $$= n + \delta - s\big[f(x(\psi)) - x(\psi)f'(x(\psi))\big]$$

$$\frac{d^2\dot{\psi}}{d\psi^2} = M''(\psi)$$

(12b)      $$= sxf'' \frac{dx}{d\psi} > 0$$

Now consider the equation

(13)    $$n + \delta - s\big[f(x(\psi)) - x(\psi)f'(x(\psi))\big] = 0$$

It may or may not possess a solution. To make this clear, let us write

$$H = (x/z)[f'(x) + \psi[n - sr(x)]$$

where $r(x) \equiv f(x) - xf'(x)$ is the rental rate of capital. We have assumed that if $\psi=0$ then $H$ or, equivalently, $xf'(x)$ reaches a maximum at some positive and finite x. It follows that both $\lim_{x \to 0} xf'(x)$ and $\lim_{x \to \infty} xf'(x)$ are finite. Similarly we have assumed that, for small and negative $\psi$, $H$ reaches a maximum at positive and finite x, implying that $\lim_{x \to \infty} r(x)$ is finite. It follows that equation (13) has a solution if and only if $\delta \le sr(\infty) - n$. We must consider separately the case in which the condition is satisfied (Case 1) and the case in which it is not satisfied (Case 2).

**Case 1: $\delta \le sr(\infty) - n$**  Denoting by $\psi^\delta$ the solution to (13), it is apparent that $z^e < x(\psi^\delta)$ and that

$$\dot{\psi}\,\big|_{\psi = \psi^\delta} = M(\psi^\delta)$$

$$= x(\psi^\delta)f'(x(\psi^\delta)) > 0$$

Moreover, from (12), $\psi^\delta$ minimizes $M(\psi)$; hence $\psi$ is positive everywhere above AB'BCC'D. In particular,

$$\lim_{\psi \to \infty} M(\psi) = \infty$$

and

$$\lim_{s\psi \to C} M(\psi) = B$$

where

$$C \equiv \lim_{x \to \infty} \left[ \frac{1 - \theta_1(x)}{\sigma_1(x)} \right]^{-1} - 1 < 0$$

and B is positive and finite. The latter result requires proof. As $s\psi$ goes to C, which is negative, x goes to infinity. We already know that as x goes to infinity, $r(x) \equiv f(x) - xf'(x)$ goes to a positive and finite number. In view of (9), then, the proof will be complete if it can be shown that

$$\lim_{x \to \infty} xf'(x) = 0$$

Let $v \equiv K/N = 1/x$ and let $g(v)$ be output per capita, so that $g'(v)$ is the marginal product of capital and $g(v) - vg'(v)$ the marginal product of labour. Then

$$xf'(x) = [g(v) - vg'(v)]/v = g(v)/v - g'(v)$$

and

$$\lim_{x \to \infty} xf'(x) = \lim_{v \to 0} [g(v)/v - g'(v)] = 0$$

and B is revealed to be $(C/s)[n + \delta - sr(\infty)]$, which is finite.

The properties of the function $M(\psi)$ are displayed in Figure 7(a).

**Case 2: $\delta > sr(\infty) - n$**  By means of a similar argument it can be shown that, in this case, $M(\psi)$ has the properties depicted by Figure 7(b). In this case, of course, there is no $\psi$ such that $M'(\psi) = 0$. Moreover, B is negative, the curve $M(\psi)$ cutting the horizontal axis at, say, $\psi_1 < 0$. It is easy to show that the greater the rate of discount the smaller is the absolute value of $\psi_1$.

Consider now the region of full employment, below AB'BCC'D in

## Figure 7(a)

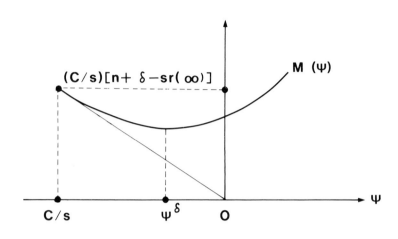

$$\delta \lessgtr sr(\infty) - n$$

**Figure 7(b)**

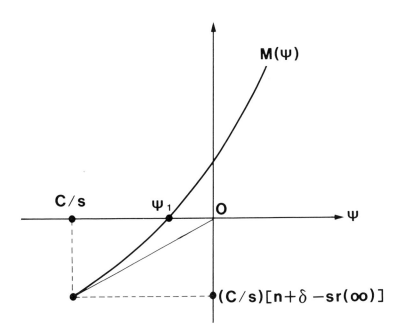

$\delta > sr(\infty) - n$

Figure 6. From (11), the locus $\dot{\psi} = 0$ is described by

$$0 = z^2 f''(z) + \psi\{(n + \delta) - s[f(z) - zf'(z) + z^2 f''(z)]\}$$

$$(14) \qquad = \frac{\theta(z)}{\sigma(z)} f(z)[1 - \theta(z)] + \psi\{(n + \delta) - sf(z)[1 - \theta(z)][1 - \theta(z)/\sigma(z)]\}$$

Suppose that $z = z^e$. Then, from (14), we obtain a corresponding value of $\psi$, which we call $\psi^\infty$:

$$(15) \qquad \psi^\infty = \frac{(z^e)^2 f_1''(z^e)}{\delta - s(z^e)^2 f_1''(z^e)}$$

On the other hand, given that $z = z^e$, the value of $\psi$ such that the constraint $x \leq z$ just binds is given by

$$\frac{1}{s\psi + 1} = \frac{1 - \theta_1(z^e)}{\sigma(z^e)}$$

Denote this value by $\psi^e$. Then

$$(16) \qquad \psi^e = \frac{1}{s}\left[\frac{\sigma(z^e)}{1 - \theta_1(z^e)} - 1\right]$$

If $\psi^\infty$ is more negative than $\psi^e$ then, clearly, there is an intersection of the loci $\dot{\psi} = 0$ and $\dot{z} = 0$ in the region of full employment. On the other hand, if $\psi^\infty$ is less negative than $\psi^e$ then the locus $\dot{\psi} = 0$, given by (14), meets CC' above C' and only the segment to the left of CC' is relevant. (To the right of CC' the constraint binds and (14) is no longer the equation of the locus $\dot{\psi} = 0$.) Subtracting (15) from (16), and simplifying,

$$(17) \qquad \psi\bigg|_{(16)} - \psi\bigg|_{(15)} = \frac{1}{[\delta + (s/\sigma_1)\theta_1(1 - \theta_1)f_1]}\left[\frac{\delta\sigma_1}{s(1 - \theta_1)} + \theta_1 f_1 - \frac{\delta}{s}\right]$$

From the definition of $z^e$, it is independent of $\delta$. Hence there is a critical positive value of $\delta$,

$$\delta^* \equiv \frac{s\theta_1(z^e)f_1(z^e)}{1 - \frac{\sigma_1(z^e)}{1 - \theta_1(z^e)}}$$

such that the second square-bracketed term in (17) is negative or positive if and only if $\delta$ is greater or less than $\delta^*$. If $\delta$ is sufficiently small $(\delta < \delta^*)$ then (17) is positive and the locus $\dot{\psi} = 0$ cuts $z = z^e$ below G, as does QQ' in Figure 6. It is now straightforward to construct the complete phase diagram. Figure 8 is based on the assumption that $\delta$ is small, that is, $\delta \leq sr(\infty) - n$. In that case, there is a non-trivial steady state at R. Evidently R is a saddlepoint, and the optimal solution is represented by R and the stable arms R'R and R''R. As the figure makes clear, after finite time (possibly at $t = 0$) the optimal point enters the region of full employment and stays there; that is, after finite time the union permanently withdraws from intervention and full employment prevails thereafter. Whether there is an initial phase during which the union sets a wage above the competitive level depends on the initial labour : capital ratio.

Much the same description applies to Figure 9, which has been constructed on the assumption that $\delta$ is large $(\delta > sr(\infty) - n)$ but not very large $(\delta < \delta^*)$. Qualitatively, the optimal trajectories of Figure 9 differ from their counterparts in Figure 8 only in allowing for an initial phase of declining $\psi$ when $z_0$ is large.

Figure 10, on the other hand, illustrates the case in which the union subjects the future to a very high rate of discount $(\delta > sr(\infty) - n$ and $\delta > \delta^*)$ and, in particular, attaches little weight to the effect of its current wage demands on accumulation and future labour productivity. In that case, there is only the trivial steady state. Along the optimal trajectory z goes to infinity, that is, the capital : labour ratio goes to zero. As the figure makes clear, after finite time (possibly at $t = 0$) the optimal point enters the region of unemployment; thereafter, the optimal point stays in that region, the union intervenes at each moment and unemployment is endemic.

We have considered in some detail the case in which $z^e > \tilde{x}_1$. However that assumption was for concreteness only. It had no bearing on our conclusions. For the sake of completeness, however, we note that if $z^e \in (\bar{x}_1, \tilde{x}_1)$ then the locus $\dot{z} = 0$ loses its horizontal segment (as in Figure 11); that if $z^e \in (\tilde{x}_2, \bar{x}_2)$ then the locus has only a finite horizontal segment (as in Figure 12); and that if $z^e \in [\bar{x}_2, \bar{x}_1)$ then the locus becomes a band (as in Figure 13). In the last of these three cases, if there exists a non-trivial steady state then there is a continuum of them; which steady state will be "chosen" by the economy depends on its initial position. In terms of Figure 13, if $z_0 < \bar{x}_2$ then

# Figure 8

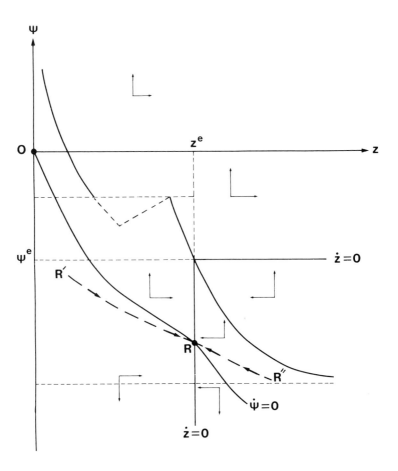

δ small

**Figure 9**

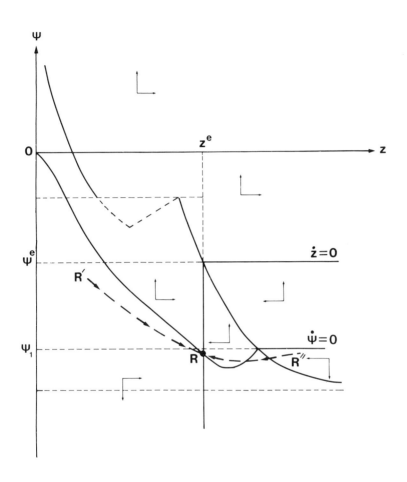

$\delta$ large but not very large

## Figure 10

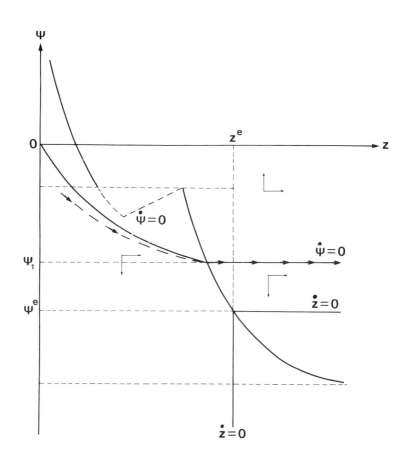

$\delta$ very large

Figure 11

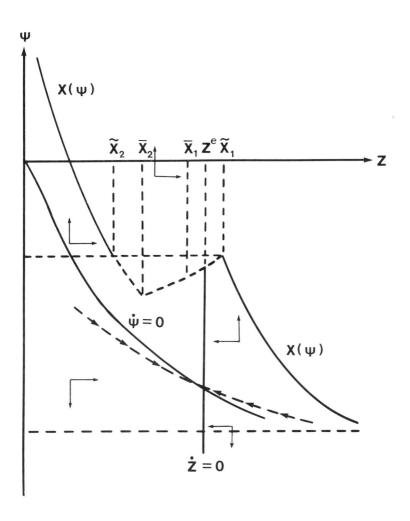

## Figure 12

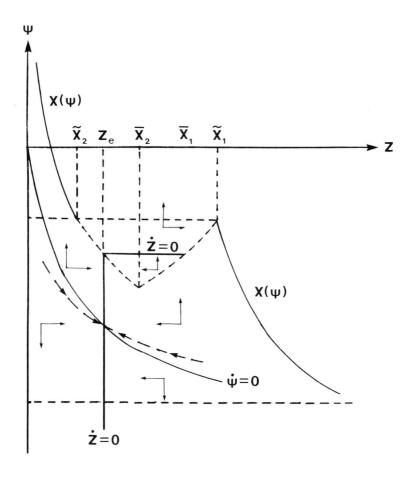

Figure 13

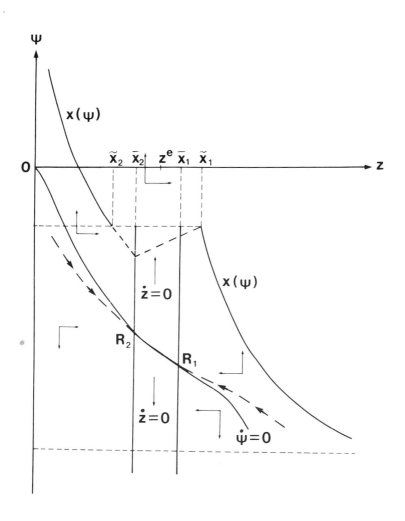

the optimal point approaches $R_2$ from the left; if $z_0 > \bar{x}_1$ then the optimal point approaches $R_1$ from the right; and if $\bar{x}_2 \leq z_0 \leq \bar{x}_1$ then the optimal point is stationary. Thus when $z^e \in [\bar{x}_2, \bar{x}_1)$, the union-ridden economy is conservative in the sense that, if the initial labour : capital ratio is low (high) then it will be low (high) in the steady state.

Whatever the value of $z^e$, however, the following proposition can be asserted.

PROPOSITION: Given the positive rate of population growth n, there is always a critical positive rate of union time preference $\delta^* + n$ such that for $\delta < \delta^*$ there is a non-trivial steady state and such that for $\delta > \delta^*$ (that is, for a sufficient degree of union myopia) there is only the trivial steady state in which the capital : labour ratio is zero. (a) In any non-trivial steady state (i) factors are fully employed and (ii) only the relatively labour-intensive first good is produced if $z^e > \bar{x}_1$, only the relatively capital-intensive second good is produced if $z^e < \bar{x}_2$, and both goods are produced if $z^e \in (\bar{x}_2, \bar{x}_1)$. Any non-trivial steady state outside the interval $[\bar{x}_2, \bar{x}_1]$ is locally stable. Depending on the initial factor endowment ratio $z_0$, the optimal path may traverse one or both of the alternative patterns of specialization on the way to the steady state. (b) Any trivial steady state is stable. Along the path to extinction, and after finite time, only the relatively labour-intensive first good is produced.

## 4.    ACCOMMODATING AN ECONOMIC MIDDLE CLASS

It has been assumed that there are just two categories of income-earners, homogeneous workers who receive only wage income (and therefore do not save) and homogeneous capitalists who earn no wage income. However the Proposition remains valid under much broader conditions. Thus, fairly obviously, nothing changes if there are several categories of more-or-less imperfectly substitutable and non-saving workers, one of which forms a union. Of greater interest, the Proposition remains true if homogeneous capitalists all earn wage income. Indeed the Proposition remains true if only a subset of capitalists earn wage income, provided that the two categories of capitalists save at the same rate. In other words the Proposition survives the introduction of an economic middle class which earns both wage and interest income.

To provide a detailed demonstration that this is so would be tedious, for such a demonstration would follow very closely the reasoning of Section 3. Instead we shall describe the revised problem and derive the counterparts of equations (8)–(11), leaving to the reader the task of providing the further details of a formal proof. Notice first, however, that whether all or only a subset of capitalists work makes no difference to the working of the economy, provided that the two categories of capitalists save at the same rate; for, under that provision, it makes no difference to total savings how a given lump of wage income is distributed among the capitalists. Suppose then, without loss, that all capitalists work. Suppose also that the labour provided by capitalists is perfectly substitutable for the labour of pure workers. (The latter assumption could be dispensed with, at the price of some additional complications.) The labour force is now composed of two parts, workers $\bar{N}(t)$ and capitalists $\bar{M}(t)$, both growing at the constant proportional rate n. The GNP function is then

$$Y = F(N + \bar{M}, K)$$

$$= KF((N/K) + (\bar{M}/K), 1)$$

$$= Kf(x + m)$$

where $m \equiv \bar{M}/K$. As in earlier sections, $x \equiv N/K$ and $z \equiv \bar{N}/K$. Since $\bar{N}$ and $\bar{M}$ change at the same rate,

$$m = \alpha z \quad (\alpha > 0, \text{ a constant})$$

The equation of capital accumulation is then

$$\dot{K} = s\left\{K[f(x + m) - (x + m)f'(x + m)] + \bar{M}f'(x + m)\right\}$$

so that

$$\dot{K}/K = s[f(x + m) - xf'(x + m)]$$

$$= s[f(x + \alpha z) - xf'(x + \alpha z)]$$

and

$$\dot{z}/z = n - s\left[f(x + \alpha z) - xf'(x + \alpha z)\right]$$

Thus the task of the union is to solve

(P′)    $\max\limits_{<x(t)>} \int_0^\infty \exp(-\delta t)(x/z)f'(x+\alpha z)\, dt$

s.t.    $z \geq x$

$\dot{z} = n - s\left[f(x + \alpha z) - xf'(x + \alpha z)\right]$

Finally, from the first-order conditions for (P′) one obtains, by familiar methods, the counterparts to (8)–(11).

**Regime I: $z \geq x(\psi)$**

(8′)    $\dot{z} = z\{n - s[f(x + \alpha z) - xf'(x + \alpha z)]\}$

(9′)    $\dot{\psi} = xf'(x + \alpha z) + \psi\{\delta + n - s[f(x + \alpha z) - (x + \alpha z)f'(x + \alpha z)]\}$

$+ \alpha xz(1 + \psi s)f''(x + \alpha z)$

**Regime II: $z < x(\psi)$**

(10′)    $\dot{z} = z\{n - s[f(z + \alpha z) - zf'(z + \alpha z)]\}$

(11′)    $\dot{\psi} = \psi\{\delta + n - s[f(z + \alpha z) - (z + \alpha z)f'(z + \alpha z)]\}$

$- z^2(1 + \alpha)(1 + \psi s)f''(z + \alpha z)$

## 5.    OPTIMAL SAVING BY CAPITALISTS

In Section 2 it was shown that if at all points of time capitalists save the same proportion of their income, whatever the rate of return to capital, and if certain auxiliary assumptions are made then, in the long run, it is suboptimal for workers to exercise their market power. However the assumption that capitalists mechanically save a constant proportion of income is quite special. One wonders therefore whether the finding of long-run impotence recurs under more plausible hypotheses.

Suppose, conventionally, that each price-taking capitalist spreads his saving over time in whatever manner maximizes the present value of the stream of instantaneous utility. A choice must then be made between alternative solution concepts; in particular, a choice must be made between the concept of an open-loop-Stackelberg equilibrium and the concept of a feedback-Stackelberg equilibrium. Under the assumptions of Section 2, the two solution sets coincide; under our present, more sophisticated assumption about saving, that is not so. In general, open-loop-Stackelberg equilibria are time-inconsistent and therefore require the supporting assumption that labour can commit itself to its dynamic policies at the outset.[3] It therefore seems more reasonable to focus on feedback-Stackelberg equilibria which, by construction, are time-consistent. However, in the present context, the set of feedback-Stackelberg equilibria coincides with the set of feedback-Nash equilibria, which will be the subject matter of Chapter 7.[4] Readers who wish to pursue this topic immediately may skip Chapter 6 and proceed to Chapter 7.

## FOOTNOTES

1. In the present chapter we extend the analysis of Kemp and Long (1986, 1987) by allowing for trade with the rest of the world.

2. Section III.8 is an exception. However the interactions of growth and union policy, the focus of attention in the present chapter, were there completely ignored.

3. Open-loop-Stackelberg equilibria for a closed economy are discussed by Kemp and Long (1989). They showed that, subject to some mild restrictions on the marginal utility of capitalists, and ignoring a razor's-edge case, labour remains powerless to improve its lot in the long run.

4. For a proof that, in the present context, the set of feedback-Stackelberg equilibria coincides with the set of feedback-Nash equilibria, see Chapter 7, Appendix 2.

## APPENDIX

## PROOF THAT CURVE BC IN FIGURE 4 IS MONOTONE

Curve BC is generated by the equation

(A1)   $F(z,\psi) \equiv H(x_2(\psi),\psi) - H(z,\psi) = 0$

Differentiating (A1) we obtain

(A2)   $\left. \dfrac{d\psi}{dz} \right|_{F=0} = -\left[ \dfrac{\partial F}{\partial z} \right] + \left[ \dfrac{\partial F}{\partial \psi} \right]$

where

(A3)   $-\dfrac{\partial F}{\partial z} = (1 + \psi s)f'(z)\left[ \dfrac{1}{1 + \psi s} - \dfrac{1 - \theta(z)}{\sigma(z)} \right]$

and, resorting to the envelope theorem,

(A4)   $\dfrac{\partial F}{\partial \psi} = -s\left\{ [f(x_2(\psi)) - x_2(\psi)f''(x_2(\psi))] - [f(z) - zf'(z)] \right\}$

Consider expression (A3). Since $\psi$ is between $\psi_0$ and $\tilde{\psi}$ on BC, $(1 + \psi s)^{-1} > \tilde{\xi}$ . From Figure 3, therefore, $(1 + \psi s)^{-1} > \tilde{\xi} > (1 - \theta(z))/\sigma(z)$ when $(\psi,z)$ is on BC. Hence (A3) is positive.

Now consider (A4). The function $f(x) - xf'(x)$ is increasing in x when x is between $\tilde{x}_2$ and $\bar{x}_2$; and $x_2(\psi) < \bar{x}_2 < z$ when $(\psi,z)$ is on BC. It follows that $f(x_2(\psi)) - x_2(\psi)f'(x_2(\psi))$ is smaller than $f(z) - zf'(z)$ if $(\psi,z)$ is on BC. Hence (A4) is positive.

We have shown that, on BC, both (A3) and (A4) are positive. It follows that (A2) is positive on BC, as was to be proved.

CHAPTER SIX

# A DIFFERENTIAL GAME BETWEEN THE
# LABOUR UNIONS OF DIFFERENT COUNTRIES

## 1. INTRODUCTION

In Chapter IV we examined the pattern of international trade and indebtedness between countries in each of which there is a powerful labour union. It is a feature of the model developed there that each union perceives itself as standing in a strategic relationship to the other union. However the earlier analysis is entirely static. It ignores the implications of the unions' wage policies for the rate of capital accumulation in each country, as well as the feedback from accumulation to the formation of union policies.

In the present chapter we develop a model of international trade and investment, where in each country there is a rational labour union which allows for the impact of its wage policies on savings decisions everywhere. Of course, the small-country analysis of Chapter V is valid whether or not there is a foreign union. Our task, then, is to rework Chapter V under the revised assumption that neither country is small and on the understanding that there is a union in each of them.

Our chief finding is that, in the long run, all unions are impotent; that is, the small-country result of Chapter V is shown to hold in a large-country context also.

## 2. THE MODEL

In this section we assemble the raw materials of our later analysis, and introduce some assumptions.

As in Chapter IV, there are two trading countries (the home country and the foreign country), two factors of production (capital and labour), and two produced and tradeable commodities. Now, however, we must be more definite about the attributes of the two commodities. Thus throughout the present chapter it will be assumed that the first is a pure consumption good and the second a pure investment good. As in earlier chapters, the first commodity is the numeraire.

There is a no-joint-products, constant-returns technology, the same for each country. As usual, the first commodity is assumed to be relatively labour-intensive. Each factor of production is perfectly mobile between sectors within a single country. In addition, capital can move freely and costlessly from country to country. This last assumption, together with the assumption of uniform technology, implies that production is everywhere incompletely specialized (or incipiently so) and that factor rewards are everywhere the same. In effect, we are dealing with a single closed economy in which one market (the labour market) is dominated by duopolists (the two unions) which sell a single homogeneous commodity (labour) and each of which is subject to a steadily changing capacity constraint (the total work force under its control).

As in Chapter V it is assumed that workers do not save and that, in each country, capitalists save a uniform and constant proportion of their incomes. Each work force grows at the constant and positive rate n. For concreteness, but without essential loss of generality, it is assumed that the home country has the larger work force; that is, if $\beta \equiv \bar{N}^*/\bar{N}$ then $0 < \beta < 1$. Each union discounts at the constant and positive rate $\rho$.

The home union seeks to maximize the time-separable utility functional

$$\int_0^\infty Nw \exp(-\rho t)\, dt = \int_0^\infty (N/\bar{N})w\bar{N}(0)\exp(-(\rho-n)t)\, dt$$

$$= \int_0^\infty (x/z)w \exp(-\delta t)\, dt$$

where $\delta \equiv \rho - n$, $x \equiv N/(K + K^*)$, $z \equiv \bar{N}/(K+K^*)$ and, by choice of units, $\bar{N}(0) = 1$. Notice that, in this chapter, x and z are given new definitions. Similarly, the foreign union seeks to maximize

$$\int_0^\infty N^* w \exp(-\rho t)dt = \int_0^\infty (x^*/z^*)w\bar{N}^*(0)\exp(-\delta t)\, dt$$

$$= \int_0^\infty (x^*/z)w \exp(-\delta t)\, dt$$

Adapting equation (2.81), we obtain the market-clearing condition

(1)     $sr(p) = pr'(p) + pw'(p)(x + x^*)$

the solution to which is $p(x + x^*)$. Moreover, the equation of accumulation can be written

(2)     $\dot{z}/z = \dot{z}^*/z^* = n - sr(p)$

Hence the task of the home union is to find

(P$_1$)    $\max\limits_{x} \int_0^\infty (x/z)w(p(x + x^*))\exp(-\delta t)\,dt$

        s.t. $\dot{z}/z = n - sr(p(x + x^*))$

           $z \geq x \geq 0$

and the task of the foreign union is to find

(P$_2$)    $\max\limits_{x^*} \int_0^\infty (x^*/z)w(p(x + x^*))\exp(-\delta t)\,dt$

        s.t. $\dot{z}/z = n - sr(p(x + x^*))$

           $\beta z = z^* \geq x^* \geq 0$

The Lagrangeans associated with (P$_1$) and (P$_2$) are, respectively,

$$L = (x/z)w(p(x + x^*)) + \mu z[n - sr(p(x + x^*))] + \lambda(z - x)$$

and

$$L^* = (x^*/z)w(p(x + x^*)) + \mu^* z[n - sr(p(x + x^*))] + \lambda^*(\beta z - x^*)$$

and the necessary conditions are

(3)     $\partial L/\partial x = (x/z)w'p' + w/z - \mu zsr'p' - \lambda = 0$

(4)     $\partial L^*/\partial x^* = (x^*/z)w'p' + w/z - \mu^* zsr'p' - \lambda^* = 0$

(5)     $\dot{\mu} = \delta\mu - \partial L/\partial z - (\partial L/\partial x^*)x^{*'}$

        $= \delta\mu + (x/z^2)w - \mu(n - sr) - \lambda - (x/z)w'p' - \mu zsr'p']x^{*'}$

(6)     $\dot{\mu}^* = \delta\mu^* - \partial L^*/\partial z - (\partial L^*/\partial x)x'$

        $= \delta\mu^* + (x^*/z^2)w - \mu^*(n-sr) - \beta\lambda^* - [(x^*/z)w'p' - \mu^* zsr'p']x'$

(7)     $\dot{z} = z(n - sr)$

(8)     $z - x \geq 0$ , $\lambda(z - x) = 0$ , $\lambda \geq 0$

(9)     $\beta z - x^* \geq 0$ ,     $\lambda^*(\beta z - x^*) = 0$ ,     $\lambda^* \geq 0$

where $w' \equiv dw/dp$, $r' \equiv dr/dp$, $p' \equiv dp/d(x + x^*)$, $x' \equiv dx(z)/dz$ and $x^{*'} \equiv dx^*(z)/dz$. Notice the terms $(\partial L/\partial x^*)x^{*'}$ and $(\partial L^*/\partial x)x'$ in (5) and (6), respectively; these terms register the *indirect* effect on the value of a country's Lagrangean of a change in the value of the state variable, where the line of causality runs through the other country's control.

There are four possible regimes or modes:

(a) $z > x$  and $\beta z > x^*$     (unemployment everywhere)

(b) $z > x$  and $\beta z = x^*$     (unemployment at home, full employment abroad)

(c)  $z = x$  and $\beta z > x^*$     (full employment at home, unemployment abroad)

(d)  $z = x$  and $\beta z = x^*$     (full employment everywhere)

However, given the uniformity of preferences and technical information across countries, and given the assumption that the home country has the larger work force, it is clear that Regime (c) will never be observed.   We therefore may concentrate on the three remaining regimes.

**Regime (a): $z > x$, $\beta z > x^*$**  From (8) and (9), $\lambda = \lambda^* = 0$.  Hence (3) and (4) reduce to

(10)   $(x/z)w'p' + w/z - \mu z sr'p' = 0$

and

(11)   $(x^*/z)w'p' + w/z - \mu^* z sr'p' = 0$

and, therefore, (5) and (6) to

(12)   $\dot{\mu} = \delta\mu + (x/z^2)w - \mu(n - sr) + (w/z)x^{*'}$

and

(13)   $\dot{\mu}^* = \delta\mu^* + (x^*/z^2)w - \mu(n - sr) + (w/z)x'$

Let $\psi \equiv \mu z^2$ and $\psi^* \equiv \mu^* z^2$.  Then, from (7), (12) and (13),

(14)    $\dot{\psi} = wx + \psi(\delta + n - sr) + zwx^{*'}$

and

(15)   $\dot{\psi}^* = wx^* + \psi^*(\delta + n - sr) + zwx'$

Equations (7), (10), (11), (14) and (15) make up the dynamic system of Regime (a). Writing the system in full detail, and recalling that $\delta \equiv \rho - n$, we have

(7a)   $\dot{z} = z[n - sr(p(x + x^*))]$

(10a)  $xw'(p(x+x^*))p'(x+x^*) + w(p(x+x^*)) - \psi sr'(p(x+x^*))p'(x+x^*) = 0$

(11a)  $x^*w'(p(x+x^*))p'(x+x^*) + w(p(x+x^*)) - \psi^* sr'(p(x+x^*))p'(x+x^*) = 0$

(14a)  $\dot{\psi} = w(p(x+x^*))x + \psi[\rho-sr(p(x+x^*))] + zw(p(x+x^*))x^{*\prime}(z)$

(15a)  $\dot{\psi}^* = w(p(x+x^*))x^* + \psi^*[\rho-sr(p(x+x^*))] + zw(p(x+x^*))x'(z)$

**Regime (b): $z > x$, $\beta z = x^*$**   From (8), $\lambda = 0$; hence (10) continues to hold. From (10) and the fact that $\beta z = x^*$ (which implies that $x^{*\prime} = \beta$), (5) reduces to

(16)   $\dot{\mu} = \delta\mu + (x/z^2)w - \mu(n - sr) + \beta(w/z)$

Hence, recalling the definition of $\psi$,

(17)   $\dot{\psi} = (\rho - sr)\psi + (x + \beta z)w$

On the other hand, applying (4) to (6),

(18)   $\dot{\mu}^* = \delta\mu^* + (x^*/z)w - \mu^*(n - sr) - \beta[(x^*/z)w'p' + w/z -$

$\mu^* zsr'p'] - [(x^*/z)w'p' - \mu^* zsr'p']x'$

so that, recalling the definition of $\psi^*$,

(19)   $\dot{\psi}^* = \psi^*(\rho - sr) - p'z(\beta zw' - \psi^* sr')(\beta + x')$

Eqs. (7), (10), (17) and (19) form the dynamic system of Regime (b). Written in detail, the system is:

(7b)   $\dot{z} = z[n - sr(p(x + \beta z))]$

(10b)  $xw'(p(x+\beta z))p'(x+\beta z) + w(p(x+\beta z)) - \psi sr'(p(x+\beta z))p'(x+\beta z) = 0$

(17b)  $\dot{\psi} = [\rho - sr(p(x + \beta z))]\psi + (x + \beta z)w(p(x + \beta z))$

(19b)  $\dot{\psi}^* = [\rho - sr(p(x + \beta z))]\psi^*$

$\qquad - p'(x + \beta z)z[\beta zw'(p(x + \beta z)) - \psi^* sr'(p(x + \beta z))] [\beta + x'(z)]$

**Regime (d): $z = x$, $\beta z = x^*$**  In this regime (5) and (6) reduce to

(20)  $\dot{\mu} = \delta\mu - (n - sr)\mu - (1 + \beta)(w' - \mu zsr')p'$

and

(21)  $\dot{\mu}^* = \delta\mu^* - (n - sr)\mu^* - (1 + \beta)(\beta w' - \mu^* zsr')p'$

From the definitions of $\psi$ and $\psi^*$ we then calculate that

(22)  $\dot{\psi} = (\rho - sr)\psi - (1 + \beta)(w'z - \psi sr')zp'$

and

(23)  $\dot{\psi}^* = (\rho - sr)\psi^* - (1 + \beta)(w'\beta z - \psi^* sr')zp'$

Eqs. (7), (22) and (23) form the dynamic system associated with Regime (d).  In full detail, the system is:

(7d)  $\dot{z} = z[n - sr(p((1 + \beta)z))]$

(22d)  $\dot{\psi} = [\rho - sr(p((1 + \beta)z))]\psi$

$\qquad - (1 + \beta)zp'((1 + \beta)z) [w'(p((1 + \beta)z))z - \psi sr'(p((1 + \beta)z))]$

(23d)  $\dot{\psi}^* = [\rho - sr(p((1 + \beta)z))]\psi^*$

$\qquad - (1 + \beta)zp'((1 + \beta)z)[w'(p((1 + \beta)z))\beta z - \psi^* sr'(p((1 + \beta)z))]$

That completes the assembly of raw materials.  It remains only to list two additional assumptions.

We have denoted by $p(x + x^*)$ the solution to the market-clearing equation (1).  We now add the assumption that

(24)  $\text{sign}\left[ \dfrac{Xp'(X)}{p(X)} \right] = \text{sign}[\theta_1 - \theta_2]$

Since

(25)  $\dfrac{Xp'(X)}{p(X)} = \dfrac{(\theta_1 - \theta_2)[(1 - s)\theta_1 + s\theta_2]}{\theta_1[1 - s(1 - \theta_2)]\sigma_1 + s\theta_2\sigma_2(1 - \theta_2) - s\theta_2(\theta_1 - \theta_2)}$

(24) holds if and only if the denominator of (25) is positive.  This is certainly the case if $\sigma_i \geq 1$ for at least one i; for example, if $\sigma_1 = \sigma_2 = 1$

then $Xp'(X)/p(X) = \theta_1 - \theta_2$ and (24) is necessarily satisfied.

## 3.    ANALYSIS

Our purpose in this section is to construct a phase diagram which clearly depicts the behaviour of the system in each of the three observable modes.

Let us concentrate for the time being on Regime (b) and the associated system of equations (7b), (10b), (17b), (19b). Our first step is to trace the locus ($\dot{z} = 0$, $z > 0$) on the $(z,\psi)$-plane. From (7b), if $\dot{z} = 0$ and $z > 0$ then

$$(26) \quad n = sr(p(X)), \qquad X \equiv x + \beta z$$

with solution $X = X^*$, say. Given any $\bar{X}$, (10b) gives the locus of points $(z,\psi)$ such that $X = \bar{X}$. The equation of this locus is

$$(27) \quad \psi = \frac{xw'(p(\bar{X}))p'(\bar{X}) + w(p(\bar{X}))}{sr'(p(\bar{X}))p'(\bar{X})}$$

$$= -\frac{w'(p(\bar{X}))}{sr'(p(\bar{X}))}\beta z + \frac{w(p(\bar{X}))}{sr'(p(\bar{X}))p'(\bar{X})}\left[\frac{p(\bar{X})w'(p(\bar{X}))}{w(p(\bar{X}))}\frac{\bar{X}p'(\bar{X})}{p(\bar{X})} + 1\right]$$

Since $w'/r' < 0$, (27) defines a positively-sloped straight line, like AFGB in Figure 1. Consider any point on that line. From (10b) with $z$ held constant, if $\psi$ falls then $x$ increases. This implies that successively higher values of $\bar{X}$ correspond to successively lower straight lines, as in Figure 2. Since $r$ is an increasing function of $X$, $\dot{z}$ is positive above the locus AFGB and negative below the locus.

As our second step, we mark out on Figure 1 that region which is consistent with Regime (b). On AFGB, $x + \beta z = X^*$. Hence $x = 0$ at G, where $z = X^*/\beta$, and $x = z$ at F, where $z = X^*/(1 + \beta)$; moreover, $x$ is decreasing along AB, with $x \geq z$ on AF and $0 \leq x \leq z$ on FG. Now consider the locus $x = z$. It must pass through F and, when $z = X^*/\beta$, it must lie below G, where $x = 0$. The locus $x = z$ is depicted as JFG'M in Figure 1. Its equation is obtained from (10b) by setting $x = z$:

$$(28) \quad \psi = \frac{zw'(p(1 + \beta)z))p'(1 + \beta)z) + w(p((1 + \beta))}{sr'(p((1 + \beta)z))p'((1 + \beta)z)}$$

## Figure 1

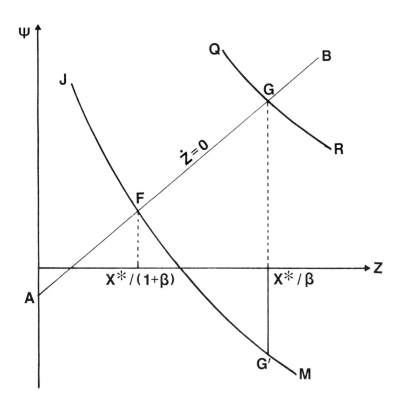

Figure 2

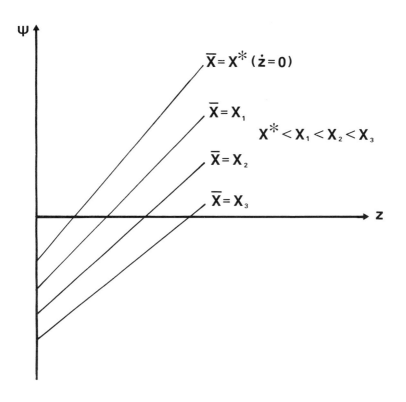

Similarly, the locus $x = 0$, represented in Figure 1 by QGR, is obtained from (10b) by setting $x = 0$:

$$(29) \quad \psi = \frac{w(p(\beta z))}{sr'(p(\beta z))p'(\beta z)} > 0$$

Thus, summarizing, all points between JFG'M and QGR are consistent with $x < z$. It remains to determine whether they are consistent with $x^* = \beta z$. From (4), the boundary separating points where $x^* < \beta z$ from points where $x^* = \beta z$ is described by

$$(30) \quad \psi^* = \frac{\beta z w'(p((1 + \beta)z))p'((1 + \beta)z) + w(p((1 + \beta))}{sr'(p((1 + \beta)z))p'((1 + \beta)z)}$$

Since $\beta < 1$, the graphs of (28) and (30) are as displayed in Figure 3. Thus it emerges that points consistent with Regime (b) must lie to the left of the locus $\psi^*(z)\big|_{(30)}$ as well as to the right of the locus $\psi^*(z)\big|_{(28)}$.

Our third step is to trace the locus $\dot\psi = 0$ and the locus $\dot\psi^* = 0$. Let us concentrate on the locus $\dot\psi = 0$ on the $(z,\psi)$-plane. Now $n - sr \geq 0$ implies that $\rho - sr > 0$. Hence $\dot\psi > 0$ on and above FG. Thus the locus $\dot\psi = 0$ lies everywhere below FG. Moreover, in a steady state, $\psi < 0$. Thus, at a steady state, $\dot\psi = 0$ and $sr = n$. From (22d), therefore,

$$(31) \quad 0 = [\delta + (1 + \beta)zp'sr']\psi - [(1 + \beta)zp'w'z]$$

Since $\mathrm{sign}\,(w') = -\,\mathrm{sign}\,(r') = -\,\mathrm{sign}\,(\theta_1 - \theta_2)$, $p'r' > 0$ and $p'w' < 0$. Hence the first square-bracketed term of (31) is positive and the second negative, implying that $\psi < 0$ in a steady state. Next we notice that, as a further implication of (22d),

$$(32) \quad \dot\psi\big|_{\psi = 0} = -\,(1 + \beta)zp'w'z \neq 0$$

Thus the locus $\dot\psi = 0$ cannot cross the horizontal axis. Finally, we show that the locus $\dot\psi = 0$ is positively sloped above FG'M in Figure 1. In view of the preceding property, we need consider only that part of the figure between FG'M and the horizontal axis. Suppose then that the locus $\dot\psi = 0$ has a negatively-sloped portion between FG'M and the horizontal axis, like CD in Figure 4. Then it must also contain a section like ABC. Combining Figures 2 and 4, one may verify that, on AB, $\psi$ declines as $\overline{X}$ increases while, on BC, $\psi$ declines as $\overline{X}$

Figure 3

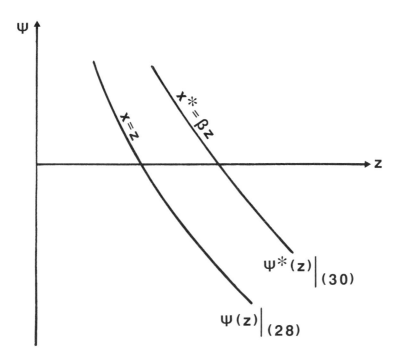

## Figure 4

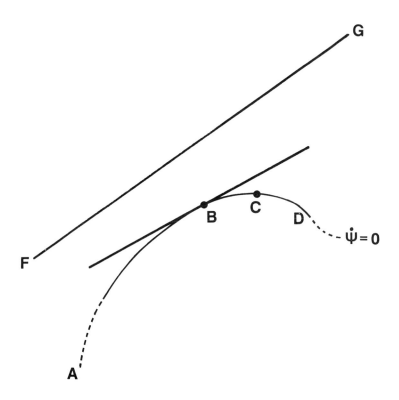

declines. Hence $d\psi/d\bar{X} = 0$ at B on $\dot{\psi}=0$. However this is impossible. For, setting $\dot{\psi} = 0$ in (17b),

(33)   $0 = [\rho - sr(p(\bar{X}))]\psi + \bar{X}w(p(\bar{X}))$

so that, differentiating,

(34)   $0 = (\rho - sr)d\psi + (-sr'p'\psi + w + \bar{X}w'p')d\bar{X}$

or, recalling (10b) and the fact that $\bar{X} = x + \beta z$,

(35)   $d\psi/d\bar{X} = \beta zw'p'/(sr - \rho) < 0$

Thus $\psi$ must decline as $\bar{X}$ increases; that is, BC in Figure 4 is impossible.

The locus $\dot{\psi}^* = 0$ has properties like those of the locus $\dot{\psi} = 0$; but $\dot{\psi}^* = 0$ lies everywhere above $\dot{\psi} = 0$.

Let us now turn to the region below JFG'M in Figure 1. In that region $x = z$; hence the world economy is in Regime (d) and eqs. (7d) and (22d) prevail. From (7d) we see that, for as long as it remains in the region, z moves monotonely towards $X^*/(1 + \beta)$. Moreover, from (10b), (17b) and (22b), the locus $\dot{\psi} = 0$ is continuous at the boundary line JFG'M and lies everywhere below the horizontal axis.

We have considered Regimes (b) and (d). However for sufficiently large z there is unemployment in both countries; that is, the world economy is operating under Regime (a). As our next step, therefore, we consider the behaviour of the world economy under Regime (a) and examine the conditions which must be satisfied at the point of transition from Regime (a) to Regime (b) or (d).

Consider then the system of equations [(7a), (10a), (11a), (14a), (15a)] associated with Regime (a). Let us redefine $X \equiv x + x^*$ and $Y \equiv \psi + \psi^*$. From (10a) and (11a),

(36)   $w'(p(X))p'(X)X + 2w(p(X)) - sr'(p(X))p'(X)Y = 0$

and, from (14a) and (15a),

(37)   $\dot{Y} = w(p(X))X + [\delta - sr(p(X))]Y + zX'(z)w(p(X))$

Differentiating (36) with respect to t, we find that

(38)   $\Delta(X,Y)\dot{X} = sr'(p(X))p'(X)\dot{Y} = 0$

where

(39)   $\Delta(X,Y) \equiv \dfrac{\partial}{\partial X} [p'(X)w'(p(X))X + 2w(p(X)) - sr'(p(X))p'(X)Y]$

Since $\dot{X} = X'(z)\dot{z}$, (38) can be rewritten as

(40)   $\Delta(X,Y)X'(z)z[n - sr(p(X))] - sr'(p(X))p'(X)\dot{Y} = 0$

Substituting from (36) and (37) into (40), and rearranging terms, we obtain the differential equation

(41) $X'(z) =$

$$\dfrac{1}{z}\left[\dfrac{sr'(p(X(z)))p'(X(z))\{w(p(X(z)))X(z) + Y(X(z))[\delta-sr(p(X(z)))]\}}{\Delta(X(z),Y(X(z))(n-sr) - sr'(p(X(z)))p'(X(z))w(p(X(z)))}\right]$$

Let us denote the solution to (41) by $X(z; z_0, X_0)$, where $(z_0, X_0)$ is an initial value; and let

(42a)   $x(z) = \dfrac{1}{2} X(z; z_0, X(z_0))$

(42b)   $x^*(z) = \dfrac{1}{2} X(z; z_0, X(z_0))$

(42c)   $\psi(t) = \dfrac{1}{2} Y(X(z; z_0, X(z_0)))$

(42d)   $\psi^*(t) = \dfrac{1}{2} Y(X(z; z_0, X(z_0)))$

$[x(t), x^*(t), \psi(t), \psi^*(t)]$ defined by (42) satisfies eqs. (7a), (10a), (11a) and (15a) and therefore is a candidate for that part of the feedback-Nash equilibrium in which there is universal unemployment.

Suppose that the feedback-Nash equilibrium path makes a transition from Regime (a) to Regime (b) at time T and $z_T$. Then the path must satisfy the transversality condition

(43)   $\dfrac{1}{2}\{x(p(X))X + Y[n - sr(p(X))]\} = \delta\Lambda(z_T)z_T$

where

(44)   $\Lambda[z_T] \equiv \displaystyle\int_0^{\infty}(x/z)w \exp(-\delta t)\, dt$

is the value of the home union's utility along the equilibrium path defined by $z(0) = z_T$. If

(45)   $X(z; z_T, X(z_T)) > X^*$ for $z > z_T$

and

(46)   $X'(z; z_T, X(z_T)) \equiv \dfrac{\partial}{\partial z} X(z; z_T, X(z_T)) \Big|_{z = z_T} \leq 2\beta$

then (44) is satisfied. If (44) is satisfied, we have the feedback-Nash solution

(47a)   $x(z) = \begin{cases} \tilde{x}(z) & \text{for } 0 \leq z \leq z_T \\ \dfrac{1}{2} X(z; z_T, X(z_T)) & \text{for } z > z_T \end{cases}$

(47a)   $x^*(z) = \begin{cases} \tilde{x}^*(z) & \text{for } 0 \leq z \leq z_T \\ \dfrac{1}{2} X(z; z_T, X(z_T)) & \text{for } z > z_T \end{cases}$

where $\tilde{x}(z)$ and $\tilde{x}^*(z)$ are associated with Regimes (a) and (b). Let $z_0 > z_T$. Then the world economy passes through three phases.

Drawing together everything learned to this point, we obtain the phase diagram Figure 5. The stationary points E and E$^*$ are saddle-points.

(i) While $z_T < z \leq z_0$ there is unemployment in each country. The level of employment is the same in each country, implying that unemployment is greatest in the home country. As z approaches $z_T$, foreign unemployment goes to zero. Throughout this phase, $\psi = \psi^*$.

(ii) While $z_D < z \leq z_T$ there is unemployment in the home country only. The home rate of unemployment declines to zero as z approaches $z_D$.

(iii) While $X^*/(1 + \beta) \leq z \leq z_D$ there is full employment in both countries.

Throughout all phases, z declines monotonely. Throughout phases (ii) and (iii), $\psi < \psi^*$. Phases (i) and (ii) are of finite duration. If $z_0 < z_T$, one or both of those phases is degenerate.

Thus the long-run impotence of labour unions, which first came to light in the small-country context of Chapter V, surfaces again in a context of large trading countries. Moreover, the power of a union evaporates more quickly the smaller the work force that it serves.

Finally, it is easy to see that along the equilibrium paths of Figure 5 the eventual increase in the ratio of home to foreign employment might give rise to a change in the pattern of trade.

## Figure 5

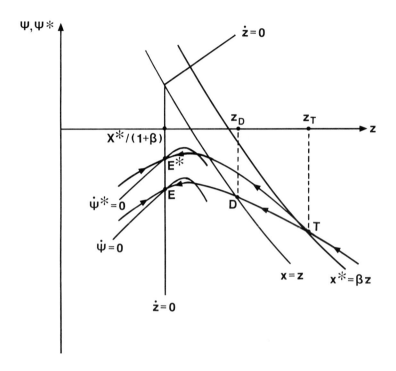

CHAPTER SEVEN

# A DIFFERENTIAL GAME BETWEEN ORGANIZED LABOUR AND ORGANIZED CAPITAL

## 1.  INTRODUCTION

In earlier chapters we have examined some of the implications of rational monopoly unionism in an otherwise competitive environment. In Chapters II and III the union was depicted as exercising its market power in an economy with a fixed stock of capital. In Chapter V, on the other hand, the union was placed in an economy which regularly adds to its stock of capital a fixed proportion of capitalists' income. In that dynamic setting, the union was obliged to temper its policies in the light of their effects on the community's rate of saving.

In the present chapter we modify the analysis of Chapter V by allowing for the possibility that capitalists as well as workers are organized. The savings ratio of the capitalists then ceases to be a constant parameter, becoming instead a variable control the setting of which is chosen by the capitalists at each moment. The labour union continues to set the minimum wage rate or, equivalently if the minimum wage is binding, the level of employment.

Evidently the workers' union and the capitalists' club find themselves in a strategic relationship. Indeed we proceed to formulate a differential game with the two organizations as players. The game has a single state variable z, the labour:capital endowment ratio, which is assumed to be amenable to observation by both players without cost or delay. The information available to each player at any moment of time is limited to the current value of the state variable; thus, in the terminology of Basar and Olsder (1982, p. 212), the information pattern of the game is "feedback perfect state." The motion of z is determined by the familiar differential equation

$$\dot{z} = z\{n - s[f(x) - xf'(x)]\}$$

The controls are, of course, x for the union and s for the club. The level at which x is set at any moment is determined by the union's strategy

$$x = x(z,t)$$

Similarly, the level at which s is set at any moment is determined by the club's strategy

$$s = s(z,t)$$

Finally, the pay-off for any player is the integral of its discounted consumption. Thus the pay-off for the labour union is

$$\int_0^\infty \exp[-\delta_w t] Nw \, dt$$

where $\delta_w$ is the workers' rate of time preference less the rate of growth of the work force n and is assumed to be positive; and the pay-off for the capitalists' club is

$$\int_0^\infty \exp[-\delta_r t](1 - s)Kr \, dt$$

where $\delta_r$ is the capitalists' rate of time preference less the rate of growth of the work force and is assumed to be positive. To keep matters simple it will be assumed henceforth that $\delta_w = \delta_r = \delta > 0$. It will be our business to discover the properties of the feedback-Nash equilibrium of the game, where the latter is characterized by a pair of strategies such that, given the strategy of one player, the other player has no incentive to change its strategy.

The conclusions of Chapter V prove to be highly sensitive to the formation of an employers' club. Let $x^*$ be the static optimum value of x (so that $x^*$ maximizes $xf'(x)$ and either $x^* = x_1^*$ or $x^* = x_2^*$). It will be shown that, if a feedback-Nash equilibrium exists, it is unique and consists of the strategies

(1a)   $x(z,t) = \begin{cases} z \text{ if } z < x^* \\ x^* \text{ if } z \geq x^* \end{cases}$

(1b)   $s(z,t) = 0$ for all $t \geq 0$ and all $z \geq 0$

Thus, provided only that the initial endowment ratio $z_0$ is not less than $x^*$, in equilibrium the union *always* exercises its market power, holding the aggregate employment : capital ratio at $x^*$; and in equilibrium capitalists *never* save, that is, there is a permanent strike of savers, implying that the labour : capital endowment ratio goes to infinity and that, after finite time, only the relatively labour-intensive good is produced.

These conclusions contrast sharply with those of Lancaster (1973), the pioneer in analysis of this kind, and of Pohjola (1985). Along the equilibrium paths which emerge from their analyses there is an initial phase during which capital is accumulated. However Lancaster assumed that labour is never a limiting factor and Pohjola, while recognizing that the labour supply might become a binding constraint, failed to allow for it in his formal analysis.

In Section 2 we derive necessary and sufficient conditions for the existence of a feedback-Nash equilibrium and then show that, if those conditions are satisfied, the equilibrium is unique and consists of the strategies (1a) and (1b). The argument is long and intricate and will not be to the taste of all readers. For those who do not insist on seeing every tack hammered home, we have provided an appendix (Appendix 1) in which it is shown, in a relatively straightforward way, that if the conditions for existence are known to be satisfied then the strategies (1a) and (1b) form a Nash equilibrium; after reading the appendix, they can return to the main text at Section 3.

## 2.   ANALYSIS

### Preliminary Considerations

In this preliminary subsection we define our differential game, derive the conditions which must be satisfied by a feedback-Nash equilibrium, and then recast those conditions in a form suitable for further analysis.

Our differential game is defined by the pair of control problems

$(P_w)$   $\max\limits_{<x(t)>}$   $V_w \equiv \int_0^\infty \exp(-\delta t)(x/z)f'(x)\,dt$

s.t.   $x \le z$

$\dot{z} = z\{n - s[f(x) - xf'(x)]\}$

$z(0) = z_0$, given

and

$(P_r)$   $\displaystyle\max_{<x(t)>}$   $V_r \equiv \int_0^\infty \exp(-\delta t)(1/z)(1 - s)[f(x) - xf'(x)]\,dt$

s.t.   $0 \leq s \leq 1$

$\dot{z} = z\{n - s[f(x) - xf'(x)]\}$

$z(0) = z_0,$ given

where, at each moment t, each player knows the value of $z(t)$.

The necessary conditions for a Nash equilibrium can be expressed in terms of the Hamiltonians

$$H^w(x, z, \mu_w; s) \equiv (x/z)f'(x) + \mu_w z\{n - s[f(x) - xf'(x)]\}$$

$$H^r(s, z, \mu_r; x) \equiv (1/z)(1 - s)[f(x) - xf'(x)] + \mu_r z\{n - s[f(x) - xf'(x)]\}$$

and Lagrangeans

$$L^w \equiv H^w + \lambda_w(z - x)$$

$$L^r \equiv H^r + \lambda_r(1 - s)$$

associated with $(P_w)$ and $(P_r)$:

(2)   $H^w\big(x(z,t), z, \mu_w; s(z,t)\big) \geq H^w\big(x, z, \mu_w; s(z,t)\big)$ for any x
such that $0 \leq x \leq z$

(3)   $H^r\big(s(z,t), z, \mu_r; x(z,t)\big) \geq H^r\big(s, z, \mu_r; x(z,t)\big)$ for any s
such that $0 \leq s \leq 1$

(4)   $L^w_x = H^w_x - \lambda_w = 0$

(5)   $\lambda_w \geq 0,\quad z - x(z,t) \geq 0,\quad \lambda_w[z - x(z,t)] = 0$

(6)   $L^r_s = H^r_s - \lambda_r = 0$

(7)   $\lambda_r \geq 0,\quad 1 - s(z,t) \geq 0,\quad \lambda_r[1 - s(z,t)] = 0$

(8)   $\dot{z} = z\{n - s(z,t)[f(x(z,t)) - x(z,t)f'(x(z,t))]\}$

$\dot{\mu}_w = \delta\mu_w - L^w_z$

$\quad = \delta\mu_w - [(H^w_x - \lambda_w)x_z(z,t) + H^w_z + \lambda_w + H^w_s s_z(z,t)]$

(9)   $\quad = \delta\mu_w + (1/z^2)\{x(z,t)f'(x(z,t)) - \mu_w z^2[n - s(z,t)(f(x(z,t))$

$\quad\quad - x(z,t)f'(x(z,t)))]\} - \lambda_w + \mu_w z\,[f(x(z,t)) - x(z,t)f'(x(z,t))]\,s_z(z,t)$

$$\dot{\mu}_r = \delta\mu_r - L_z^r$$

$$= \delta\mu_r - [(H_s^r - \lambda_r)s_z(z,t) + H_z^r + H_x^r x_z(z,t)]$$

(10) $$= \delta\mu_r + (1/z^2)\{[1 - s(z,t)][f(x(z,t)) - x(z,t)f'(x(z,t))]$$

$$- \mu_r z^2[n - s(z,t)(f(x(z,t)) - x(z,t)f'(x(z,t)))]\}$$

$$+ (1/z)\{[1 - s(z,t)] - \mu_r z^2 s(z,t)\}x(z,t)f''(x(z,t))x_z(z,t)$$

where $H_x^w \equiv \partial H^w/\partial x$, $L_x^w \equiv \partial L^w/\partial x$, $x_z(z,t) \equiv \partial x(z,t)/\partial x$, etc. The last terms on the right-hand sides of (9) and (10) contain the partial derivatives $s_z(z,t)$ and $x_z(z,t)$, respectively. Those terms describe the "cross effects" discussed by Clemhout and Wan (1979); they separate closed-loop from open-loop equilibria and make it difficult to find closed-loop solutions. In our particular case, however, progress can be made.

Consider inequalities (2) and (3). Differentiating $H^w$ with respect to x, we obtain

$$H_x^w = \frac{f'(x)}{z}\left\{1 - (1 + s\mu_w z^2)\left[\frac{1 - \theta(x)}{\sigma(x)}\right]\right\}$$

This equation is of the same form as (V.6). In view of (a)–(d) on page 190, then,

(11) $$x(z,t) = \min\{z, x(\mu_w z^2; s)\}$$

where the function $x(\mu_w z^2; s)$ is defined on page 192. (There, however, the parameter s is suppressed.) Similarly, differentiating $H^r$ with respect to s, we obtain

$$H_s^r = -(1/z)(1 + \mu_r z^2)[f(x) - xf'(x)]$$

so that, if both x and z are positive,

(12) $$s(z,t) = \begin{cases} 0 \text{ if } 1 + \mu_r z^2 > 0 \\ 1 \text{ if } 1 + \mu_r z^2 < 0 \end{cases}$$

But if $s(z,t)$ is determined by (12) then $s_z(z,t) = 0$ and the "cross effect" in (9) vanishes; moreover (11) can be re-written as

(12) $$x(z,t) = \begin{cases} \min\{z, x(\mu_w z^2; 0)\} \text{ if } 1 + \mu_r z^2 > 0 \\ \min\{z, x(\mu_w z^2; 1)\} \text{ if } 1 + \mu_r z^2 < 0 \end{cases}$$

Denoting $\mu_w z^2$ and $\mu_r z^2$ by $\psi_w$ and $\psi_r$, respectively, and recalling that $s_z(z,t) = 0$, (9), (10) and (11′) can be re-written as

$$\dot{\psi}_w = z^2\dot{\mu}_w + 2\mu_w z\dot{z}$$

$$= x(z,t)f'(x(z,t)) + \psi_w\{(\delta - n) + s(z,t)[f(x(z,t)) - x(z,t)f'(x(z,t))]\}$$

$$- \lambda_w z^2 + 2\psi_w\{n - s(z,t)[f(x(z,t)) - x(z,t)f'(x(z,t))]\}$$

$$(9')\qquad = x(z,t)f'(x(z,t)) + \psi_w\{(\delta + n) - s(z,t)[f(x(z,t)) - x(z,t)f'(x(z,t))]\}$$

$$- \lambda_w z^2$$

$$\dot{\psi}_r = z^2\dot{\mu}_r + 2\mu_r z\dot{z}$$

$$(10')\qquad = [1 - s(z,t)][f(x(z,t)) - x(z,t)f'(x(z,t))]$$

$$+ \psi_r\{\delta - n - s(z,t)[f(x(z,t)) - x(z,t)f'(x(z,t))]\}$$

$$+ z[1 - s(z,t) - s(z,t)\psi_r]x(z,t)f''(x(z,t))x_z(z,t)$$

and

$$(11'')\quad x(z,t) = \begin{cases} \min\{z, x(\psi_w; 0)\} \text{ if } 1 + \psi_r > 0 \\ \min\{z, x(\psi_w; 1)\} \text{ if } 1 + \psi_r < 0 \end{cases}$$

where

$$\lambda_w = (1/z)f'(x(z,t))\left\{1 - (1 + s(z,t)\psi_w)\left[\frac{1 - \theta(x(z,t))}{\sigma(x(z,t))}\right]\right\}$$

Now consider the pair of differential equations (8) and (9′). The solution $(z(t), \psi_w(t))$ depends on the initial condition $(z_0, \psi_w(0))$, but $\psi_w$ does not depend on z. Similarly, the solution $(z(t), \psi_r(t))$ to the pair of equations (8) and (10′) depends on the initial condition $(z_0, \psi_r(0))$, but $\psi_r$ does not depend on z. Thus $\psi_w$ and $\psi_r$ are functions of time but not of the current value of the state variable. Hence (11″) can be rewritten in its turn as

$$(11''')\quad x(z,t) = \begin{cases} \min\{z, x(\psi_w(t); 0)\} \text{ if } 1 + \psi_r(t) > 0 \\ \min\{z, x(\psi_w(t); 1)\} \text{ if } 1 + \psi_r(t) < 0 \end{cases}$$

It follows that if $z > x(\psi_w(t); 0)$ and $1 + \psi_r(t) > 0$ or if $z > x(\psi_w(t); 1)$ and $1 + \psi_r(t) < 0$ then either $x(z,t) = x(\psi_w(t); 0)$ or $x(z,t) = x(\psi_w(t); 1)$; that is, $x(z,t)$ depends exclusively on t and does not depend on z. This in turn implies that $x_z(z,0) = 0$, so that the "cross effect" in (10) vanishes. On the other hand, if $z \leq x(\psi_w(t), 0)$ then, from (11'''), $x(z,t) = z$; that is, $x(z,t)$ depends exclusively on $z$ and does not depend on $t$. In this case $x_z(z,t) = dz/dz = 1$.

Let us pause to summarize the foregoing argument.

($\alpha$) Suppose that $1 + \psi_r > 0$. Then $s = 0$ and $x = \min \{z, x(\psi_w; 0)\}$, where $x(\psi_w; 0) = x_2^*$.

($\alpha$-1) If $z > x_2^*$ then $x = x_2^*$ and any candidate equilibrium must satisfy the system of equations

$$\dot{z} = nz$$

(13)    $$\dot{\psi}_w = x_2^* f'(x_2^*) + (\delta + n)\psi_w$$

$$\dot{\psi}_r = f(x_2^*) - x_2^* f'(x_2^*) + (\delta + n)\psi_r$$

($\alpha$-2) If $z \leq x_2^*$ then $x = z$ and

$$\dot{z} = nz$$

(14)    $$\dot{\psi}_w = -z^2 f''(z) + (\delta + n)\psi_w$$

$$\dot{\psi}_r = f(z) - zf'(z) + z^2 f''(z) + (\delta + n)\psi_r$$

($\beta$) Suppose that $1 + \psi_r < 0$. Then $s = 1$ and $x = \min \{z, x(\psi_w; 1)\}$.

($\beta$-1) If $z > x(\psi_w; 1)$ then $x = x(\psi_w; 1)$ and

$$\dot{z} = z\{n - [f(x(\psi_w; 1)) - x(\psi_w; 1)f'(x(\psi_w; 1))]\}$$

(15)    $$\dot{\psi}_w = x(\psi_w; 1)f'(x(\psi_w; 1)) + \psi_w\{(\delta + n) - [f(x(\psi_w; 1))$$
$$- x(\psi_w; 1)f'(x(\psi_w; 1))]\}$$

$$\dot{\psi}_r = \psi_r\{(\delta + n) - [f(x(\psi_w; 1)) - x(\psi_w; 1)f'(x(\psi_w; 1))]\}$$

($\beta$-2) If $z \leq x(\psi_w; 1)$ then $x = z$ and

$$\dot{z} = z\{n - [f(z) - zf'(z)]\}$$

(16)    $$\dot{\psi}_w = -z^2 f''(z) + \psi_w\{(\delta+n) - [z^2 f''(z) + f(z) - zf'(z)]\}$$

$$\dot{\psi}_r = \psi_r\{(\delta + n) - [z^2 f''(z) + f(z) - zf'(z)]\}$$

Once $(z_0, \psi_w(0), \psi_r(0))$ is given, a complete trajectory can be pieced together from (13)–(16). Let us call such a trajectory a Pontryagin path.

That completes our preliminary analysis. As our next step, we show that there is no Nash equilibrium if $r(x_2^*) > \delta + n$.

*There is no equilibrium if* $r(x_2^*) > \delta + n$

Consider the construction of phase diagrams in the $(z, \psi_r)$-plane.

**LEMMA 1:** No Pontryagin path such that $1 + \psi_r < 0$ for all $t \geq 0$ can be an equilibrium path.

**PROOF** If, along some Pontryagin path, $1 + \psi_r < 0$ for all $t$ then $s = 1$ for all $t$, that is, capitalists consume nothing for all $t$. Capitalists therefore have an incentive to depart from that path. ◊

Suppose that $r(x_2^*) = f(x_2^*) - x_2^* f'(x_2^*) > \delta + n$. From the third member of (13), for given $z > x_2^*$,

$$\lim_{\psi_r \to -1^+} \dot{\psi}_r = \dot{\psi}_r \Big|_{\psi_r = -1} = r(x_2^*) - (\delta + n) > 0$$

From the third member of (14), on the other hand, $\dot{\psi}_r \Big|_{\psi_r = -1} < 0$ for sufficiently small $z$. To verify that this is so, notice first that, when $z$ is very small, only the second good is produced, that is, $f(z) = pf_2(z)$ and $f(z) - zf'(z) = pf_2(z)[1 - zf'(z)/f_2(z)]$; second, that since the elasticity of factor substitution of each good is less than unity, $1 - zf'(z)/f_2(z)$ goes to zero with $z$; and, third, that $z^2 f''(z) \leq 0$. It is clear, then, that there exist $\underline{z}$ and $\overline{z}$ such that

(i)   $0 < \underline{z} \leq \overline{z} < x_2^*$

(ii)  $\dot{\psi}_r \Big|_{\psi_r = -1} > 0$ for any $z > \overline{z}$

(iii) $\dot{\psi}_r \Big|_{\psi_r = -1} < 0$ for any $z < \underline{z}$

Hence Figure 1 is a possible phase diagram when $r(x_2^*) > \delta + n$. (The figure is drawn on the assumption that $\underline{z} = \overline{z}$, that is, that $r(z) + z^2 f''(z) = \delta + n$ has a unique solution. However nothing in the subsequent argument rests on that assumption.) Notice that, if $\psi_r > -1$, $z$ always increases at the growth rate $n$.

The remaining possibilities need not detain us. If $r(x_2^*) < \delta + n$, $\dot{\psi}_r \Big|_{\psi_r = -1}$ is always negative and Figure 2 is a possible phase diagram; and, if $r(x_2^*) = \delta + n$, Figure 3 is a possible phase diagram.

**LEMMA 2:** If $z_0 \in [0, x_2^*]$ then no Pontryagin path starting below the path FC in Figures 1–3 can be a Nash equilibrium path.

# Figure 1

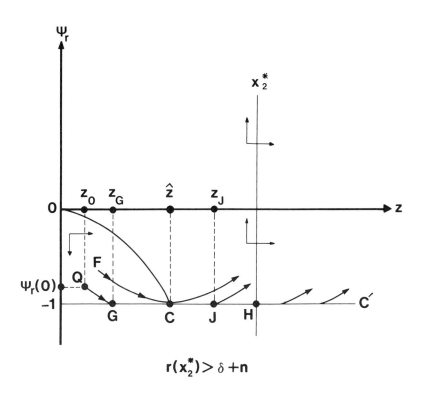

$$r(x_2^*) > \delta + n$$

## Figure 2

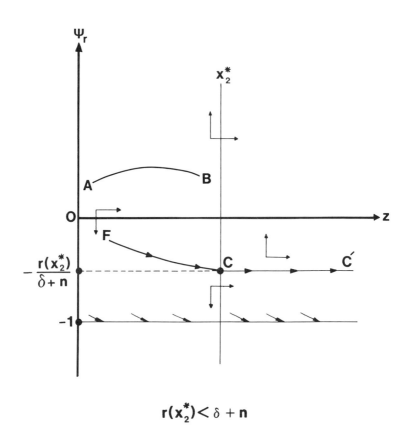

$$r(x_2^*) < \delta + n$$

Figure 3

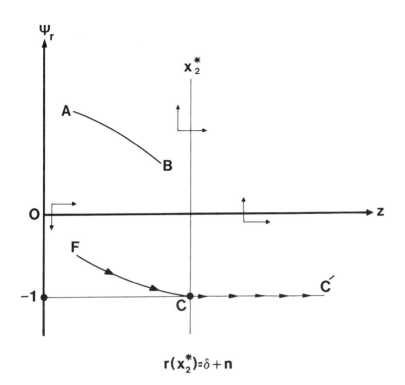

$$r(x_2^*)=\delta + n$$

**PROOF** Consider a Pontryagin path which starts at $(z_0, \psi_r(0))$, below the path FC and such that $z_0 \in [0, x_2^*]$. The conclusion of the lemma is obviously true in the case illustrated by Figure 2.

Let us consider the case illustrated by Figure 1. Suppose that $1 + \psi_r(0) > 0$ and that the path under consideration crosses $\psi_r = -1$ twice, first at G when $t = t_0$ and then, from below, at J when $t = t_1$. Let us denote by $x^A(z,t)$ and $s^A(z,t)$ the decision rules associated with the given path and by $z^A(t,z_0)$ the solution to the differential equation (8) generated by $x^A(z,t)$ and $s^A(z,t)$. Then, clearly, $z^A(t_0,z_0) = z_G$ and $z^A(t_1,z_0) = z_J$. Now let us construct a new decision rule

$$s^N(z,t) = \begin{cases} s^A(z,t) \text{ for all } z \in (0, z_G] \\ 0 \text{ for all } z \in (z_G, z_J] \\ s^A(z,t) \text{ for all } z \in (z_J, \infty) \end{cases}$$

Thus, in terms of Figure 4, $s^N(z,t)$ coincides with $s^A(z,t)$ except in the shaded region on which $s^N(z,t) = 0$. Let us denote by $z^N(t,z_0)$ the solution to (8) generated by $x^A(z,t)$ and $s^N(z,t)$. In Figure 4 the graph of $z^N(t,z_0)$ is depicted as QGJ'H'D' while the graph of $z^A(t,z_0)$ is depicted as QGJHD. As the figure makes clear, (i) at each moment during an initial phase ending at $t_0$, capitalists' cumulated discounted consumption is the same with the decision rules $x^A(z,t)$ and $s^A(z,t)$ as with the rules $x^A(z,t)$ and $s^N(z,t)$. Moreover, (ii) capitalists' cumulated discounted consumption is positive on GJ', with the decision rules $x^A(z,t)$ and $s^N(z,t)$, but zero on GJ, with the decision rules $x^A(z,t)$ and $s^A(z,t)$. Finally, comparing J'D' with JD, we see that, for any $z_H \geq z_J$, $t_{J'H'} < t_{JH}$; hence

$$(1/z)[f(x_2^*) - x_2^* f'(x_2^*)]\exp(-\delta t_{J'H'})$$

$$> (1/z)[f(x_2^*) - x_2^* f'(x_2^*)]\exp(-\delta t_{JH}),$$

that is, (iii) above $z_H$ the pair of strategies $(x^A(z,t), s^N(z,t))$ is superior to the pair $(x^A(z,t), s^A(z,t))$. In view of (i)–(iii),

$$V_r(z_0, x^A(z^A(t,z_0),t), s^A(z^A(t,z_0),t), z^A(t,z_0))$$

$$< V_r(z_0, x^A(z^N(t,z_0),t), s^N(z^N(t,z_0),t), z^N(t,z_0))$$

which implies that the pair of decision rules $(x^A(z,t), s^A(z,t))$ is not an equilibrium solution.

# Figure 4

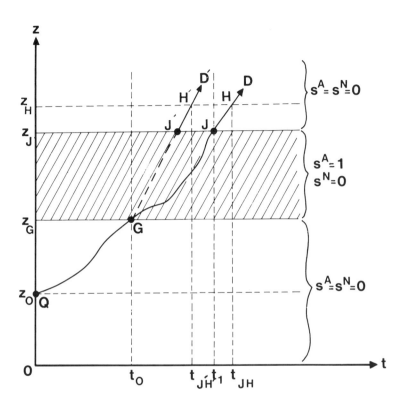

The case in which $r(x_2^*) = \delta + n$, illustrated by Figure 3, can be subjected to a similar argument. ◊

Applying the foregoing lemmata to Figures 1–3, two things become clear.

(I) It is impossible for s to change from zero to one along an equilibrium path; that is, paths like QG in Figure 1 are not equilibrium paths.

(II) Along an equilibrium path either s is always zero or s changes once, from one to zero; that is, if T is any point in time at which s changes from one to zero and if T = 0 means that s = 0 at t = 0 then T is uniquely determined. In view of systems (13)–(16), the unique T does not depend on z(T), although it does depend on the initial condition $(z_0, \psi_w(0), \psi_r(0))$.

Notice that (I) and (II) are valid whatever the relative values of $r(x_2^*)$ and $(\delta + n)$.

**PROPOSITION 1:** If $r(x_2^*) > \delta + n$, the differential game has no equilibrium solution.

**PROOF** Suppose that there is a Nash equilibrium $\{s^e(t,z), x^e(t,z)\}$ when $r(x_2^*) > \delta + n$. In the game under consideration, time t appears only in the players' objective functions; hence the equilibrium is time-invariant and can be written $\{s^e(z), x^e(z)\}$. (See Clemhout and Wan (1985, p. 551).) Let us denote by $z^e(t,z_0)$ the solution to the differential equation

$$\dot{z} = z\{n - s^e(z)[f(x^e(z)) - x^e(z)f'(x^e(z))]\}$$

$$z(0) = z_0$$

In view of (I) and (II) there is a unique value of z, say $\tilde{z}$, such that, along the optimal path, $s^e(z)$ changes from one to zero at $z = \tilde{z}$; let $\tilde{T}^e(z_0)$ be the time at which the switch takes place. Consider Figure 1. From (I) and (II) again, the equilibrium path eventually must enter the region $x_2^*HC'$, say at time $T^e$, where $T^e$ may be zero and depends on $z_0$; thereafter, $x = x_2^*$. If the equilibrium path crosses HC', $T^e$ must be equal to $\tilde{T}^e$; and if the path crosses $x_2^*H$, $T^e$ must be greater than $\tilde{T}^e$. Thus $T^e \geq \tilde{T}^e$; and, for any $t \geq T^e$, $s^e(z) = 0$ and $x^e(z) = x_2^*$.

Now choose some value of t, say $T^*$, which is sufficiently larger than $T^e$, and consider the following strategy for capitalists:

$$(17) \quad \tilde{s}(z,t;\Delta t) = \begin{cases} s^e(z) \text{ for all } t \in [0,T^*] \\ \bar{s} \in ((\delta + n)/r(x_2^*), 1) \text{ for all } t \in (T^*, T^*+\Delta t) \\ s^e(z) \text{ for all } t \in [T^*+\Delta t, \infty) \end{cases}$$

(In Figure 5, $x^e(z) = x_2^*$ on zDBH and $T^e$ is determined by the intersection of the path $z_0B$ and the horizontal line DBH.) Denote by $V_r^{\Delta t}$ the value of $V_r$ associated with $(\tilde{s}(z,t;\Delta t), x^e(z))$. Then

$$V_r^{\Delta t} = \int_0^{T^*} \exp(-\delta\tau) \frac{[1 - s^e(z^e(\tau,z_0))]}{z^e(\tau,z_0)} r\big(x^e(z^e(\tau,z_0))\big) d\tau$$

$$(18) \qquad + \int_{T^*}^{T^*+\Delta t} \exp(-\delta\tau) \frac{1 - \bar{s}}{z_{\Delta t}^e(\tau,z_0)} r\big(x^e(z_{\Delta t}^e(\tau,z_0))\big) d\tau$$

$$+ \int_{T^*+\Delta t}^{\infty} \exp(-\delta\tau) \frac{[1-s^e(\tilde{z}^e(\tau,z_0))]}{\tilde{z}^e(\tau,z_0)} r\big(x^e(\tilde{z}^e(\tau,z_0))\big) d\tau$$

where $z_{\Delta t}^e$ is the solution to the differential equation

$$(19) \quad \dot{z} = z\big\{n - \bar{s}[f(x^e(z)) - x^e(z)f'(x^e(z))]\big\}$$

for $\tau \in (T^*, T^* + \Delta t)$ with $z_{\Delta t}^e(T^*, z_0) = z^e(T^*, z_0)$, and where $\tilde{z}^e(\tau, z_0)$ is the solution to the differential equation

$$(20) \quad \dot{z} = z\big\{n - s^e(z)[f(x^e(z)) - x^e(z)f'(x^e(z))]\big\}$$

for $\tau \in (T^* + \Delta t, \infty)$ with $\tilde{z}^e(T^* + \Delta t, z_0) = z_{\Delta t}^e(T^* + \Delta t, z_0)$.

Consider (20). When $t = T^*$ the path is at point M in Figure 5. Since $\overline{MA}$ (= $z^e(T^*, z_0)$) is greater than $\overline{OD}$, $x^e(z)$ must be equal to $x_2^*$ at $T^* + \varepsilon$, where $\varepsilon$ is positive and sufficiently small. Thus, for as long as $t \ (> T^*)$ is in a sufficiently small neighbourhood of $T^*$, (20) can be written as

$$(21) \quad \dot{z} = z\{n - \bar{s}r(x_2^*)\} < 0$$

for $\bar{s} > (\delta+n)/r(x_2^*)$. After $T^*$, $z$ monotonely decreases. If we take $\Delta t$ sufficiently small, the path of $z$ is like MM' in Figure 5, so that, at $t = T^* + \Delta t$, $\overline{M'F}$ (= $z_{\Delta t}^e(T^* + \Delta t, z_0)$) is still greater than $\overline{OD}$, which implies that, at M', $x^e(z) = x_2^*$. Thus, for $t \in [T^* + \Delta t, \infty)$, (20) becomes

$$(22) \quad \dot{z} = z\big\{n - s^e(z)[f(x_2^*) - x_2^*f'(x_2^*)]\big\}$$

Figure 5

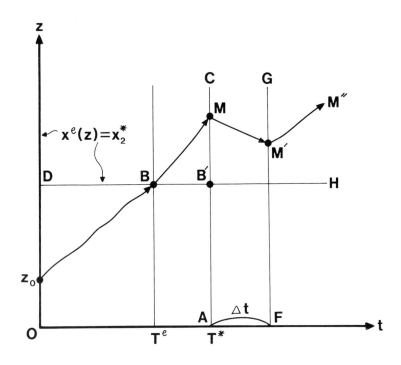

On zDOAB′C: $\tilde{s}(z,t;\Delta t) \equiv s^e(z)$

On CBAFG: $\tilde{s}(z,t;\Delta t) \equiv \bar{s}$

On GFt: $\tilde{s}(z,t;\Delta t) \equiv s^e(z)$

$z_0$BM: solution to $\dot{z}=z\left\{n-s^e(z)\left[f(x^e(z)-x^e(z)f'(x^e(z))\right]\right.$
        with $z(o)=z_0$

As we have noticed, however, if $x^e(z) = x_2^*$ then $s^e(z) = 0$; hence (22) reduces to

(22')  $\dot{z} = nz$

Let us summarize the foregoing argument. For $t \in [T^*, T^* + \Delta t)$, the movement of $z$ is determined by

(23)  $\dot{z} = z[n - \bar{s}r(x_2^*)]$

with $z(T^*) \equiv z^e(T^*, z_0)$; and for $t \in [T^* + \Delta t, \infty)$ the movement is determined by

(24)  $\dot{z} = nz$

Thus, from (23),

(25)  $z(t) = z(T^*)\exp[-(\bar{s}r(x_2^*) - n)(t - T^*)]$  for $t \in [T^*, T^* + \Delta t)$

and, from (24),

(26)  $z(t) = z(T^*)\exp[-(\bar{s}r(x_2^*) - n)\Delta t]\exp[n(t - (T^* + \Delta t))]$

$\qquad$ for $t \in [T^* + \delta t, \infty)$

From (18), therefore,

(27)  $V_r^{\Delta t} = \Gamma + \displaystyle\int_{T^*}^{T^* + \Delta t} \frac{\exp(-\delta\tau)(1 - \bar{s})r(x_2^*)}{z(T^*)\exp[-(\bar{s}r(x_2^*) - n)(\tau - T^*)]}\, d\tau$

$\qquad + \displaystyle\int_{T^* + \Delta t}^{\infty} \frac{\exp(-\delta\tau)\exp[-n(\tau - (T^* + \Delta t))]r(x_2^*)}{z(T^*)\exp[-(\bar{s}r(x_2^*) - n)\Delta t]}\, d\tau$

$\qquad = \Gamma + \dfrac{(1 - \bar{s})r(x_2^*)}{z(T^*)\exp[(\bar{s}r(x_2^*) - n)T^*]} \displaystyle\int_{T^*}^{T^* + \Delta t} \exp[(\bar{s}r(x_2^*) - (\delta + n))\tau]\, d\tau$

$\qquad + \dfrac{r(x_2^*)}{z(T^*)} \exp[nT^* + \bar{s}r(x_2^*)\Delta t] \displaystyle\int_{T^* + \Delta t}^{\infty} \exp[-(\delta + n)\tau]\, d\tau$

$$= 1^{'} + \frac{(1 - \overline{s})r(x_2^*)\{\exp[(\overline{s}r(x_2^*) - (\delta + n))\Delta t] - 1\}}{z(T^*)[\overline{s}r(x_2^*) - (\delta + n)]}$$

$$+ \frac{r(x_2^*)}{z(T^*)} \frac{\exp[nT^* + \overline{s}r(x_2^*)\Delta t]}{(\delta + n)} \exp[-(\delta + n)(T^* + \Delta t)]$$

$$= \Gamma + \frac{(1 - \overline{s})r(x_2^*)\{\exp[(\overline{s}r(x_2^*) - (\delta + n))\Delta t] - 1\}}{z(T^*)[\overline{s}r(x_2^*) - (\delta + n)]}$$

$$+ \frac{r(x_2^*)}{z(T^*)} \frac{\exp[(\overline{s}r(x_2^*) - (\delta + n))\Delta t - \delta T^*]}{(\delta + n)}$$

where

$$\Gamma \equiv \int_0^{T^*} \exp(-\delta\tau) \frac{[1 - s^e(z^e(\tau,z_0))]}{z^e(\tau,z_0)} r(x^e(z^e(\tau,z_0))) \, d\tau$$

Differentiating (27) with respect to $\Delta t$, and evaluating at $\Delta t = 0$, we obtain

$$\frac{d}{d(\Delta t)} V_r^{\Delta t} \bigg|_{\Delta t = 0} = \frac{r(x_2^*)}{z(T^*)} \left[ (1 - \overline{s}) + \frac{\overline{s}r(x_2^*) - (\delta + n)}{\delta + n} \exp(-\delta T^*) \right]$$

$$= \frac{r(x_2^*)}{z(T^*)(\delta + n)} \{(1 - \overline{s})(\delta + n) + [\overline{s}r(x_2^*) - (\delta + n)]\exp(-\delta T^*)\}$$

which, since $1 > \overline{s} > (\delta + n)/r(x_2^*)$, is positive. It follows that, if $\Delta t > 0$ is sufficiently small, the pair of strategies $(\tilde{s}(z,t; \Delta t), x^e(z))$ is superior to the pair $(s^e(z), x^e(z))$, a contradiction.                                    ◊

*Existence and uniqueness of equilibrium when $r(x_2^*) \leq \delta + n$*

At this point we describe in broad outline the route we shall follow in our further search for an equilibrium path. First, we shall take any non-negative T and suppose that $s = 1$ for all $t \in [0,T]$ and that $s = 0$ for all $t \in (T, \infty)$. Then, subject to this constraint, as well as the inequality $z \geq x$, we shall solve the union's problem, thus obtaining the union's decision rule $x_T(z,t)$. Once $x_T(z,t)$ is obtained, we shall formulate the problem confronting the capitalists' club, which is to maximize cumulated discounted consumption subject to the union's decision rule $x_T(z,t)$ by choosing the point in time, say $T^*(T)$, at which s changes from one to zero. In general, $T \neq T^*$. However, by definition of a Nash equilibrium, $T = T^*$ in equilibrium. We therefore seek a T such that $T = T^*(T)$.

Let us begin, then, with the problem

$(P'_w)$  $\max_{<x>} \int_0^\infty \exp(-\delta t)(x/z)f'(x)\, dt$

s.t.  $z \geq x$

$$\dot{z} = \begin{cases} z\{n - [f(x) - xf'(x)]\} \text{ for all } t \in [0,T] \\ nz \text{ for all } t \in (T,\infty) \end{cases}$$

$$\left. \begin{array}{l} z(0) = z_0 > x_2^* \\ \\ T \geq 0 \end{array} \right\} \text{ given}$$

which can also be rewritten as

$(P''_w)$  $\max_{<x>} \int_0^\infty \exp(-\delta t)(x/z)f'(x)\, dt$

$\qquad\qquad + [\exp(nT)/z(T)] \int_T^\infty \exp[-(\delta+n)t]xf'(x)\, dt$

s.t.  $z \geq x$

$\dot{z} = z\{n - f(x) - xf'(x)]\}$ for all $t \in [0,T]$

$$\left. \begin{array}{l} z(0) = z_0 > x_2^* \\ \\ T \geq 0 \end{array} \right\} \text{ given}$$

And let us denote by $z^{e1}$ the solution to $n - [f(z) - zf'(z)] = 0$. ($z^{e1}$ is a special case of $z^e$ which, in Chapter V, was defined as the solution to $n - s[f(z) - zf'(z)] = 0$.) In the sequel we shall confine our attention to the case in which $z^{e1} > x_2^*$; this is for concreteness only—none of our conclusions depends on it. Then,

$z\{n - [f(x_2^*) - x_2^* f'(x_2^*)]\} > 0$ if $z \geq x_2^*$

Hence $z_0 > x_2^*$ implies that $z(T) > x_2^*$. Consider now the truncated problem

$$\max_{<x>} \ [\exp(nT)/z(T)] \int_T^\infty \exp[-(\delta + n)t]xf'(x)\,dt$$

$$\text{s.t.} \quad z(T)\exp[n(t - T)] \geq x$$

Since $z(T) > x_2^*$, the solution to the problem is obviously $x = x_2^*$ for all $t \in [T, \infty)$; if the capitalists do not save, it is optimal for the union to maximize the wage bill at each instant. Hence the maximum value of the integral is

$$\frac{\exp(-\delta T)}{z(T)(\delta + n)} \ x_2^* f'(x_2^*)$$

and $(P_w'')$ can be again rewritten as

$$(P_w''') \quad \max_{<x>} \int_0^T \exp(-\delta t)(x/z)f'(x)\,dt + \frac{\exp(-\delta T)}{z(T)(\delta + n)} \ x_2^* f'(x_2^*)$$

$$\text{s.t.} \quad z \geq x$$

$$\dot{z} = z\{n - [f(x) - xf'(x)]\}$$

$$\left.\begin{array}{l} z(0) = z_0 > x_2^* \\[2mm] T \geq 0 \end{array}\right\} \text{ given}$$

Associated with $(P''')$ are the Hamiltonian

$$\tilde{H}(x, z, \mu) \equiv (x/z)f'(x) + \mu z\{n - [f(x) - xf'(x)]\}$$

and the Lagrangean

$$\tilde{L} \equiv \tilde{H} + \lambda(z-x)$$

The necessary conditions for a solution are

$$\tilde{H}(x, z, \mu) \geq \tilde{H}(x^*, z, \mu) \text{ for any } x^* \text{ such that } 0 \leq x^* \leq z$$

$$(28) \quad \partial\tilde{L}/\partial x = [f'(x)/z] \left\{ 1 - (1 + \mu z^2) \left[ \frac{1 - \theta(x)}{\sigma(x)} \right] \right\} - \lambda = 0$$

$$\lambda \geq 0, \quad z - x \geq 0, \quad \lambda(z - x) = 0$$

and the transversality condition

$$(29) \quad \mu(T) = -\frac{1}{(z(T))^2} \frac{\exp(-\delta T)}{(\delta + n)} \ x_2^* f'(x_2^*)$$

Letting $\mu z^2 \equiv \psi_w$, one may verify that the Pontryagin paths generated by (28) are described by (15) and (16), and that the transversality condition (29) becomes

$$(29') \quad \psi_w(T) = - \frac{\exp(-\delta T)}{(\delta + n)} x_2^* f'(x_2^*)$$

Recalling the argument of Chapter V, one can easily obtain the phase diagram consisting of the Pontryagin paths generated by (28). Defining

$$\delta^{*1} = \frac{\theta_1(z^{e1}) f_1(z^{e1})}{1 - \dfrac{\sigma_1(z^{e1})}{1 - \theta_1(z^{e1})}}$$

we obtain Figures 6 and 7 if $\delta^{*1} > \delta$ and Figure 8 if $\delta^{*1} < \delta$. (Figure 6 is associated with the case in which $\delta \leq r(\infty) - n$, Figure 7 with the case in which $\delta > r(\infty) - n$.)

Consider Figure 6. With the exception of the horizontal "transversality" line AD''B, which is the graph of

$$(30) \quad \psi_w = - \frac{\exp(-\delta T)}{(\delta + n)} x_2^* f'(x_2^*)$$

the loci of Figure 6 have the same interpretations as the similarly-labelled loci of Figures V.8–10. Suppose that the initial value $z_0$ is less than $z^{e1}$. Any Pontryagin path starting from the vertical segment D''D', except for point D', arrives at the horizontal line AD''B. Let us denote by m the period of time that it takes to move from D''D' to AD''B. At D'', of course, $m = 0$; and, as the initial point moves along D''D' towards D', m diverges to $+\infty$. Hence there exists a unique point on D''D', say M, such that it takes exactly T units of time to move from M to AD''B. Thus the optimal trajectory can be depicted by MQ'Q in Figure 6.

In Figure 9 the solid directed lines form a family of optimal trajectories, one for each value of T. Each trajectory ends on the locus bc of points like Q in Figures 6–8. The locus is determined by (30) and the two additional equations

$$(31) \quad z = z(T, z_0, \psi_w(0))$$

and

# Figure 6

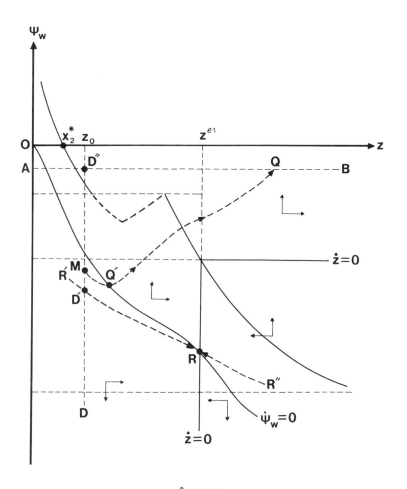

$\delta$ **small**

Figure 7

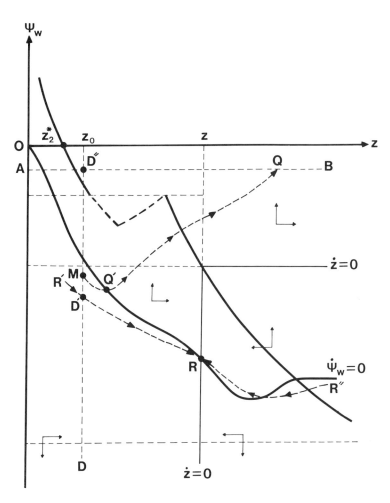

δ large but not very large

# Figure 8

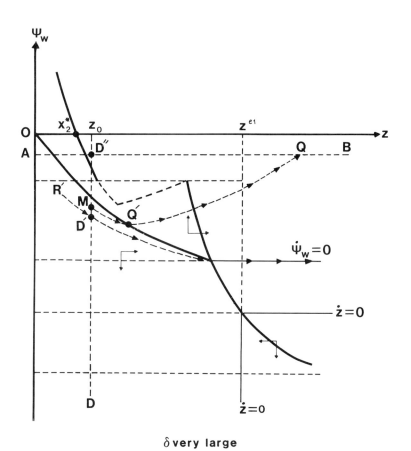

$\delta$ **very large**

Figure 9

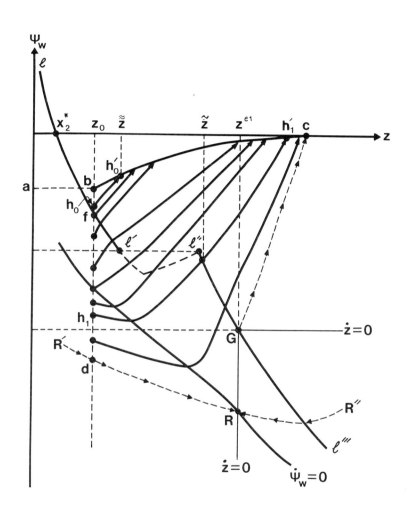

(32)   $\psi_w = \psi_w(T, z_0, \psi_w(0))$

where $(z(\ ), \psi_w(\ ))$ is the solution to the system of differential equations composed of the first and second members of (15) and the initial condition $(z_0, \psi_0(0))$.

Inspection of Figure 9 yields a decision rule $x(z,t)$ for each of the optimal trajectories. As an example, consider the trajectory $h_0 h'_0$ which starts on segment bf. Denoting by $T_0$ the period of time needed to move from $h_0$ to $h'_0$, the decision rule is

$$(33) \qquad x_{T_0}(z,t) = \begin{cases} x(\psi_w(t); 1) \text{ for all } t \in [0,T_0] \\ x_2^* \text{ for all } t \in (T_0, \infty) \end{cases}$$

See Figure 10.   As a second example, we have the trajectory $h_1 h'_1$ which starts on segment fd.   Denoting by $T_1$ the period of time needed to move from $h_1$ to $h'_1$, the decision rule is

$$(34) \quad x_{T_1}(z,t) = \begin{cases} z \text{ for all } t \in [0,t^1) \\ x(\psi_w(t); 1) \text{ for all } t \in [t^1, T_1] \\ x_2^* \text{ for all } t \in (T_1, \infty) \end{cases}$$

where $t^1$ is determined by

$$\tilde{z} = x(\psi_w(t^1); 1)$$

and $\tilde{z}$ lies at the intersection of the trajectory $h_1 h'_1$ and the graph of $x = x(\psi_w; 1)$, as in Figure 9. See Figure 11.

Given a decision rule like $x_{T_0}(z,t)$ or $x_{T_1}(z,t)$, say $x_T(z,t)$, one can formulate the capitalists' problem

$$(35) \quad \max_{T^*} \ V_r = \int_{T^*}^{\infty} \exp(-\delta t)[1/z_T(t,z_0)][f(x_T - x_T f'(x_T)] \, dt$$

where $x_T \equiv x_T(z_T(t,z_0), t)$ and $z_T(t, z_0)$ is the solution to the differential equation

$$(36) \quad \dot{z} = \begin{cases} z\{n - [f(x_T(z,t)) - x_T(z,t)f'(x_T(z,t))]\} & \text{for all } t \in [0,T^*] \\ zn \text{ for all } t \in (T^*, \infty) \end{cases}$$

In view of (36), (35) can be rewritten as

$$(35') \quad \max_{T^*} \ V_r =$$

$$[\exp(nT^*)][1/nz_T(T^*, z_0)] \int_{T^*}^{\infty} \exp[-(\delta + n)t] \left[ f(x_T - x_T f'(x_T) \right] dt$$

Figure 10

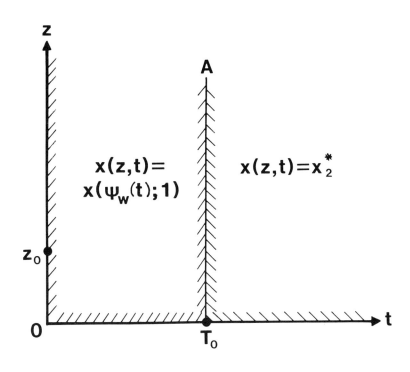

## Figure 11

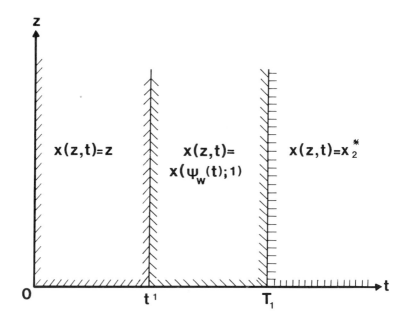

where $x_T = x_T(z_T(T^*, z_0) \exp[n(t - T^*)], t)$. Let us denote by $T_e^*$ the solution to (35'). Since the decision rule $x_T(z,t)$ depends on T, so does $T_e^*$: $T_e^* = T_e^*(T)$. It follows that if we manage to find a fixed point $T = T_e^*(T)$ then we shall have found an equilibrium of the game.

Differentiating $V_r$ in (35') with respect to $T^*$, we obtain

$$(37) \quad \frac{\partial V_r}{\partial T^*} =$$

$$\frac{\partial}{\partial T^*} \left\{ \frac{\exp(nT^*)}{nz_T(T^*, z_0)} \int_{T^*}^{\infty} \exp[-(\delta+n)t] \left[ f(x_T(z_T(T^*, z_0) \exp(n(t-T^*)), t)) \right. \right.$$

$$\left. - x_T(z_T(T^*, z_0) \exp(n(t-T^*)), t) f'(x_T(z_T(T^*, z_0) \exp(n(t-T^*)), t)) \right] dt \right\}$$

$$= \frac{-\exp(nT^*)}{[nz_T(T^*, z_0)]^2} \left\{ \dot{z}_T(T^*, z_0) \int_{T^*}^{\infty} \exp[-(\delta+n)t][f(x_T)-x_T f'(x_T)] \, dt \right.$$

$$+ z_T(T^*, z_0)[f(x_T(z_T(T^*, z_0), T^*)) - x_T(z_T(T^*, z_0), T^*) f'(x_T(z_T(T^*, z_0), T^*))]$$

$$\times \exp[-(\delta+n)T^*] + z_T(T^*, z_0)[\dot{z}_T(T^*, z_0) - nz_T(T^*, z_0)] \exp(-nT^*)$$

$$\left. \times \int_{T^*}^{\infty} \exp(-\delta t) x_T f''(x_T)(\partial x_T/\partial z) \, dt \right\} + \frac{\exp(nT^*)}{z_T(T^*, z_0)} I$$

where

$$I \equiv \int_{T^*}^{\infty} \exp[-(\delta + n)t][f(x_T) - x_T f'(x_T)] \, dt$$

Now

$$\dot{z}_T(T^*, z_0) = \begin{cases} nz_T(T^*, z_0) & \text{from the right} \\ nz_T(T^*, z_0) - [f(x_T) - x_T f'(x_T)] z_T(T^*, z_0) & \text{from the left} \end{cases}$$

Hence the right-hand derivative is

$$(38a) \quad \left. \frac{\partial V_r}{\partial T^*} \right|_{T^* = T^+} = - \frac{\exp(nT^*)}{nz_T} [f(x_T) - x_T f'(x_T)] < 0$$

and the left-hand derivative is

$$\frac{\partial V_r}{\partial T^*}\bigg|_{T^*=T^-} =$$

$$-\frac{\exp(nT^*)}{(z_T)^2}\left\{-z_T[f(x_T)-x_Tf'(x_T)]\,\frac{\exp(-\delta-n)T}{n+\delta}\,[f(x_2^*)-x_2^*f'(x_2^*)]\right.$$

$$+\frac{z_T[\exp(-\delta-n)T]}{n+\delta}\,(n+\delta)[f(x_T)-x_Tf'(x_T)]\right\}$$

so that

(38b)  $\text{sign}\,\dfrac{\partial V_r}{\partial T^*}\bigg|_{T^*=T^-} = -\,\text{sign}\,[(n+\delta)-r(x_2^*)] < 0$

It follows from (38) that $T^* = T$ does not maximize $V_r$, and this in turn implies that there is no equilibrium solution with $T > 0$. By a similar argument, if $T = 0$ then $\partial V_r/\partial T^* < 0$ for any $T^* \geq 0$. It follows that if $T = 0$ then $T^* = 0$ maximizes $V_r$; that is, $0 = T_e^*(0)$. In terms of Figure 9, if the initial condition is $z_0$ then the equilibrium is represented by point b. The decision rules chosen by the labour union and the capitalists' club are, respectively,

(39a)  $x(z,t) = \min\,[x_2^*,z]$

and

(39b)  $s(z,t) = 0$ for all $(z,t) \geq 0$

One may verify that if $(z_0,\psi_0)$ is inside the region $x_2^*fl'l''Gz^{el}\widetilde{\widetilde{z}}zx_2^*$ in Figure 9 then the above pair of decision rules is the equilibrium of the game.

*Remark*  In fact, the pair of decision rules (39) is the equilibrium of the game even if $(z_0,\psi_0)$ lies below $x_2^*fl'l''Gz^{el}\widetilde{\widetilde{z}}zx_2^*$, provided that $x_2^* < z_0 < z^{el}$. Consider Figure 12, in which the locus of terminal points is $bh_0'c$. We seek to evaluate the sign of $\partial V_r/\partial T^*$ at points like $h_0'$. To this end, consider the terms within the braces of equation (37). The first two terms are positive, as in the more restricted case. Since the point $h_0'$ lies in the area of full employment, the decision rule at $h_0'$ must be $x_T = z$, so that $\partial x_T/\partial z = 1$. Hence the third term is

$$z_T(T,z_0)[\dot z_T(T,z_0)-nz_T(T,z_0)]\exp(-nT^*)x_2^*f''(x_2^*)\,\frac{\exp(-\delta T)}{\delta}$$

Figure 12

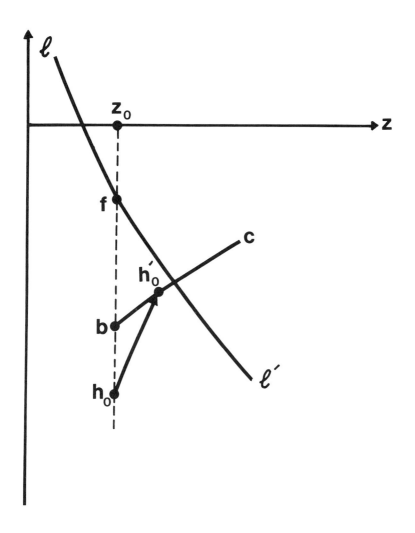

Applying (36), we see that this term is non-negative. Hence the expression in braces in (37) is positive and $\partial V_r / \partial T^* |_{T^* = T}$ is negative at $h'_0$.

Let us turn our attention to the case in which $z_0 > z^{el}$. Consider Figure 13. The figure is drawn on the assumption that

$$\psi_w^{el} < -x_2^* f'(x_2^*)/(\delta + n)$$

where $\psi_w^{el}$ is defined as the solution to $z^{el} = x(\psi_w; 1)$; $-x_2^* f'(x_2^*)/(\delta+n)$ corresponds to $Pz_0$ in the figure. Displayed in the figure are several trajectories, $a_1 a_2$, $b_1 b_2$, $c_1 c_2$, $d_1 b_1 b_2$ and $d_2 a_1 a_2 a_3$, each associated with a different T ($a_1 a_2$ with the lowest T) and each ending on the locus of terminal points $Pa_2 b_2 c_2 b_3 a_3 Q$ determined by (30)–(32). Now consider $T^*$. It is obvious from inspection of the figure that $\dot z(T^*, z_0) > 0$ on $Pa_2 b_2 c_2 b_3 a_3 Q$; that is, $\dot z(T^*, z_0) > 0$ if $T = T^*$. Thus (37) is negative at $T = T^*$. Hence $T^*$ which maximizes $V_r$ coincides with T only if T $= 0$. Thus, as in the case $z_0 < z^{el}$, in Nash equilibrium $T = T^*(T)$ at T $= 0$; (39) is the equilibrium pair of decision rules.

That leaves for consideration the case in which $z_0 > z^{el}$ and

$$\psi_w^{el} > -x_2^* f'(x_2^*)/(\delta + n)$$

Consider Figure 14, in which $Pz_0$ corresponds to $-x_2^* f'(x_2^*)/(\delta+n)$ and the locus of terminal points determined by (30)–(32) is depicted as $Pa_2 b_2 Q'' Q' c_2 d_2 Q$. Each of the trajectories $a_1 a_2$, $b_1 b_2$, $c_1 c_2$, $d_1 d_2$ is associated with a different T, $a_1 a_2$ with the lowest. Consider $T^*$. It is a remarkable feature of the present case that, on part of the locus of terminal points, $\dot z_T(T, z_0)$ is negative. Does this mean that $\partial V_r / \partial T^* |_{T^* = T}$ may be positive?

Consider any point on $Pa_2 b_2 Q'' Q'$, say $b_2$, with co-ordinates denoted by $(z_b, \psi_{wb})$. Suppose that it takes $T_b$ units of time to move from $b_1$ to $b_2$. Then from (37) and the argument of pp. 261-62 we can calculate $\partial V_r / \partial T^* |_{T^* = T_b}$ and show that it is negative. Thus we can be sure that $T = 0$ is the equilibrium of the game.

We have confined our attention to the case in which the union has only a slight time preference; that case is illustrated by Figure 6. However our main conclusions are the same in the remaining cases, which are illustrated by Figures 7 and 8.

Figure 13

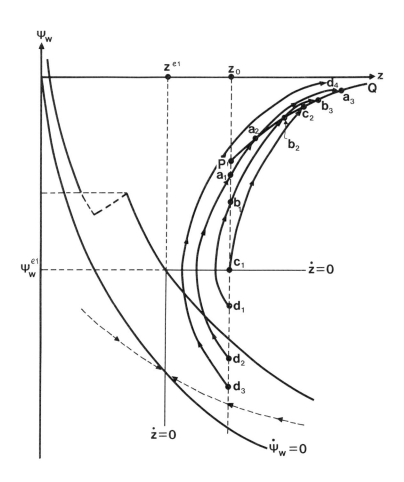

## Figure 14

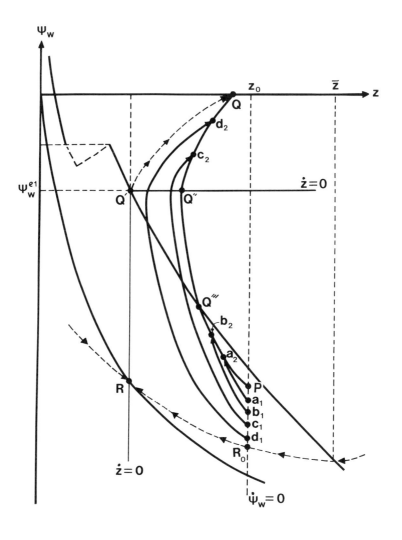

**PROPOSITION 2:**  If $r(x_2^*) \leq \delta + n$, there is a unique feedback-Nash equilibrium. Along the equilibrium path, (i) the union always exercises its market power, exception made of an initial finite period if $z_0 < x_2^*$, and (ii) the employers' club saves nothing.

## 3.    POSSIBLE NEXT STEPS

It has been shown that, if time preference is not too strong, there is a unique feedback-Nash equilibrium in which $x(z,t) = \min \{z, x_2^*\}$ and $s(z,t) = 0$. In that equilibrium the economy stagnates with zero capital formation and an ever-growing rate of unemployment.

Evidently the theory suggests too much and should be modified. Three kinds of modification come to mind.

*Solution concept*  We have assumed that, in addition to its own preferences and technical capabilities, each player knows only the current value of the state variable; and, given that assumption, it seemed natural to confine our attention to Nash equilibria.  Alternatively, we might endow one or both of the players with a richer supply of information and consider other solution concepts.  The Stackelberg solution concept has been popular in static economic contexts and has been employed in situations bearing some similarity to the one studied in this chapter; see Pohjola (1983) and Başar et al. (1985).  However the open-loop-Stackelberg solution concept is relevant only if the leader can plausibly pre-commit its policy, and it is difficult to see how that might be done in the employer-employee confrontation.  Moreover, in the present context, the set of feedback-Nash solutions coincides with the set of feedback-Stackelberg solutions if the labour union serves as leader; see Appendix 2.  It remains to consider the outcome of a game in which the capitalists' club serves as leader.

*A third player*  One might change the cast of players by adding a landowners' club or by adding the government.  The latter possibility has been explored by Driffil (1985) and Hersoug (1985).  (In their papers, the government *replaces* the capitalists' club.)  However it is unreasonable to treat the government as an independent player, in parity with the labour union and the capitalists' club; for the government has itself been elected by members of the union and the club.

*A more general economy*   Our game has been played in the restricted context of a small open economy without access to an international capital market. To abandon these restrictions seems to be the most promising next step. Notice however that if a small country has free access to the world capital market then the union has no market power and our problem evaporates. Access to the world capital market can be introduced only if, simultaneously, the small-country assumption is dropped.

# APPENDIX 1

## DIRECT PROOF THAT IF A FEEDBACK-NASH EQUILIBRIUM EXISTS THEN THE PAIR OF STRATEGIES $(x(z,t) = \min\{z,x^*\}$, $s(z,t) \equiv 0)$ IS A FEEDBACK-NASH EQUILIBRIUM

It is convenient to define $k \equiv K/\bar{N} = 1/z$, $v \equiv K/N = 1/x$ and $Y \equiv g(v) = f(x)/x$; in particular, $v_i^* \equiv 1/x_i^*$ $(i = 1, 2)$ and $k^{e1} \equiv 1/z^{e1}$, where $z^{e1}$ is the solution to $n - [f(z) - zf'(z)] = 0$. Then the rental of capital can be expressed as $r(v) \equiv g'(v) = f(x) - xf'(x)$ and the wage rate as $w(v) \equiv g(v) - vg'(v) = f'(x)$. For concreteness it is assumed that $x_2^*$ (rather than $x_1^*$) maximizes $xf'(x)$, that is, that $v_2^*$ maximizes $[g(v) - vg'(v)]/v$; nothing depends on that assumption. Let $r^* \equiv r(v_2^*)$.

Attention is confined to piece-wise continuous strategies.

*The case $r^* < \delta+n$*

Until further notice it is assumed that $r^*$ is less than the rate of time preference $\delta + n$. It will be shown that, under that assumption, the strategies

(A1a) $\bar{v}(k,t) = v(k) = \begin{cases} k & \text{if } k > v_2^* \equiv 1/x_2^* \\ v_2^* & \text{if } k \leq v_2^* \end{cases}$

and

(A1b) $\bar{s}(k,t) = 0$ for all $k \geq 0$ and all $t \geq 0$

are a feedback-Nash equilibrium.

We begin by observing that if $s(k,t) = 0$ identically then the wage demands of the union have no effect on capital accumulation and the union can do no better than set the employment:capital ratio at its static optimal level $\max\{k,v_2^*\}$. The proof that (A1a) and (A1b) are an equilibrium will then be completed by showing that, if the union follows the strategy $v(k) = \max\{k,v_2^*\}$, the capitalists' club can do no better than set $s(k,t) = 0$ identically.

Let us further define

$$\phi(k) \equiv \begin{cases} kr^* & \text{if } k \leq v_2^* \\ kg'(k) < kr^* & \text{if } k > v_2^* \end{cases}$$

In terms of this notation, the capitalists' problem is to find

$$\max_{<s(t)>} \int_0^\infty \exp(-\delta t)(1 - s)\phi(k) \, dt$$

$$\text{s.t. } 0 \leq s \leq 1$$

(A2)                $\dot{k} = s\phi(k) - nk$

$$k(0) = k_0, \text{ given}$$

Let us assume that $\phi(k)$ is concave, as in Figure A1. Then the capitalists' problem is formally identical to a bang-bang control problem encountered in the analysis of optimal economic growth; see Shell (1967).

The Hamiltonian associated with the capitalists' problem is

(A3)   $H = (1 - s)\phi(k) + \psi[s\phi(k) - nk]$

From (A3) we see immediately that

$$s = 0 \quad \text{if } -1 + \psi < 0$$

(A4)   $s = 1 \quad \text{if } -1 + \psi > 0$

$$s \in [0,1] \quad \text{if } -1 + \psi = 0$$

and

(A5)   $\dot{\psi} = (n + \delta)\psi - (1 - s + \psi s)\phi'(k)$

where $\psi$ is the costate which is associated with (A2) and which there-fore indicates the current utility value of additional capital. We proceed to construct the phase diagram in $(k,\psi)$-space.

*The locus $\dot{\psi} = 0$* Suppose that $k \leq v_2^*$. Then $\phi'(k) = r^*$ and (A5) reduces to

(A5′)   $\dot{\psi} = (n + \delta - sr^*)\psi - (1 - s)r^*$

Figure A1

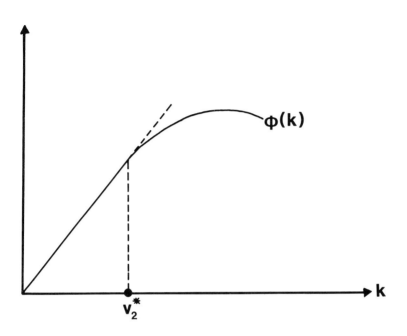

It follows that if $\psi > 1$ (so that $s = 1$) then $\dot\psi = (n + \delta - sr^*)\psi$; and that if $\psi < 1$ (so that $s = 0$) then $\dot\psi = (n + \delta)\psi - r^*$. Thus, defining $\psi^* = r^*/(\delta+n)$, we see that $\dot\psi \gtreqless 0$ if and only if $\psi \gtreqless \psi^*$.

Suppose alternatively that $k > v_2^*$, so that $\phi'(k) < r^*$. In this case, if $\psi > 1$ (so that $s = 1$) then $\dot\psi = (n + \delta - \phi')\psi > (n + \delta - r^*) > 0$; and if $\psi < 1$ (so that $s = 0$) then $\dot\psi = (n + \delta)\psi - \phi'$, so that $\dot\psi = 0$ if $\psi = \phi'(k)/(n+\delta)$.

The foregoing information is summarized by Figure A2.

*The locus $\dot k = 0$*   If $r(k^{e1}) > r^*$, that is, if $k^{e1} < v_2^*$ then, at all points of time, $v > k^{e1}$ and $\dot k < 0$. Thus, recalling Figure A2, we obtain Figure A3(a) as the phase diagram. In this case it is optimal to set $s = 0$ always. Thus, discounted back to $t = 0$, the consumption loss associated with a pulse of saving at rate $s = 0$ during the short interval $[0,\Delta t]$ is, approximately,

$$L = sK_0r^* \int_0^{\Delta t} \exp(-(\delta + n)t)\,dt$$

$$= sK_0r^*[1 - \exp(-(\delta + n)\Delta t)]/(\delta + n)$$

and the consumption gain attributable to the additional capital $\Delta K = sK_0r^*(\Delta t)$ is, approximately,

$$G = sK_0(r^*)^2(\Delta t) \int_{\Delta t}^{\infty} \exp(-(\delta + n)t)\,dt$$

$$= sK_0(r^*)^2(\Delta t)\exp(-(\delta + n)\Delta t)/(\delta + n)$$

Hence the net gain is, approximately,

(A6)   $G - L = sK_0r^*\{r^*(\Delta t)\exp(-(\delta+n)\Delta t)-[1-\exp(-(\delta+n)\Delta t)]\}/(\delta+n)$

Dividing by $\Delta t$ and taking the limit,

(A7)   $\displaystyle \lim_{\Delta t \to 0} \frac{G - L}{\Delta t} = \frac{1}{\delta + n}[r^* - (\delta + n)] < 0$

The same inequality emerges when the pulse of saving occupies the interval $[t,\Delta t]$, $t > 0$. It follows that no path lying everywhere above the locus $\dot\psi = 0$ can be optimal, for, along such a path, eventually $\psi > 1$ and $s = 1$. Nor can any path which eventually lies below the locus $\dot\psi = 0$ be optimal, for along such a path $\psi$ eventually is negative. Thus the optimal path is as indicated by Figure A3(a).

# Figure A2

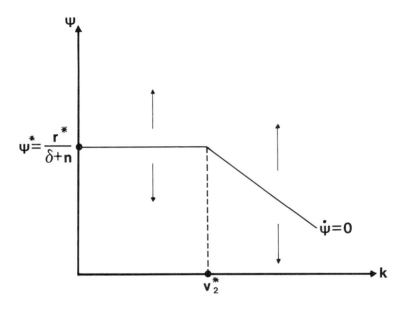

## Figure A3(a)

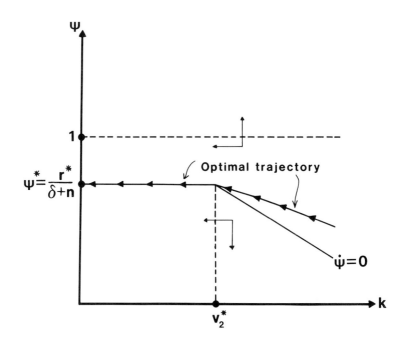

$$r^*<r(k^{e1}),r^*<\delta+n$$

## Figure A3(b)

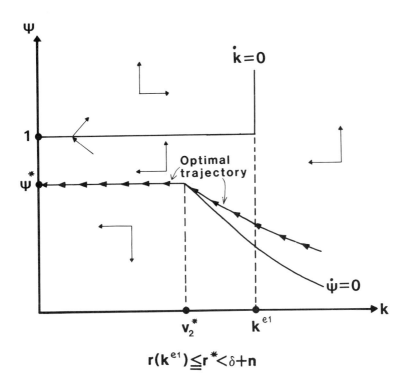

$$r(k^{e1}) \leqq r^* < \delta + n$$

Suppose, alternatively, that $r^* \geq r(k^{el})$, that is, that $k^{el} \geq v_2^*$, as in Figure A4. Then, as (A2) and Figure A4 make clear, $\dot{k} = 0$ if and only if *either* $k = k^{el}$ and $s = 1$ *or* $k < k^{el}$ and $s = nk/\phi(k) < 1$. Figure A3(b) is the phase diagram. No path above the locus $\dot{\psi} = 0$ can be optimal, for along such a path $s = 1$ after finite time; and, as we have noted, no path which eventually lies below $\dot{\psi} = 0$ can be optimal. Hence the optimal path is as depicted by Figure A3(b), with $s = 0$ always.

That completes our demonstration that if $r^* < \delta + n$ then the strategies (A1a) and (A1b) are a feedback-Nash equilibrium. It remains to consider the possibility that $r^* = \delta + n$.

*The case $r^* = \delta + n$*

In this singular case, $g'(k^{el}) = n < \delta + n = r^*$; hence $k^{el} > v_2^*$ and Figure A5 is the phase diagram. It will be shown that

(A8a)  $\bar{v}(k,t) = v(k) = \max \{v_2^*, k\}$

(A8b)  $\bar{s}(k,t) = s(k) = \begin{cases} 0 \text{ if } k > v_2^* \\ n/r^* \text{ if } k \leq v_2^* \end{cases}$

is a Nash equilibrium. Suppose that the union is known by the capitalists to have adopted strategy (A8a). If at any point in time $k > v_2^*$, it is optimal for the capitalists to set $s = 0$; for if at that point $s > 0$ then, as Figure A5 makes clear, thereafter $s = 1$, which is suboptimal. After a finite interval of time, therefore, $k \leq v_2^*$ and $v = v_2^*$. Suppose that after that interval the capitalists set $s$ below $n/r^*$, thus allowing $k$ to fall. By a calculation similar to the one which produced (A6), it can be shown that the consumption gain associated with such a move is outweighed by the cost. Thus (A8b) is optimal, given (A8a).

Suppose now that the capitalists are known by the union to have adopted strategy (A8b). If $k > v_2^*$ there is no incentive to set $v > k$; there is no incentive to do so when $s = 0$ identically, hence there is no incentive to do so when the capitalists adopt a strategy which allows saving in some states. Similarly, if $k \leq v_2^*$, there is no incentive to set $v > v_2^*$. Moreover, if $k \leq v_2^*$, there is no incentive to set $k \leq v < v_2^*$, for that would reduce the wage bill while failing to induce a compensating increase in the rate of investment.

Thus, summarizing, if $r^* = \delta + n$ then strategies (A8a) and (A8b) are a Nash equilibrium.

## Figure A4

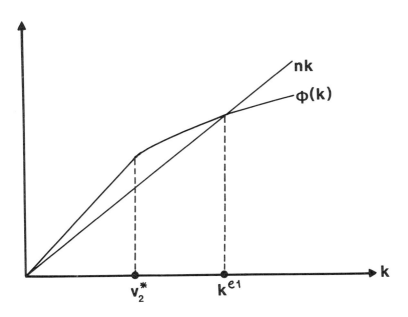

## Figure A5

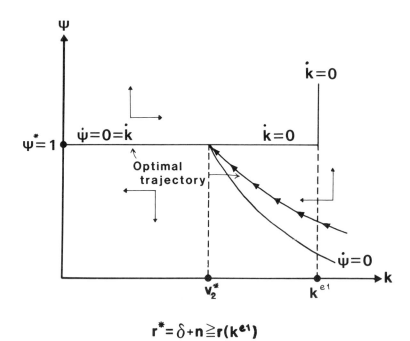

$$r^* = \delta + n \geqq r(k^{e1})$$

# APPENDIX 2

## THE IDENTITY OF THE FEEDBACK-NASH AND FEEDBACK-STACKELBERG SOLUTIONS WHEN THE LABOUR UNION LEADS

If the workers lead and the capitalists follow, the feedback-Stackelberg solution may be written

(B1)
$$s(x,z,t)$$
$$x(z,t)$$

However time t appears only in the players' objective functions. Hence we may apply to (B1) an argument originally formulated by Clemhout and Wan (1985, p. 551) and suppress t:

(B1′)
$$s(x,z)$$
$$x(z)$$

The reaction function of the capitalists is defined as

$$\arg \max_{s \in [0,1]} H^r$$

$$= \arg \max_{s \in [0,1]} \left\{ \frac{1}{z}(1-s)(f(x) - xf'(x)) + \mu_r z[n - s(f(x) - xf'(x))] \right\}$$

Differentiating $H^r$ with respect to s, we obtain

$$H^r_s = \frac{1}{z}[f(x) - xf'(x)][1 + \mu_r z^2]$$

Hence

$$s \begin{cases} = 0 \\ \in [0,1] \text{ if and only if } \mu_r z^2 \gtreqless -1 \\ = 1 \end{cases}$$

and s(x,z) is seen to be *independent* of x.

It follows that (B.1) can be re-written as

$$(B1'') \quad \begin{array}{c} s(z) \\ x(z) \end{array}$$

which coincides with the feedback-Nash solution.

We note that Basar *et al.* (1985) consider a game of Lancaster (1973) type and, by means of dynamic programming, show that, if the workers lead, the feedback-Stackelberg solution coincides with the feedback-Nash solution. The explanation in their case is the same as in ours: the capitalists' reaction function is such that their strategy is independent of the workers' control.

# REFERENCES

Amano, A. (1977), Specific factors, comparative advantage and international investment, *Economica* 44, 131-144.

Basar, T. and A. Haurie (1984), Feedback equilibria in differential games with structural and modal uncertainties, in J.B. Cruz, Jr, ed., *Advances in Large Scale Systems*, Vol. 1, 163-201. Greenwich, CT, JAI Press.

Basar, T. and G.J. Olsder (1982), *Dynamic Noncooperative Game Theory*. New York, Academic Press.

Basar, T., A. Haurie and G. Ricci (1985), On the dominance of capitalists'leadership in a "feedback-Stackelberg" solution to a differential game model of capitalism, *Journal of Economic Dynamics and Control* 9, 121-125.

Bhagwati, J.N. and T.N. Srinivasan (1971), The theory of wage differentials: Production response and factor price equalization, *Journal of International Economics* 1, 19-35.

Brecher, R.A. (1974a), Minimum wage rates and the pure theory of international trade, *Quarterly Journal of Economics* 88, 98-116.

Brecher, R.A., (1974b), Optimal commercial policy for a minimum wage economy, *Journal of International Economics* 4, 139-149.

Brock, W.A. and S.P. Magee (1978), The economics of special interest politics: the case of a tariff, *American Economic Review* 68, 246-250.

Brock, W.A. and S.P. Magee (1980), Tariff formation in a democracy, in J. Black and B. Hindley, eds., *Current Issues in Commercial Policy and Diplomacy*. Papers of the Third Annual Conference of the International Economics Study Group, 1-9. London, Macmillan for the Trade Policy Research Centre.

Chan, K.S. (1978), The employment effects of tariffs under a free exchange rate regime, *Journal of International Economics* 8, 414-424.

Clemhout, S. and H.Y. Wan, Jr. (1979), Interactive economic dynamics and differential games, *Journal of Optimization Theory and Applications* 27, 7-30.

Clemhout, S. and H.Y. Wan, Jr. (1985), Cartelization conserves endangered species? in G. Feichtinger, ed., *Optimal Control Theory and Economic Analysis*, vol. 2, 549-568. Amsterdam, North-Holland Publishing Company.

Das, S.P. (1982), On the effect of a tariff on employment under flexible exchange rates, *Journal of International Economics* 12, 165-168.

Driffill, J. (1985), Macroeconomic stabilization policy and trade union behaviour as a repeated game, *Scandinavian Journal of Economics* 87, 300-326.

Eichengreen, B.J. (1981), A dynamic model of tariffs, output and employment under flexible exchange rates, *Journal of International Economics* 11, 341-359.

Eichengreen, B.J. (1983), Protection, real wage resistance and employment, *Weltwirtschaftliches Archiv* 119, 429-451.

Ethier, W. (1972), Non-traded goods and the Heckscher-Ohlin model, *International Economic Review* 13, 132-147.

Findlay, R. and S. Wellisz (1982), Endogenous tariffs, the political economy of trade restrictions, and welfare, in J.N. Bhagwati, ed., *Import Competition and Response*, 223-234. Chicago, University of Chicago Press.

Fishlow, A. and P. David (1961), Optimal resource allocation in an imperfect market setting, *Journal of Political Economy* 69, 529-546.

Gorman, W.M. (1958), Tariffs, retaliation, and the elasticity of demand for imports, *Review of Economic Studies* 33, 133-162.

Gylfason, T. and A. Lindbeck (1986), Endogenous unions and governments. A game-theoretic approach, *European Economic Review* 30, 5-26.

Haberler, G. (1933), *The Theory of International Trade with its Applications to Economic Policy*. London, William Hodge and Company.

Haberler, G. (1950), Some problems in the pure theory of international trade, *Economic Journal* 60, 223-240.

Hagen, E.E. (1958), An economic justification of protectionism, *Quarterly Journal of Economics* 72, 496-514.

Herberg, H. and M.C. Kemp (1971), Factor market distortions, the shape of the locus of competitive outputs, and the relation between product prices and equilibrium outputs, in J.N. Bhagwati et al., eds., *Trade, Balance of Payments and Growth*. Papers in International Economics in Honor of Charles P. Kindleberger, 22-48. Amsterdam, North-Holland Publishing Company.

Herberg, H. and M.C. Kemp (1972), Growth and factor market "imperfections," *Zeitschrift für die Gesamte Staatswissenschaft* 128, 590-604.

Herberg, H., M.C. Kemp and S.P. Magee (1971), Factor market distortions, the reversal of relative factor intensities, and the relation between product prices and equilibrium outputs, *Economic Record* 47, 518-530.

Hersoug, T. (1985), Workers versus government — who adjusts to whom? *Scandinavian Journal of Economics* 87, 270-292.

Johansson, P.-O. and K.-G. Löfgren (1980), The effects of tariffs and real wages on employment in a Barro-Grossman model of an open economy, *Scandinavian Journal of Economics* 80, 167-18 .

Johannson, P.-O. and K.-G. Löfgren (1981), A note on the employment effects of tariffs in a small open economy, *Weltwirtschaftliches Archiv* 117, 578-583.

Johnson, H.G. (1954), Optimal tariffs and retaliation, *Review of Economic Studies* 21, 142-153.

Jones, R.W. (1971), Distortions in factor markets and the general equilibrium model of production, *Journal of Political Economy* 79, 437-459.

Jones, R. and R. Ruffin (1977), Protection and real wages: the neoclassical ambiguity, *Journal of Economic Theory* 14, 337-348.

Kemp, M.C., Y. Kimura and K. Okuguchi (1977), Monotonicity properties of a dynamical version of the Heckscher-Ohlin model of production, *Economic Studies Quarterly* 28, 249-253.

Kemp, M.C. and Y. Kimura (1978), *Introduction to Mathematical Economics*. New York, Springer-Verlag.

Kemp, M.C. and N.V. Long (1982), The efficiency of competitive markets in a context of exhaustible resources, in W. Eichhorn et al., eds., *Economic Theory of Exhaustible Resources*, 205-211. Würzburg, Physica-Verlag.

Kemp, M.C. and N.V. Long (1986), Union power in the long run: the case of concave utility, University of New South Wales.

Kemp, M.C. and N.V. Long (1987), Union power in the long run, *Scandinavian Journal of Economics* 89, 103-113.

Kemp, M.C. and N.V. Long (1989), Union power in the long run: the case in which capitalists save optimally, IFO-Studien. To be published.

Kemp, M.C. and K. Shimomura (1984a), Labour unions and foreign investment, University of New South Wales.

Kemp, M.C. and K. Shimomura (1984b), Labour unions and the theory of international trade, University of New South Wales. Read to the Sydney meeting of the Econometric Society, August 1984.

Kemp, M.C. and K. Shimomura (1985a), Do labour unions drive out capital?, *Economic Journal* 86, 1087-1090.

Kemp, M.C. and K. Shimomura (1985b), A neglected corner: labour unions and the pattern of international trade, University of New South Wales. To appear in a volume of essays in honour of Joan Robinson, edited by G.R. Feiwel.

Kemp, M.C. and H.Y. Wan, Jr. (1974), Hysteresis of long-run equilibrium from realistic adjustment costs, in: G. Horwich and P.A. Samuelson, eds., *Trade, Stability and Macroeconomics*. Essays in Honor of Lloyd A. Metzler, 221-242. New York, Academic Press.

Komiya, R. (1967), Non-traded goods and the pure theory of international trade, *International Economic Review* 8, 132-152.

Kumcu, M.E. (1985), The theory of commercial policy in a monetary economy with sticky wages, *Journal of International Economics* 18, 159-170.

Lancaster, K. (1973), The dynamic inefficiency of capitalism, *Journal of Political Economy* 81, 1092-1109.

Magee, S.P. (1976), *International Trade and Distortions in Factor Markets.* New York, Marcel Dekker.

Okuguchi, K. (1976), Product price change and intersectoral re-allocation of specific factors, *Economic Record* 52, 497-504.

Ohlin, B. (1931), Protection and non-competing groups, *Weltwirtschaftliches Archiv* 33, 30-45.

Pazner, E.A. and A. Razin (1980), Competitive efficiency in an overlapping-generation model with endogenous population, *Journal of Public Economics* 13, 249-258.

Pencavel, J. (1985), Wages and employment under trade unionism: microeconomic models and macroeconomic applications, *Scandinavian Journal of Economics* 87, 197-225.

Pohjola, M. (1983), Nash and Stackelberg solutions in a differential game model of capitalism, *Journal of Economic Dynamics and Control* 6, 173-176.

Pohjola, M. (1985), Growth, distribution and employment modelled as a differential game, in G. Feichtinger, ed., *Optimal Control Theory and Economic Analysis,* vol. 2, 581-591. Amsterdam, North-Holland.

Ruffin, R. and R. Jones (1977), Protection and real wages: the neoclassical ambiguity, *Journal of Economic Theory* 14, 337-348.

Scitovsky, T. (1942), A reconsideration of the theory of tariffs, *Review of Economic Studies* 9, 89-110.

Shell, K. (1967), Optimal programs of capital accumulation for an economy in which there is exogenous technical change, in K. Shell, ed., *Essays on the Theory of Optimal Economic Growth,* 1-30. Cambridge, Mass., MIT Press.

Wagstaff, P. (1975), Consensus tariff policy, *Economic Record* 51, 105-108.

Wickström, B.-A. (1986), Transfers, collective goods, and redistribution, in D. Bős and C. Seidl, eds., *Welfare Economics of the Second Best*, Supplementum 5 to Zeitschrift fūr Nationalōkonomie, 259-280. Vienna, Springer-Verlag.

# INDEX